Kings of the Forest

Kings of the Forest

The Cultural Resilience of
Himalayan Hunter-Gatherers

Jana Fortier

University of Hawai'i Press
Honolulu

© 2009 University of Hawai'i Press
All rights reserved
Printed in the United States of America

14 13 12 11   6 5 4 3 2

Library of Congress Cataloging-in-Publication Data

Fortier, Jana.
 Kings of the forest : the cultural resilience of Himalayan
hunter-gatherers / Jana Fortier.
     p.   cm.
 Includes bibliographical references and index.
 ISBN 978-0-8248-3322-0 (hard cover : alk. paper)—
ISBN 978-0-8248-3356-5 (pbk. : alk. paper)
   1. Raute (Nepalese people)—Social life and customs.
2. Raute (Nepalese people)—Ethnobiology.   3. Human
ecology—Nepal.   4. Hunting and gathering societies—
Nepal.   5. Nepal—Social life and customs.   I. Title.
   DS493.9.R38F67   2009
   305.895′4—dc22

                                              2008052138

University of Hawai'i Press books are printed on acid-free
paper and meet the guidelines for permanence and
durability of the Council on Library Resources.

Designed by the University of Hawai'i Press production staff
Printed by The Maple-Vail Book Manufacturing Group

In memory of Man Bahadur Raute, 1933–2008

ŋāna harha-o biya mītou, ŋā-shi 'nā-'ay.

Your spirit with us, we are happy together.

Contents

Acknowledgments ix

Conventions xi

1 Introduction 1

2 Encounters 13

3 Who Are the Rautes? 24

4 Forests as Home 57

5 Monkey's Thigh Is the Shaman's Meat 75

6 Let's Go to the Forest and Eat Fruit 100

7 Economy and Society: A Complex Mix 114

8 The Children of God 142

9 Cultural Resilience: The Big Picture 159

Appendix 171

Notes 187

Glossary 195

References 199

Index 211

Acknowledgments

I would like to thank a number of people, including my colleagues and students, who have provided hours of comments and advice that shaped the topics and ideas presented in this book. The Nepali language materials especially have been fine-tuned with the help of my research assistants Rekha Lohani, Gyaneshwor Karki, and Bisnu Pariyar. As a result of their advice and assistance this book is better written and researched. Without the comfort of my home-stay families, headed by Yogeshwor Karki and Harsha Narayan Dhaubhadel, research would have been impossible. Fieldwork and writing was supported by gratefully received grants from the Wenner-Gren Foundation For Anthropological Fieldwork, the National Endowment for the Humanities, and the U.S. Department of State Fulbright Program.

Finally, I thank my family. My parents, Ross and Ann Fortier, kindly lent me their lake cabin for me to write in; my grandmother Alvera Fortier listened patiently to chapter sketches; and my husband, Paul S. Goldstein, and daughter, Sarah, gave me the love, inspiration, and patience I needed to carry out months of field research and writing.

Conventions

Nepali terms are transliterated from the *devanāgāri* script conventionally in accordance with Indological tradition. Vowels include *a, e, i, o, u*
with a macron (ā) over long vowels except for word final vowels, which
are pronounced as a short vowel in Nepali. Vowels are pronounced as in
Spanish with the *a, e, i, o,* and *u* sounds as in the words *mama, hey, meet,
oh,* and *tune.* Dipthongs include *ai* and *au.* The Raute ethnic group's name
is thus pronounced *Rāu-tey.* Names of most places and ethnic groups are
written in common English form, such as "Raute" rather than "Rāuṭe" and
"Jajarkot" rather than "Jājārkoṭ." For exceptional orthographic conventions,
see van Driem 2001, and for common Nepali spelling conventions, see
Turner 1931.

Nepali consonants in this text include:

k	kh	g	gh	ŋ
c	ch	j	jh	
ṭ	ṭh	ḍ	ḍh	ṇ
t	th	d	dh	n
p	ph	b	bh	m
y	r	l	v	
ś		ṣ	s	
		h		

The western Nepali dialects are somewhat different from the standard
written Nepali format. When the dialect format is contextually relevant,
words are spelled phonetically with the written Nepali form in parentheses.

Raute is an unwritten Tibeto-Burman language. Transcriptions are
based on a broad phonetic form. Transliterations are based on conventions
established by Matisoff 2003 and Van Driem 2001. Vowels are short and
long (a, ā).

Consonants are written:

k	kh	g	ŋ	ʼ
c	ch	j	ṇ	
t	th	d	n	
p	ph	b	m	ɱ
ts	tsh	dz	w	
y	r	l		
s	ś	ṣ	h	

The /ʼ/ represents a glottal stop, as in the English word "oh-oh." The ŋ represents the sound in the English word "sing." Retroflexed sounds such as /ṭ/ are made by touching the tip of the tongue to the roof of the mouth while saying the sound. The sibilant /ś/ sounds like the English "**ship**." A few consonants (m, n, r, l) may be voiceless, sounding to English speakers as if the speaker is breathlessly saying the sound, as in the name Rhiannon. Voiceless consonants are represented by an 'h' next to the voiceless sonorant, such as the Raute words *mhu-ta* (tail) or *horh* (ancestral spirit).

1

Introduction

Ten thousand years ago, all the people in the world lived on wild plants and animal foods. They were hunters and gatherers who collected food rather than produced it. Even though the practice of hunting and gathering was universal, there were many cultural and technological variations in foraging that were determined by differences in the environment, wildlife resources, cultural technology, surrounding polities, and prevailing patterns of trade with others. From the perspective of the human species, this was a highly successful way to live.

Even with the rise of agriculture, hunting and gathering did not simply wither away. Only five hundred years ago, with the beginning of European incursions into other countries, people who relied upon food collecting rather than food production continued to occupy almost half of the world. Hunters and gatherers, also known as foragers, occupied all of Australia, most of North America, and large areas of South America, Africa, and Asia. But by the turn of the twentieth century, while dozens of foraging societies remained viable, most others had been encapsulated into surrounding dominant agrarian regimes. Post-foraging societies, many located in North America and Australia, were subject to intense pressures to assimilate, and many faced the imminent demise of their cultures and languages. They were pressed to settle down, learn the dominant language, attend majority culture schools, and intermarry into other families. These assimilative measures largely succeeded, yet memories of foraging lifestyles have persisted and have even formed the basis of indigenous people's political movements worldwide as they struggle to preserve their cultural autonomy.

As the twenty-first century or, from an environmental perspective, the eleventh millennium of the Holocene begins, we can see all contemporary foraging societies being assimilated into agrarian state systems on every continent of the world. Will such absorption by agrarian societies bring about the complete demise of the foraging way of life? In the mid-1960s, participants in the first conference about hunting-and-gathering societies (the "Man the Hunter" Conference) believed they were witnessing the last throes of sovereignty and survival among such groups as the Bushmen of southern Africa. Yet, in the most recent hunter-gatherer studies conferences, contemporary foragers have demonstrated their cultural resiliency. In this book, "cultural resiliency" refers to the ability to hold on to traditional beliefs and practices in the face of constant pressures to assimilate exerted by a dominant society.

Foraging societies are those that base their subsistence upon food collecting. Both historical and contemporary foragers have trade relations with food producers such as farmers or herders, but their societies are based upon hunting, gathering, and/or fishing. In the last generation, we find that foraging peoples may not have sovereignty but are nonetheless surviving the onslaughts of cultural hegemony by agrarian societies. Many contemporary foraging societies may be familiar to readers. Some of these include the Arctic-dwelling Inuits, Aleuts, and Samis; subarctic-dwelling Beaver,

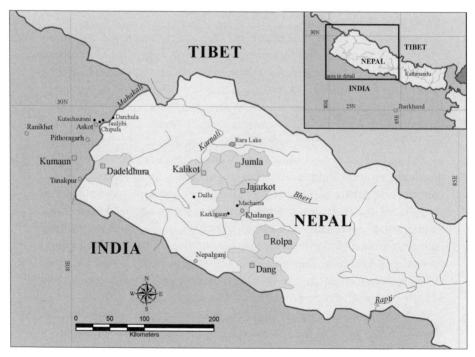

The Raute area showing locations mentioned in the text. Map by Alice E. Brewster.

Mayn Bahadur Kalyal has come to trade a large wooden bowl, known as a *koshi*, with the villagers of Khalanga, the capital of Jajarkot District, Nepal.

Dogrib, and Carrier Indians; desert-dwelling Bushmen (Ju/'hoansi), Mission Indians of California, and Australian aboriginals; temperate forest-dwelling Anishinabe (Chippewa), Coeur d'Alene, and Nez Perce; plains dwellers such as the Dakota, Kiowa, and Crow; and subtropical forest peoples of Asia such as the Batek, Andamanese, and Birhor.

This book is about one of these foraging societies that has managed to survive in the monsoon rainforests of western Nepal. The Rautes, who call themselves "kings of the forest," represent a society of hunter-gatherers who subsist on langur and macaque monkeys, wild yams, and rice traded from local farmers. They wander in forests where monkeys can be found, and thus they migrate from river valleys of a thousand-foot-high altitude up to the middle Himalayan ridges reaching nine thousand feet, wherever they can successfully hunt and gather. To supplement hunting their "little brothers," as they refer to monkeys, the Rautes gather over ninety edible plants from the Himalayan forests that are untrammeled by roads or airstrips. To maintain this lifestyle, Rautes live in temporary camps that are hidden away from the villagers in the most remote forest glades. In the wet monsoon summers they camp at the highest altitudes, while during the dryer, cooler winters they migrate to the lower subtropical forest zones. Like many foraging societies, Rautes situate themselves in the optimum ecological niche in order to take advantage of the most natural resources.

Like other contemporary foragers worldwide, Rautes face the very real problems of deforestation, population encroachment by majority societies, language domination, and the political hegemony of the surrounding Nepalese society. Rather than dwelling upon these social problems, however, this book focuses upon the foragers' strategies of cultural resilience. As Nepali villagers continue to denounce Rautes as fearsome *ban mānche* (forest men), how have the remaining Raute communities survived amidst immense pressures to settle them in villages? In this book, I consider the challenges involved in maintaining cultural resilience from the nomadic Rautes' point of view and try to illuminate the choices that promote that resiliency. These questions require us to examine in detail the beliefs and practices of people who collect food rather than produce it through agriculture or pastoralism.

The population of Rautes and their cultural and linguistic relatives who live in the Nepal/India border region is estimated to be about 700 Rautes, 2,500 Rajis, and 2–3,000 Banrajis. The name "Raute" derives from a Nepali word, *rāut*, meaning a person who commands respect, such as a man known for his bravery or a member of nobility. The name "Raut" has been used by high-caste families to infer that they are "princely" or that their ancestors were the sons of princes. Similarly, the name "Raji" means "little king," and Rajis emphasize that they should be treated fairly by caste Hindus because they bear this name. The name "Banraji" means "little kings of the forest," and it too has a story associated with it. Regardless of their various favored ethnic names, all of the Rautes, Rajis, and Banrajis share close linguistic and cultural features. They all speak dialects of the Raute language that have 70–90 percent intelligibility among speakers;[1] they are all historically nomadic hunter-gatherers; and they all share other cultural features, such as the same kinship systems. The subject of this book is the easternmost nomadic community, a roving population of about 150 Rautes who travel throughout western Nepal. They live in one band that occasionally splinters into separate hunting groups as they migrate in search of monkeys to hunt. This group is one of the last that has not been forcibly settled by government officials, and its members take pride in their nomadic existence.

Although the book focuses upon the nomadic Rautes, occasionally I compare them with their Raji and Banraji neighbors. Historically, the Banrajis also were forest-dwelling monkey hunters, but they have been forcibly settled by the Indian government. Today they no longer hunt monkeys, but continue to hunt porcupines, bats, and deer. Despite being settled, the Banrajis display a resolute independence and are unwilling to assimilate into the surrounding lifestyle of local Hindu farmers. The lives of the various foraging communities are similar, yet they also differ. Some of these differences stem from the political impacts of the dominant society. The governments of Nepal and India have inherited diverse colonial histories; they pursue different forest policies, and the contingencies of such varied histories deeply affect contemporary hunter-gatherers. Nepal, for its part, has imposed little colonial pressure upon the nomadic Rautes. The Rajis and Banrajis living in far-western Nepal, however, have experienced more pressure to settle, even receiving land parcels from the government of Nepal. These communities have subsequently lost their lands to elite farmers, and many of their families now survive through tenant farming combined with part-time foraging. The Banrajis living on the Indian side of the border have faced the most forcible government-led settlement drives. Many of their land allotments are leases of forestland rather than arable farmland. Thus the Banrajis, too, inhabit a netherworld between farming and foraging, with highly depleted forest resources and few prospects for successful adoption of farming.

Unlike the Raji and Banraji, the nomadic Rautes who are the subject of this book have managed to avoid forcible assimilation. They have not settled in villages, have not assimilated many Hindu ideas, and continue their full-time nomadic journeys throughout western Nepal, hunting langur and macaque monkeys. This book seeks to understand the resilience of these Rautes and their perception of themselves as a unique society. They are unique not only because of their foraging lifestyle but because they valorize that lifestyle as the "children of God," a deity who wishes Rautes to be nomadic monkey hunters. Embodied in the sun, their solar deity holds the ultimate responsibility for life. Pointing to the sun, one Raute said: "Berh is our God and you see him as the sun. The stars are his temple. Stones have broken, earth has fallen apart, trees have fallen down, but the sun is always like this." In our search to understand the cultural autonomy and resilience of the Rautes, we shall consider how their belief systems form a foundation for their nomadic hunting existence.

Necessarily, Rautes must migrate through a secular world, with farmers' political intrigues and fights over land, timber, and other resources swirling all around them. Having no word in their own language for "farmer," Rautes refer to the surrounding sedentary Nepali farmers as *maŋa*, a term derived from the ancient Tibetan word *mang*, meaning an elder brother, an elite, a ruler, an official (Benedict 1972, 189; Matisoff 2003, 601). *Maŋa* captures the essence of how Rautes see farmers in relation to themselves. With the knowledge that *maŋa* wield an enormous amount of political power over them, Rautes defer to them and ask them for permission to camp in forests controlled by villagers. While Rautes value their foraging lifestyle, they do so knowing that they are but one strand in a larger web of nature and society that is the lower Himalayas.

Finding Importance in Hunter-Gatherer Lives

For many of us who live in a fast-paced postindustrial world, the lives of a few hundred hunter-gatherers might seem irrelevant, simply a cultural curiosity to be noted in passing. What could be important about foragers? What meaning could they have for us living in an era of globalization? For some, there may be nothing compelling about an endangered culture that is teetering on the brink of extinction. Ironically, the fact that animal species such as pandas, leopards, and tigers, as well as many plant species, are endangered is of great concern to most people. The links between species in a system of biodiversity is something many of us readily can grasp. But because human symbiotic relationships are so complex and delicately intertwined, most people have trouble appreciating the importance of human diversity and the role played by food collectors in the web of biodiversity. Raute lives afford us a good example of the meshing of society and nature, for they directly rely on many natural resources, including water, trees, monkeys, forest edibles, and even goods obtained from villagers such as iron, cloth, and grain. In symbiotic fashion, villagers appreciate having monkeys hunted out of their fields, as they are crop predators and can eat a grain harvest down to nearly nothing. Yet farmers also believe that the langur monkey is an incarnation of the Hindu deity Hanuman, and thus loathe hunting monkeys themselves. As a result, when Rautes hunt monkeys, farmers are relieved of this need. Farmers and Rautes are thus linked in a symbiotic web of resource exchange. In other words, the relationship of Raute-monkey-villager is part of a system of biocultural diversity, in that within it intrinsic ties exist between human and environmental diversity. When these factors change, for example when monkeys have been mostly hunted out of a given forest, Rautes move their camps to another forest locale. The nomadic monkey hunters work in concert with changing environmental conditions. Hunter-gatherer lives such as that of the Rautes thus can provide us with important insights into the biocultural diversity that exists between society and nature in the Himalayas. Unfortunately, just at the very moment in history when we have truly begun to value biocultural diversity on this planet, we are losing it. At the exact time when people in complex societies such as our own desperately need to understand how to promote cultural diversity, few technologically simple societies like that of the Rautes remain to teach us about the nuances of particular environments.

In broad perspective, it can help us to hold up the behaviors of hunter-gatherers as a kind of mirror reflection of our own social lives. For example, hunter-gatherer sociality has formed the foundation of studies of human sharing (Blurton-Jones 1984; Hawkes 1987; Hill et al. 1987). Sharing of meat, material goods, and prestige involves intricate rules of social exchange that can be best studied in small-scale societies. Further, hunter-gatherer studies have contributed to ecological studies of diet choices (Charnov 1976; Hawkes et al. 1982; Winterhalder and Smith 1981). When we want to know if humans need certain kinds of diets rich in protein, carbohydrates, or fat, we can study diet among foragers, as human diets historically were based on foraging rather than farming. Studies of contemporary hunter-gatherers have even contributed to understanding human violence (Kent 1989; Knauft 1990). Study of small-scale societies can help to untangle the complicated conditions that lead to violence, such as sedentism, overcrowding, resource distribution problems, and so on. From such studies, it is clear that contemporary hunter-gatherers can help us understand our more complex selves in addition to simply documenting the range of human and cultural diversity.

Writing about Raute Lives

This research began with an innocent enough suggestion made by a Nepali development worker in western Nepal. In 1986, I was doing field research among farmers in Jajarkot District, a rural setting that has now become an area of Maoist political upheaval. In Jajarkot, farmers talked about their recent encounters with Rautes, who had traversed the district in 1985. As I listened, a seed was planted that later grew into a desire to study the people who lived in the forests and how they managed to maintain their unique lifestyle. For the next ten years I continued to do research on Nepalese farming systems, returned to Jajarkot several times, and wrote about agricultural labor relations as the subject of my Ph.D. dissertation. When that project was completed, I felt ready to explore a new dimension of sociality, one located in the same place but based on hunting and gathering rather than on farming systems.

In 1997 I returned to Jajarkot District, this time to study forager economic systems rather than farming systems. What I found among the band of 140 Rautes was not simply an egalitarian foraging people, but an egalitarian foraging people that was embedded within a larger economic system based on Hindu codes of hierarchy. It became clear to me that, although many researchers had focused on foragers, they had often missed seeing how the broader social and political environment shapes forager sociality. Since I was knowledgeable about the world of Hindu farmers, I decided to use that knowledge to situate Rautes within this broader social environment. In the process of doing so, I found that Raute lives are part of a larger web of Himalayan social life that is similar to the lives of other indigenous peoples and hunter-gatherers worldwide but is also contingent upon Himalayan historical events.

Raute material culture was and is technologically simple, based on the multifunctional use of nets, axes, and a small variety of wooden implements. Yet Raute lives are forged within a historically and geographically contingent Asian context that has made their form of foraging unique. In fact, their social life is based upon a highly complex and delicate balance maintained within the overall social and physical environment.

Unlike most foragers, Rautes have also devised strategies of cultural resilience to help them maintain their autonomy. According to an anthropological definition, "resilience" refers to the ability of a system or society to undergo change while still maintaining its basic elements or relationships. I became intrigued by the ways in which Rautes ingeniously borrowed and transformed elements from the larger society, incorporating them in a unique "Raute" fashion in order to preserve a way of life that was stamped out in most other parts of the world a century ago. While Rautes at first may appear to be "primitive," much to the contrary their choices are guided by contemporary insights into the larger surrounding complex society. Rautes represent a thread of simplicity woven into the larger social fabric of Nepalese society. Like cultural groups such as the Romany Gypsies in Europe, Rautes choose to live a highly communal and nomadic lifestyle that rejects the accoutrements of a settled agrarian one. Unlike that of the Romany Gypsies, however, the Raute way of life revolves around hunting monkeys and gathering wild yams from the forest. Rautes can thus be viewed in comparative perspective with other nomadic societies, but the essense of their sociality is something wonderfully unique.

Each of the following chapters represents an aspect of Raute sociality that I found particularly important. As I struggled to learn and appreciate what it means to live as a Raute forager, I found several recurring themes. These include a stress on the forest as home and on monkey hunting and yam foraging as fundamental ways of getting food, and a dualistic viewpoint of self versus others, family versus strangers, forest versus village. In Chapter 2 I write in a narrative fashion about some of these themes in order to introduce readers to the Rautes and to local farmers in Jajarkot District. While the surrounding Hindu farmers play a minor role throughout the book, they are not homogeneous characters, and Rautes meet many different kinds of Nepali people during their sojourns. I was impressed by the range of farmers' opinions about these foragers, and each chapter presents the mixed feelings they have about the Rautes.

In Chapter 3, I explore Raute identity in the light of Nepalese history and politics. Rautes represent a radical "other" amidst millions of Hindu farmers. For Rautes even to assert that they are a unique ethnic group is sometimes a dangerous political gesture. Using Goffmanesque impression management, they claim that they are just like farmers, except that they live in forests rather than in villages. Using this political strategy of claiming to be similar yet different enables Rautes to protect themselves from the daily urgings toward assimilation disguised as "social upliftment" that are proffered by local farmers.

In Chapter 4, I ask a simple question, "Where do Rautes live?" Considering the fact that Rautes are nomads, the answer is complex, for they live everywhere and nowhere. It turns out that not only is the question of place difficult, but the question of Raute ideas of natural and cultural places is also complex, because they conceive of forests as cultural places. For them, forests are a sacred home, while places outside of forests, such as villages, represent the uncivilized wilderness. It is this inversion of nature and culture that is the most difficult for farmers to understand and accept. They are generally upset that Rautes have no interest in settling down in villages to raise livestock or farm.

Chapters 5 and 6 delve into hunting and gathering as the basis of the Raute economy. In Chapter 5, I describe how Rautes hunt "little brother" monkey and how God, who demands that they hunt monkey, blesses this symbolic cannibalism. As Rautes note, "The monkey's thigh is our shaman's meat," adding that their shamans call the monkeys into their nets and, with the blessings of God, dispatch and consume them as their main source of protein. Chapter 6 explores the other half of Raute economic well-being, which is devoted to collecting wild yams, fruits, and greens in the forests: as Rautes are fond of singing, "Let's go to the forest and eat wild fruits!" Forest foraging represents an important aspect of subsistence, and the more wild yams, fruits, and greens the Rautes can gather, the less they have to rely on bartering with villagers for grain.

Rautes see hunting as the very heart of their lifestyle, yet they also acknowledge that trade with farmers is essential. Chapter 7 explores Raute subsistence as based upon two spheres of exchange—one symmetrical, the other asymmetrical. Among each other, Rautes share food, clothing, tools, and labor, and this forms the basis of their egalitarian society. But in dealing with farmers, Rautes have developed the wily ways of the stranger/ trader and employ patronage, begging, the "hard sell," pilfering, and fictive kinship as strategies to obtain the maximum amounts of grain and goods. In particular, I was fascinated by the ways in which these asymmetrical exchange strategies indirectly supported their sphere of symmetrical exchange among each other.

Chapter 7 also explores how Rautes manufacture and exchange items for trade. All contemporary hunter-gatherers need to trade for items they cannot produce themselves. Rautes trade wooden bowls for grain, iron, and cloth. Such work takes up roughly one-third of some mens' work time. To better determine the flows of work time and value, I converted food received during trading into calories and labor time. Using this "energy input-output" analysis, I estimated the amount of food calories Rautes need in order to get a better picture of how they survive. For example, their band of about 150 people must consume roughly 300,000 calories per day. For people who have no storage facilities and produce no daily surpluses, this means that Rautes must successfully forage, hunt, and trade nearly every day in order to feed everyone. Is this difficult? The anthropologist Marshall Sahlins described hunter-gatherers as the "original affluent society," meaning that they had more leisure time than farmers. Rautes may not live in such an "affluent" leisured condition, but nevertheless they do claim that "wild yams are still easy to dig" and they are loath to take up farming. Chapters 5, 6, and 7, then, represent the fundamental aspects of Raute life.

Chapter 8 turns to the ideological aspects of the cultural resilience of the Rautes, which are just as important to maintaining their lifestyle. Their religious cosmology is radically different from that of high-caste Hindus. Rautes worship the sun and moon, as well as spirits of animals and ancestors,

Four Raute elders sit and chat *(left to right)*, Mayn, Jasbir, Man Bahadur, and Karna Bahadur, during a dance performance in Karkigaun, Jajarkot District, Nepal. Although Man Bahadur was the leader who negotiated with outsiders, Jasbir was the oldest and most respected Raute leader in 1997.

in what can be described as a sacred and sentient ecology. Using a handful of elder men and women to intercede with God, Rautes follow the lead of their shamans, who have mastered the arts of trance, shaking, and reaching out to communicate with deities and spirits. Yet Rautes resist telling Hindu farmers about their beliefs and practices; instead, Rautes refashion Hindu stories in order to entertain—and deceive—inquiring villagers.

In conclusion, I review broader issues that have been important to hunter-gatherer studies and to anthropology in general. Among these, I consider why investigation of biocultural diversity is so important, and why the study of contemporary foragers has moved away from an evolutionary focus on the ideal hunter-gatherer to a renewed interest in hunter-gatherer diversity.

In keeping with the wishes of the Raute people, this book is intended solely to inform, not for other purposes such as to "aid the development" of

Rautes. Rautes abhor the programs devised by international development agencies; they wish to choose their own destiny. Raute elder Man Bahadur understood that ethnographic writing about his people might possibly encourage others to try to acculturate the Rautes. Nevertheless, he told me, "Go and teach your students in America about us." But he also cautioned me that there are many people who do not understand the Raute lifestyle, and such people pressure Rautes to settle down and take up farming. If there is one development strategy I advocate, it is to leave the Rautes alone. After reading this book, it is my hope that people will relinquish any idea of acculturating Rautes to an agrarian way of life. Rautes do not want to be the object of development, and they have no wish to become farmers. Their cultural resilience consists of continuing to live in forest camps, not in villages. Rautes stress that they wish to live in the same way their ancestors lived.

2

Encounters

"We hunt monkey. Can you live with that?"
—Man Bahadur, during a confrontation with a village leader

In the middle of a rural district town in Nepal, a Hindu servant boy ran up to me. Breathless, he blurted out, "The Raute is there, hurry up!" I ran back to my host family's house and found a Raute elder, named Mayn Bahadur, sitting in a chair. He had sparkling eyes and a noticeable twitch running along his cheek. He smiled at me from across the courtyard and beckoned me forward. I told him about my desire to study with the Raute, and we talked about the need to preserve their way of life.

Most Americans know Nepal as a country of the towering Himalayas. In fact, it extends from Mount Everest all the way down to the plains of the Ganges River basin, encompassing an incredibly diverse range of habitats and animals. Nepal is home to more than one hundred different ethnic groups who speak languages other than Nepali, including the most unusual people in their midst, the last surviving hunter-gatherers of the Himalayas. With the ever-encroaching onset of modernization, however, this culture is threatened with assimilation into Nepal's largely Hindu society.

In Jajarkot, one of western Nepal's most isolated districts and where my research with Rautes and Nepalese farmers took place, over a hundred thousand people scratch a living from the steep green Himalayan foothills. The farmers are Hindu and their mother tongue Nepali, a language closely related to Hindi. The residents of Jajarkot live far from the capital, Kathmandu, and even with its large population, the district lacks roads, electricity, an airstrip, and most other modern conveniences. Most people raise just enough grain and dairy products to feed their own families. Occasionally, when villagers travel to India for the winter to work as migrants, they will bring something to sell, such as bamboo baskets, woolen blankets, butter, honey, forest medicinals, or morel mushrooms. To survive the uncertainties of subsistence farming, neighbors help each other by lending plow animals, money, and daily labor.

Years before, these local farmers had first told me of an enigmatic forest people who appeared in Jajarkot about once every twelve years. In the midst of Hindu Nepal, where monkeys are considered as sacred as cows, these nomads known as Rautes say that God gives them monkeys to hunt. They catch and kill rhesus and langur monkeys, using axes and nets that they spread out between the trees. Yet at the same time Rautes claim that monkeys are their little brothers. In fact, Rautes feel that they are dependent on the forest for almost all of their needs, and they constantly move into new forests to hunt monkeys. Many farmers have tried to persuade the Raute to settle down in villages "like civilized Nepalese" rather than live in the forest "like animals," but they refuse. They claim that they do not have the habit of staying in one place, do not know how to farm or herd animals, and will never send their children to school. One farmer told me that he had given the Rautes two pregnant goats and explained how to manage them. "The next time I saw them," he said, "they claimed that the goats had died. What a waste." "Listen," he added, "they may not know how to farm, but they're part of our Nepali culture. They're like our country's inner organs, they are the original people here. Truly, they represent a national treasure. And they may have knowledge about the forest. We can learn from them. They can learn from us."

Finally, here in the district bazaar, I had encountered the Raute elder named Mayn. Calling himself the "King of the Forest," he told me that "without the forest, there is no life." As if his wise saying deserved a reward, Mayn then asked me for new shoes, showing me the hole worn in the sole of his canvas shoe. Later, I would learn that asking for my help was his way of finding out if I would commit myself to being his patron while he moved through this part of the country. In Nepal, a patron is someone wealthy and influential who helps aspiring friends accomplish their goals. Like the Hindu farmers, the Rautes, too, solicit the wealthy men of each village, hoping to gain access to community forest resources. Mayn wanted to solicit my friendship, money, and protection. At the time, I only knew that this was my only opportunity to get to know this elusive Raute man. I offered to buy him a new pair of shoes, and we walked down to the main bazaar. They cost 165 Nepali rupees, equal to U.S.$2.75. Mayn thought for a minute, then explained, "My wife doesn't need shoes, women don't need to wear villager things. But my son should have a pair too."

I'd been warned by farmers about the Rautes' habit of demanding i
in exchange for their carved wooden wares or even their conversation.
wanted to make each exchange count, and so far I hadn't learned much of
anything about the Rautes. Stalling, I sent Mayn to fetch his son so we could
measure his shoe size. When they returned, however, a crowd of curious
villagers had gathered, chatting eagerly while Mayn listened and nodded.
Wishing they would let Mayn talk more, I watched with fascination the
encounter of the Nepali villagers and the Raute hunter-gatherer.

Shortly after I met Mayn, I was summoned by other Rautes who had
come into the bazaar. As the afternoon monsoon rains began to fall, I met
them at the local agriculture office. Several Raute women had blistered and
cut their toes while walking barefoot down the steep rocky trails and they
asked me to bandage their feet. Mayn knew that I should lance the blisters
first, so he gave me the large safety pin that he wore on his shirt like a badge.
Rather than being concerned about the antibiotic cream and their wounds,
the Raute women looked more excited about wearing bright white strips
of cloth, and Mayn even had me bandage his arthritic knee. As I stooped
to clean and bandage their feet, I wondered, "Am I playing the role of researcher, nurse, patron, or servant?"

As I applied bandages, the Rautes talked quietly among themselves. Like
water bubbling down a stream, a Raute woman named Hira murmured
to her relatives. Their strange language sounded musical and exotic, but
since the Raute language has not been studied by any Nepalese or foreign
researcher, no one but the Rautes can understand the language they call
khāmci (meaning "our talk"). I felt somewhat overwhelmed by the thought
of trying to understand the language and a people so secretive about themselves. As I would learn, Rautes have good reasons for being secretive, because most people in Nepal would have them assimilate into the dominant
culture. After four months, and after I had developed a relationship with
them based on the trust that I would not try to change them, I learned
much of their culture and language.

When everyone's feet were cleaned and dressed, one of the agriculture
office workers, a resourceful woman named Nandakali, called the Rautes
for lunch. She offered them some late-morning lentils and rice dāl-bhāt,
asking them to come inside and eat. Yet they refused. Unwilling to enter a
stranger's house, they were also reluctant to eat outside like low-caste un-
touchables. "Ke garne," as Nepalis say: "What to do?" Nandakali came out
to the porch and set huge plates of cooked lentils and boiled rice nearby.
From across the courtyard, another Nepali woman spitefully commented
to me, "They'll eat until the food fills them to their throats." The Raute

ie verandah began to eat the rice but without lentils.
l the *dāl-bhāt* and instead share some roasted cereal. I
people ate with their left hand, apparently unaware that
aboo among Nepalis. Questioned by the Nepalis about
rences, the Raute defended themselves, saying, "We're the
pt that we live in the forest while you live in villages." But
ites like to pretend that they're the same as the villagers,
the differences are obvious even to an outsider like myself. Before these differences could cause any difficulties, however, it was time for the Rautes to break camp and move on.

Struggles between Contrary Cultures

Each time Raute hunter-gatherers and Hindu villagers meet, their encounters reflect an ideological struggle for legitimacy. What is the right way to live? What is the right way to learn, love, eat, or die? The Raute ways of celebrating life and death differ fundamentally from those of the Hindu farmers. Rautes, for example, bury their dead in the forest, while Hindus cremate the deceased. Further, Rautes have a completely egalitarian society, living in small mobile bands without accumulating property. In contrast, Nepali villagers value extended families that live in large villages. Villagers live by the rules of Hindu caste hierarchy, in which Brahmans represent the most "pure" end of the social scale and leather workers the most impure, "untouchable" end. In nearly every way, the foraging lifestyle and habits of the Rautes contradict Nepali rules of social legitimacy. For example, farmers say that people are supposed to go to school nowadays. Why don't the Rautes send their children to school? People are supposed to live in a village. Why do the Rautes live in the forest, "like animals"? People are supposed to raise corn, wheat, rice, barley, and millet. It is unfathomable to villagers why the nomadic Rautes cannot accept farming with its "stable" sedentary lifestyle. Underlying these differences lies a notion held by farmers of what constitutes a socially acceptable neighbor: a person who has a high social caste, owns land, raises crops and animals, and practices the dharma of Hinduism.

As they migrate past the villages that dot the middle hills of Nepal, the Rautes try to accommodate the expectations of the farmers; for example, they claim to be Hindu yet know little of the intricacies of Hinduism. They also claim to be part of the social caste of nobility known as the Thakuri caste. Yet the Rautes obviously are not landed nobility. Furthermore, they don't speak Nepali as their mother tongue. And they don't even eat *dāl-bhāt*, the rice and lentil dish that is the quintessential food of Nepal. Instead, Rautes prefer to drink a mildly alcoholic grain beer (*dzyā'*) and snack on delicious handfuls of toasted wheat and wild seeds of plants such as amaranth, butternut (*Bassia butyracea*), and orchid tree (*Bauhinia purpurea*). Their toasted and ground grain and seed snacks, known as *tātā*, are similar to the tasty barley Tibetan *tsampa*. Raute women and men consume handfuls of toasted cereal while foraging in the forest during the day and drink beer each time they return to camp, sometimes mixing the beer into their ground *tātā*. But during their nomadic odyssey throughout western Nepal, Rautes hide their food and other cultural differences from local Hindu farmers. Before I worked with the Rautes, there had been only one other foreigner who published field research about them (Reinhard 1974). Even he was thrown out of their camp under threat of death after merely a few weeks of research. Nepali scholars have had the same experiences, and I felt terribly uncertain about whether Rautes would treat me any differently.

I knew it would involve difficult research, but nevertheless I felt compelled to do this field project for several reasons. I felt that Raute cultural traditions, and their very lives, did not deserve to be lost to encroaching assimilation. Their place in the landscape of Nepalese society is an important piece of the story of the ebb and flow of human migrations throughout this awesome Himalayan range. I wanted to know why these people lived in the forest and called it their home, why they were able to live as simple egalitarian hunters and gatherers when everyone else around them had embraced the harsh realities of farming and herding; and I hoped that their lives might teach those of us who live in complex, commercial, and often inhumane conditions about alternative ways of living. I don't hold out the false hope that we who live in postindustrial societies might evolve into simple egalitarian foragers, but rather that we can compare our strategies for living with those of people like the Rautes. Though I was responding to the simple urge to comprehend the range of human culture, I also wished to hold up the lives of the Rautes as a mirror in which to reflect upon my own society.

Climbing to the Rautes' Camp

The day after meeting Mayn, I hiked out of the district bazaar, with its government offices and several hundred households, and traveled to the Raute camp in the ridge-top forests. During the four months that I conducted field research with the Rautes, they moved their camps ten times as they camped in forests near three distinct village locations. The first was Khalanga, the district capital. With about two thousand residents, thirty-five government offices, five tea stalls, and a dozen shops, Khalanga was the only large town in the district. Rautes next migrated to forests near a village called Machaina, a small hilltop rest stop of only three houses. And by the end of the fall season, Rautes camped near Karkigaun, a large village of about a hundred houses, and were on their way farther west toward the next forest camp on their traditional route.

When I first met the nomadic Rautes, they had recently moved camp from forests north of the district bazaar to an area one day's walk west of there. This area the Rautes referred to in Nepali as Salli Pakha, meaning "pine fields," while the farmers called it Tarepatal, meaning "the distant leafy forest." As I began the day-long hike along a steep footpath toward the Rautes' new camp area, I spotted several types of edible greens and a local variety of raspberry. This forest was rumored to have a dense monkey population and plentiful fruits available for forage. In addition to hunting for monkeys and yams, a handful of Rautes would barter in nearby towns, where they would trade their wooden bowls for grain, tobacco, and cloth.

Machaina village was only about four miles away from the district capital, but to walk there, one had to climb two mountain ridges. From the capital at 3,000 feet, I scaled a 6,000-foot mountain ridge, then scrambled back to about 4,000 feet, and then climbed up again to a 7,500-foot mountain ridge. For nine hours, I slowly climbed the trail, chatting with my research assistant, cook, and porters. My assistant, a young woman named Rekha, was from Kathmandu and found the trail challenging yet exciting. My cook, named Krishna, and I had climbed this trail several times before. Krishna lived near Machaina and was expert at coaxing farmers into selling us chickens, garlic, potatoes, and other fresh produce. From the district bazaar I hired four young men, boys really, who were eager to earn wages for portering my equipment and five hundred pounds of precious rice. The Rautes had told me that rice was their favorite item of exchange. Krishna, Rekha, and I thus ate the rice, but more important, we used it for exchange and donations to the Rautes for their time working with me. This was not a form of bribery, but honest pay for honest work. The Raute camp needed about 300,000 calories per day in order to feed everyone, so I couldn't expect Rautes to spend their time with me rather than hunting and doing other productive work.

Local villagers could make the climb to Machaina in seven hours, and even children regularly carried twenty-five pounds of goods as they traveled. We, however, walked slowly and stopped to rest at the home of a

Nepali woman named Laksmi, who brought us cool buffalo-milk yogurt and cucumbers seasoned with salt and chili pepper. As we talked about the local news, Laksmi reminisced about when she had met the Rautes, over fifty years ago. "They came through here but wouldn't talk with anyone. I don't think they knew Nepali then. They just showed up at our courtyard one night and left a wooden bowl there, along with a piece of turban cloth. We put some grain in the bowl and some yams from our garden into the cloth. In the morning the Rautes came and wrapped everything in the cloth and left. I'll go get the bowl, we still have it."

Laksmi shuffled into the house and came back with a blackened old bowl the size of a big pumpkin. "We used this bowl to sell butter in the city of Nepalganj. With some red mud plastered on the lid to hold it tightly closed, this bowl filled with butter weighs exactly twenty pounds."

"Why isn't there even a crack in it after all these years?" I wondered. "This is made out of wood, isn't it?" "Of course," she answered. "Its supposedly made from a magnolia tree. But you can't tell what wood anymore after all these years. The butter has soaked into the wood." Laksmi rapped with her knuckles on the bowl. "See how it sounds like metal? The oil made the wood as hard as iron. This bowl was made well. If the Rautes want to give me another bowl, a good one, I'll give them some wheat for it."

"Tell me," I asked, "What have you heard about the Rautes?"

Laksmi thought for a moment. "My neighbor Kali Bahadur told me that a wealthy farmer met the Rautes recently. He wanted them to have a better life. He offered them his best planting seed on the condition that they would settle down and become farmers."

"What did the Rautes say?"

"They accepted. So the Thakuri farmer gave them one five-pound bag of corn, one bag of wheat, and one of millet too. But the Rautes didn't sow that very good seed. Instead they roasted it and then ate it! The grain was so good for planting, what a shame!"

"Well," I asked, "where were they supposed to plant the seed? They don't have any fields."

"Kali Bahadur said that people near the next mountain ridge offered to give them some land, I think," she said, shaking her head.

As we walked on, I reflected upon villager notions of merit and charity, for every Hindu and Buddhist farmer knows that by giving help to those less fortunate, one acquires religious merit. Laksmi's generosity is typical among Hindu farmers. Almost all Nepali farm families feel comfortable tithing part of their meager harvest to artisans and wandering ascetics (and landless researchers). Some Nepali villagers view the Rautes as another such itinerant caste that needs enfolding into a stable, settled community rather than as people who rationally choose a nomadic lifestyle. While wandering is frowned upon by villagers, traveling is acceptable. Many village men and women migrate to India seasonally, carrying forest medicinals there. Most medicinals, such as *bhulte* (*Nardostachys jatamansi*), an ayurvedic source product, will be sold in Indian markets. But wandering is different; it violates a deep sense of rootedness in villagers. This sensibility of place is thus violated by the nomadic perambulation of Raute monkey hunters.

Among the Rautes

Late in the day, I finally arrived in Machaina village and negotiated to rent a room above the local tea stall. This would be our house and research base since I didn't want to offend Rautes by camping next to them, a problem encountered by previous researchers. Once our group unpacked, we washed at the water tap and visited with our new neighbors. As evening fell, the monsoon mists crept across the valley below. Just then, I spotted the Raute woman Hira walking up the trail followed by her husband, Man Bahadur ("Man" rhymes with "run.") With a huge bamboo basket strapped to her head, Hira walked slowly. Man Bahadur had a smaller basket strapped to his back and led a goat that he later referred to as "the goat as big as a water buffalo." I noticed that they were carrying fifty pound loads of *dābre* (*Leptadenia reticulata*), a spinach-like green found only in the monsoon season. Obviously, the *dābre* leaf was meant for the whole Raute community to eat.

Man Bahadur saw me on the balcony of my room, and I climbed down to talk with him. He asked the tea merchant to bring us two shots of distilled rice drink and a couple of cigarettes. For Hira, I called for a small basket of apricots. Already I knew I had to provide the food and drink required of me in my new role as patron. Man Bahadur wanted to talk about trading their hand-carved wooden bowls and boxes, which are called *koshi*. My assistant Rekha wrote in her notebook that "We met with Mr. and Mrs. Man Bahadur (she is named Hira) and Mrs. Man Bahadur's sister's daughter named Sahra. I've noticed that the Raute women hardly speak. I think they hardly opened their mouths in front of their husbands but they do speak something when they are alone. But still the young Raute woman Sahra didn't say anything. When we asked her something then she just looked at us! It could be because of language problems but they seem to understand what we are talking about. Jana bought one *koshi* wooden bowl from Man Bahadur's wife and one breadboard from Sahra. Raute love to exchange their products for grain, boxes for goat, and breadboards for cloth. Sahra exchanged her breadboard with Jana for two pieces of cloth."

The following morning, we walked into Tarepatal forest to visit the Raute camp. Going down the path, after about twenty minutes I noticed that various trees—Himalayan oaks, rhododendrons, cedars, pines, and magnolia—had been cut down. Some of these trees still stood upright, but large bowl-size chunks had been hollowed out from their cores. The wood was used to make wooden bowls as well as numerous types of camp equipment. After a few more minutes of walking, we arrived at a clearing with about forty huts scattered along a small ridge. Thousands of feet below, a river rushed on its way toward the Gangetic plain of India.

Man Bahadur greeted me at the edge of camp with a warning that the other Rautes do not like visitors in camp. "But you have a place in my heart," Man Bahadur said, "so you can visit my camp." I looked at the people gathered around and saw two women talking to each other and sharing a meal out of a bowl. Another woman came toward me and asked about medicine for her relative. An old woman nearby had what people in Nepal called *ḍāḍ*; it looked like a bad case of eczema with the skin clearly being eaten away (this woman died a few weeks later). Others, however, were in good physical health and noticeably fatter than many Nepali farmers. While many Rautes came and looked us over, others simply went about their business; a man carved a wooden bowl, a girl munched on a *chapāti* bread, a woman waved her hands in the air and chatted with a neighbor.

Sitting inside Man Bahadur's hut, I was impressed by the orderliness and cleanliness of the interior. His family's cooking utensils were stacked like washed dishes in one corner. Unlike villagers' kitchenware, here everything was carved out of *mālu* (*Bauhinia* spp.), a dark wood that is called 'mountain ebony' in English. I saw ladles, drinking bowls, plates, eating bowls, cutting boards, and a bread-making board, all made of wood. The only stone object I saw was the Tibetan-style stone pestle and rectangular mortar made of *kurda*, an amorphous gray slate. Other stones were used opportunistically. A stone lying next to a hut would be appropriated for a place to sit, a place to dry the wash, a place for children to play. A hand broom made of branches lay in a shallow ditch that had been carved around the edges of the hut. A few shreds of leftover greens lay waiting to be washed down the ditch by the afternoon rains.

I knew that most people in Nepal think that living in camps in the forest is dangerous, or at least dirty and uncomfortable. Yet comparing this camp with photos of Raute camps in 1968, when researcher Johan Reinhard visited the Rautes, it seemed that the style of the huts had changed very little in thirty years. The huts housing this group of Raute were all similar, roughly eight or ten feet wide by ten or twelve feet long. Man Bahadur's hut, like the others, was roofed with *mālu* leaves woven into a tarp and draped on top of a wooden pole frame. Other huts were covered with alder branches. Adding a bit of color, worn-out cotton shawls were draped on top of some huts. Looking at photos from researcher Johan Reinhard, I did notice a few differences in hut construction. Reinhard had worked with Rautes in Surkhet, a region several days south of where I was. Here, the huts were covered with pine boughs.

For the Raute, there are certainly uncomfortable moments, such as when the monsoon rains seep through the roofs, leaches bite the children, or tigers wander near the camp. But the forest represents something very different to them than it does to villagers. As Man Bahadur said, the forest is "where God's children live." It is home, just as a village is home to sedentary Nepali farmers. During this first visit to the Raute camp, I asked one of the men if he ever wanted to live in a village, and he replied: "My heart is in living here in the forest. Besides, since the time of our ancestors, it has been just like this. The forest is fine. The wild yams are still easy to find and dig."

As with hunter-gatherers in Africa and Southeast Asia, camp moves depended on many conditions. Sometimes they moved merely five minutes away to a new slope on the mountain. At other times a splinter group would walk five hours to relocate in a forest known for dense monkey populations. Having worked for years with agriculturalists, this life of constant movement seemed strange to me. But after my season of work with the Raute, I realized that settling down was not an option for them. Even the thought of settling into a sedentary agricultural existence is disturbing to the Raute. During an interview with Man Bahadur at camp, he explained this need for the Raute to maintain their identity and way of life: "We can't marry with villagers in the village and become landowners. [He addressed a Nepali woman:] I can't marry you, for example. If I married you then I'd have to go to Kathmandu and other big cities. I would have to plow and dig like a farmer. Therefore my elder son should get married within our group. If he married a villager, he'd have to cut grass for buffalo, give service to the government, and study in schools. [He shook his head.] So that's the reason we don't marry villagers. We love our own people."

Cultural Selves and Cultural Others

During my field research with the Rautes, I came to understand that both the Nepali villagers and I used them as a mirror for understanding ourselves. They are exotic, outside the Hindu sense of social order. In their cultural differences, they present us with a distorted reflection of our own unanalyzed social world. For example, my research assistant's questions to them reflected her own experience as a high-caste Hindu woman. "When is your Dasain [a festival held during the fall in honor of the goddess Durga]?" she would ask. When a Raute didn't know when it was, her eyes would glow with fascination. How could these people claim to be Hindu and not even know when this major yearly festival occurs? It was like claiming to be Christian and being ignorant of Christmas; it simply didn't happen.

My research assistant and the other villagers found the Rautes fascinating precisely because they ignore so many of the Hindu social boundaries yet do so without appreciating the causes or consequences. To the people in Nepal, the Rautes are like children who have never learned the proper social rules. Like orphaned children, they may lose their freedom and become wards of the Nepalese state at any time. Rautes wish to get along with sedentary villagers, but they are afraid to attend schools or settle in villages. If they were to adopt village life, they would join the poorest, most exploited underclasses of Nepali society, becoming landless laborers like other recently settled hunter-gatherers in South Asia. But unlike marginalized social groups, Raute sociality is resilient, incorporating successful strategies of cultural survival that allow them to exist in a Hindu world.

3

Who Are the Rautes?

An ethnic group exists only when it runs the risk of existing.
—Michel de Certeau

We are what God gave birth to.
—Bhakta Bahadur

It is now the beginning of September and I've been meeting with Raute elders since June. I've noticed that when I ask Man Bahadur (and others) about their origins, they tell me different things. Sometimes I hear them tell the story about being related to the kings of the area. Once or twice, I've been told fables about their relationships with animals, especially with monkeys. And sometimes, like today, Man Bahadur just says that, frankly, they really don't know where they originally came from. He said, "I don't know how the Raskoti [his clan] were born. I mean, first they came from Raskot, from the head of the big Karnali River. But I don't know . . . there's a place called Raskot on the upper part of Jumla. It is said that Raskoti were born there. How did God create them? He may have created us, but how? How? Where did people come from? What do people know about it? Only God knows.

Identities

Anthropologists find classification according to subsistence types helpful for a variety of reasons, and often classify societies into food collectors (hunting, gathering, fishing) or food producers (horticulturalists, pastoralists, agriculturalists). They would thus refer to Rautes by their form of subsistence as "hunter-gatherers" or "foragers." This basic subsistence orientation would then be used as a means of cultural comparison with other food collectors, such as the South African Bushmen, central African forest peoples, Southeast Asian foragers, the Birhor of India.[1] The classification "hunter-gatherers" does fit the Rautes' own conception of themselves, for they refer to themselves as *šyāola*, which literally means "hunters." And if asked by farmers if they would like to take up farming, Rautes will reply, "No, because we hunt monkey."

Though Rautes are hunters, they more often describe themselves as a nomadic people. They explain to Nepalese villagers that they are the *bāsisthāne mānche* (from *bāsi*, meaning an inhabitant, and derived from the root words *bās*, to sit/stay; -*stan*, a place or country; *mānche* men/people). A name with multiple meanings, *bāsisthāne mānche* connotes people who originally belonged to a place. They inhabit or stay in that country; in the Rautes' case, they are the people who stay in the forests of western Nepal. By using this description, Rautes draw attention to their identity as indigenous people who are original to a place. This perhaps best captures the spirit of how they idealize themselves as a people. Calling Rautes "indigenous" also has certain advantages over other descriptors such as "hunter-gatherers," as it does not privilege the Raute's food-obtaining strategies over other markers of identity.

In our conversations, I at first tried to identify Man Bahadur as some category of forest dweller, monkey hunter, food collector, nomad, or another marker of identity. But when I listened again to our audiotaped conversations, I realized that this is unfair, that I was trying to categorize Rautes in a manner consistent with my own academic interests and categories. For Rautes, however, it is not so much a matter of *what* they are, but of *who they are in relationship to others*. They know themselves as part of a social world inhabited by humans, deities, animals-as-relatives, ancestors, and living plants, all of whom live together in forests. They do identify themselves as forest nomads whose subsistence is based upon hunting and gathering, but this is only when they compare themselves with farmers. Among each other, they identify themselves according to family roles as siblings, children, aunts, and uncles. Like other Raute groups, the nomadic Rautes identify each other mostly according to territory, naming places where other groups have settlements. The "Darchula" Rautes, for example, live in far northwestern Darchula District, Nepal. In comparing themselves with other Raute settlements, the group with whom I worked call themselves the "nomadic Rautes," or point out the name of some place where they camped recently, such as saying, "We are the Rautes who stayed in Dang District last winter."

Surrounding farmers, on the other hand, identify Rautes as a different and exotic people. Newspaper reporters from Kathmandu portray them as the "last monkey hunters of Nepal," and imagine them to be archaic primitives who need "upliftment" into agrarian society. The development agencies and the government of Nepal assign the nomadic Rautes the dubious status of "Disadvantaged Groups" (DAGs), lumping them together with women, Dalit low castes, and other small ethnic groups. The last government budget allocated twenty-six million dollars for the "upliftment" of DAGs.

Such identity markers have little to do with the Rautes' own sense of social identity. The enormous gap between what Rautes think of themselves and dominant societal characterizations stems largely from different ideas about the nature of what constitutes a "society." People in Nepal emphasize social hierarchy, sedentism, thrift, complexity, and Hindu moral codes as important aspects of Nepalese society. They see society as guided by a controlling legal authority. Most people in Nepal recognize the legitimacy of the State of Nepal and have a primordial feeling of being "Nepali." In contrast, Rautes emphasize no such social identity or nationality. For the nomadic foragers, social relations are characterized by sharing everything (among each other, not with non-Rautes) and by treating each other with equality. They express the sentiment that other forest creatures are equal, animate sentient beings, and believe in the right to each individual's freedom of choice and social autonomy. It is evident that these two divergent views constitute a fundamental disagreement between the foragers and the surrounding agrarian society concerning the very definition of a society. Given this difference in sociality, Rautes could express their true identity only at the risk of being criticized by the surrounding agrarian population.

Ironically, how we perceive another person's ethnic identity involves a complex and subjective process in which we filter information through our own ethnic identities: to know "Rauteness" is to know the Rautes in terms of our own subjective interests, cultural experiences, and historically situated knowledge. But how accurate is it to define Raute identity as seen through the prism of people who may be Nepalese or American or British? Difficult though it is to set aside our storybook images about wild savages and cavemen, we need to move beyond our own cultural myths and explore what is factually valid about Raute ethnic identity. If our goal is to reveal how Rautes see themselves and their unique ways of expressing their identity, we must strive to avoid ethnocentric perceptions, and to create a culturally relative understanding of Raute identity, gleaning it from what Rautes say about themselves.

To capture an ethnographic understanding of Raute identity is a goal worth pursuing, but this is difficult given that Rautes have no *unified* sense of identity. When we compare various Raute groups scattered across Nepal and into India, we find Rautes who fish, others who do not; Rautes who are settled, others who are not. While all Rautes speak their own distinctive language, a sense of Raute identity varies in each community; there is no single leader who enforces group identity among the scattered family groups. Unlike our societies, in which we belong because we are part of a nation, pay taxes, and follow written laws, there is no unified "Raute society." Each Raute band draws upon slightly different ways of presenting itself to others.

As is characteristic of other historically foraging peoples, Raute political power is a form of direct democracy. Rather than a hierarchical social order, it can be described as *heterarchical*, a form of social power that is distributed along a continuum of members and leaders. In such societies, political decisions cannot be enforced by elders, religious edicts, or written legal systems. Instead, people in foraging societies have to learn to be good orators, using the rhetorical power of persuasion in order to influence each other. As such, various bands of Rautes form their own decisions about how to represent their political selves to others. For example, in 1979–1980, the government of Nepal forcibly resettled a group of Rautes from the northwest corner of Nepal (Darchula District), moving them down into the middle hills of Dadeldhura (pronounced "Daddledura") District. They were given land settlements and expected to take up subsistence farming. These families began to call themselves by the surname of Rajwar, a caste name of local ruling elites.[2] After twenty years, however, most of these Rautes had lost their land to crafty Hindu farmers. By 2004, reportedly only four of 145 Raute families still owned the land assigned to them when they were pulled out of the jungle and "rehabilitated" (Pant 2004). Having lost the government land to swindling landowners, the group moved back into the forests and again began calling themselves Raute. They believed that if they were landowners, they should adopt high-caste surnames, but if they pursued forest-based subsistence, they should call themselves Rautes. Some of them petitioned the government for more land, saying that they wanted to become Rajwar farmers again. But the government ignored their requests.

Does such flexibility of identity seem strange, or even deceitful? Does it seem like a form of "devolution" to revert to hunting and gathering? To those of us who believe in fixed surnames and inflexible ethnic identity, the switch from Raute to Rajwar to Raute again seems deceitful, and to people raised in agrarian communities, reverting to forest foraging seems like a step downwards on the ladder of evolution. But many groups worldwide have adroitly moved between farming and foraging. Archaeologists who study foragers of Madagascar, for example, have traced the original inhabitants as probably having been Bantu iron-wielding farmers who migrated from Africa two millennia ago. After arriving on the island of Madagascar, these new immigrants began to hunt hippopotamus and other large mammals, yet they seem to have lost their interest in farming, or at least there is no archaeological evidence of farming until a thousand years ago (Stiles 1998). A millennium later, sailors coming all the way from Indonesia emigrated to the island today known as Madagascar, and warfare erupted. Oral histories and scant written documents indicate that some communities fled into the forests, perhaps to become the foraging Mikea people of today. Thus, over the course of two millennia, it is likely that some communities moved back and forth between farming and foraging subsistence strategies.

Pursuing different economic strategies is not unusual. Some communities in South Asia combine foraging with horticulture or herding, or engage in trade of baskets, mats, honey, and other non-timber forest products. When a community maintains two distinct cultural identities along with distinct economic practices, they have found a way to exploit two different economic niches. In situations where the foragers can retreat to a forest, they may alternate between a life among farmers and another life of foraging, and ideally, not assimilate into the dominant farming system. This type of oscillating bicultural identity was first described by anthropologist Peter Gardner, who was doing field research among a south Indian foraging community known as Paliyan (Gardner 1985). He noticed that the Paliyan adopted Hindu cultural practices while working for caste Hindus; but they adopted their own egalitarian and autonomous cultural practices when they moved back into the forests.

While biculturalism represents one strategy for cultural interaction, other scholars of northern South Asian societies describe another strategy known as *impression management* (Barth 1969; Berreman 1962; Manzardo 1982). Impression management involves creating particular effects among others by playing certain roles, conveying calculated sets of information, and, like an actor, adopting a certain pose or persona (Mintz 1963, 1362). In a recent review of his life's work, the eminent scholar Frederik Barth recalls, "We documented situations where people changed their ethnic identities under pressure, or as a result of ecologic change, or where they clung to them in minority situations by careful impression management, or used impression management to deny patent cultural differences that might have been given ethnic significance" (Barth 2007, 10).

Similarly to people occupying various ecological niches in the western Himalayas, the Rautes in Nepal do employ impression management. I recall being somewhat bemused when a Raute elder named Ratna walked into the courtyard of a Hindu farmwife one day. She seemed a bit nervous about talking with Ratna as he tried to barter one of his wooden bowls in exchange for an amount of grain that would fill the bowl. Softly, he beseeched her, "Dullu has basmati rice, but there are empty stomachs in Dailekh; Love is not a small thing, it's as big as a grain-storage tree."[3] Hearing this, the farm woman relaxed; the little saying evoked a number of meanings to which she could relate and they shared a laugh. Ratna's saying referred to Dullu, the old capital of the local kingdom. Everyone in the region had heard stories of its wealth, how there were even bathing pools there, yet the people of the Dailekh region were as flat broke and poor as the farm woman. For poor people, the most important things in life are not luxuries like swimming pools, but the basics—love and food. Just having these basics can mean the difference between a miserable and a satisfying life. In a rural farming community, crafting poetic imagery around the old-fashioned grain-storage trees was another touch of verbal art (*bhanne kala*) much appreciated in the countryside. Ratna evoked the image of love in the form of delicious grain filling up a huge tree, with its spreading branches that had been woven with mats and wooden planks into a grain bin that pests could not reach. Those grain bins set into trees were still around, and I occasionally saw them nestled like huge eagle's nests into the trees bordering a household's courtyard. By evoking this imagery, Ratna evoked the economic trust he needed to make the trade of his bowl for the farm woman's grain. Although Ratna himself doesn't store grain, he always presents an impression sympathetic to farm life in order to achieve the most favorable transactions.

Ratna cleverly employs impression management skills such as verbal art to trade with farmers, but other Rautes have different skills. Some bands do not trade bowls; some have settled down; some sell firewood and do labor for farmers; a few collect and sell honey. "Rauteness," then, varies according to many factors, such as degree of interaction with non-Raute communities, political pressures, historical territories, economic situation, and the availability of forest resources. From the point of view of the Raute band with whom I carried out research, one of the main features of "Rauteness" is being *nomadic* rather than sedentary. When they witness other Raute families living in western Nepal forming only *seminomadic* settlements, the nomadic group opines that they themselves might be the only "true" remaining Rautes. Yet others who speak dialects of the distinctive Raute language nevertheless consider themselves to be Raute. Raute identity thus exists in the light of a constantly shifting cultural landscape peopled by various kinds of foragers and post-foragers.

A Conjectured History

Rautes have no written history and claim to be unaware of their ancestral heritage more than four generations back. As one person noted: "After about three generations, we don't remember the names [of ancestors] . . . they go to the skies and there they live. They are like air." This also explains why Raute elders are irritated when people ask them about their origins. They do not know such histories and so feel that such questions are irrelevant. Brahman scholars, too, have neglected to record the ethnic histories of other local commoners. Traditional Nepalese histories contain information about royal lineages, taxes, land grants, and astrological charts, but no such ethnic histories. Like the histories of tailors, iron smiths, and small-scale farmers, Raute ethnic history must rely on clues gathered from oral histories, stories, language, and other sparse research writings.

In the nineteenth century, British colonial officers and experts surveyed the "scheduled tribes"[4] of north India (Dalton 1960; Guha 1999). While these men worked in colonial India and few traveled into western Nepal, it is nevertheless informative to look at how they categorized various peoples living outside the Hindu caste system, and how these ethnographic reports shed light on the historical conditions of Rautes in Nepal. In South Asia, various exonyms, names applied by outsiders, were given to Rautes and their neighbors who spoke similar dialects. The popular epithets included: little king (*Raji*), king's messenger (*Rawat*), forest men (*Ban mānche*), forest-eating Raut (*Ban khāne rāut*), and jungle dwellers (*Jaŋgali, Jangyali, Dzaŋgali*).[5] One nineteenth-century administrator, for example, gives the following definition for the name Rawat:

> Rawát—(from Sanskrit: *Rájá-dúta*, king's messenger) is properly a title of respect but specially applied to various classes of people. In the hills it is applied to a sub-division of the *Pujáris*, to a sub-division of the *Khasiya* Rájputs . . . one story is that they were originally cart drivers or Ahirs [hunting people]. . . . Mr. Traill classes Rawát as Rájis and considers them aboriginal. The low-caste Doms are supposed to be their poor relations. Colonel Dalton speaks of a somewhat similar tribe in Chhota Nagpur [in present-day Jharkhand, India] called *Rautiyá* who are almost certainly of Gond [Dravidian] extraction but aspire to Aryan descent. (Crooke 1890, 181)

From this description we see that the names Rawat and Raute pertain to quite different sources. The names refer to high-caste Hindus as well as low castes, hunter-gatherers, and aboriginal peoples who live in forests. To make matters more difficult, they also refer to peoples residing in a large territory of northern South Asia. Edward Dalton, also writing in the mid-nineteenth century, alludes to the powerful Rautiyá, who numbered fifteen thousand people and lived in north-central India and were "probably of the Gond family," a Dravidian-speaking people (Dalton 1960, 268). Today no oral histories remain that link the nomadic Rautes to Dravidian speakers, who occupy the entire southern half of India. The original Dravidian-language speakers are theorized to have been the people of the Indus Valley civilization, one of the world's original emergent state societies.

Today, about two million people of northern regions of the south Indian subcontinent continue to speak Dravidian languages. For example, a population of about thirty thousand Dravidian-speaking people live southeast of the Rautes, in the lowlands of Nepal. This ethnic group, known as the Kurukh people (also known as Dhangar and Oraon), however, have no ostensible ties to Rautes. They share a few words in their native languages, notably words for natural word classes such as "hill," "river," "stream," "roots," but probably not more than about 5 percent of Raute words have their origin in the Dravidian-language family.

Raute social practices do resemble those of some other Indian forest foragers. The most closely related groups culturally are the Birhor and Hill Kharia, two ethnic groups living in the Chota Nagpur Plateau, a great forested region in northern South Asia. Like Rautes, these other hunter-gatherer groups live in similar huts, worship similarly named deities, and carry out similar hunting and trading practices. For example, both Birhor and Raute love monkey hunting, make ropes and nets from *Bauhinia* shrubs, and live nomadic lives in the forests. The Birhor and Hill Kharia speak Austroasiatic languages, another major language family of the region. Rautes and Birhor have some vocabulary in common, especially for words referring to family members and to deities. The Raute supreme god of the sun, known as Berh, is also the name of the supreme god of the Kharia and Birhor. And up to 20 percent of Raute words are etymologically original to Austroasiatic words. According to philologists, during the era of Gautama Buddha circa fifth century B.C.E., Austroasiatic-speaking peoples lived in areas that are now part of the Nepalese *terai* and northern Indian state of Bihar. Even earlier evidence from ancient Sanskrit texts suggests that Austroasiatic-speaking peoples occupied northern South Asia all the way to the Indus River (Muir 1967; Wezler and Witzel 1995). Thus, western branches of Austroasiatic-speaking peoples lived in or near the territories in which Rautes currently reside.

However, the Raute language is most closely related to Tibeto-Burman (TB) languages spoken in the central Himalayas. TB represents another of the world's major language families, with more than 2.5 million speakers living in Nepal. The Raute's language overwhelmingly is composed of TB-derived vocabulary and syntax. Since prehistoric times until about seven hundred years ago, the area was occupied and governed by TB-speaking peoples. Undoubtably, the early Tibetan language, known as Proto-Tibetan, shaped the Raute language, perhaps even causing a new "layer" in the Raute ancestral language laid on top of older Austroasiatic and Dravidian language "layers." Today, while Raute cultural practices closely match those of Austroasiatic-speaking forest foragers from northern India, the Raute language is much more closely related to Tibetan.

The earliest written Hindu text that might refer to Rautes is the *Brihat Sanhita* (*Brihatsamhita*), a book written in the sixth century A.D. attributed to the mathematician Varahamihira. In this book, a people described as Rājya Kirata are mentioned as dwelling in present-day Kumaun, the current home of Banrajis. Given the language conventions of the time, the term "Rājya Kirata" would most closely mean something like the "barbaric hunters living in mountainous forests who claim royal heritage." This actually does sound a good deal like what local writers would say about Banrajis and Rautes, as they say something pretty close to that today. Thus, possibly the contemporary Banraji and Raute are the descendants of such peoples depicted as barbaric forest dwellers of the Himalayas.

For centuries afterwards, there is no known mention of Rautes or their Raji relatives. The next recorded missives come from the journals of British administrators stationed on the empire's border with Nepal. The British Commissioner to the princely state of Kumaon, for example, noted: "a small remnant, pertinaciously adhering to the customs of their ancestors, are to be found in the *Rawats* and *Rajis*. They are now reduced to about twenty families, who wander in the rude freedom of savage life, along the line of forests situated under the eastern part of the *Himalaya*, in the province [Kumaon]" (Trail 1828, 160). The Commissioner was writing from secondhand descriptions, but subsequently a British officer, Captain H. Strachey, did meet Banrajis and noted in his 1846 A.D. journal:

> The government agent caught two of the forest men, the wild men of Chilpula [ward] for my inspection.[6] I saw nothing very remarkable about them except an expression of alarm and stupidity in their faces and they are darker and otherwise

more like lowland Hindustanis than the average Hills-people of Kumaun. They manufacture wooden bowls for sale and live under temporary huts, frequently moving from place to place amidst the jungles; their principal subsistence being edible wild plants and what game they can catch, and they occasionally get presents of cooked food from the villagers. They have a dialect of their own, but some of them can communicate with their civilized neighbours in Pahari [hill] Hindu. The scanty vocabulary of the Raji language that has been collected supports the connection with the tribes of Nepal suggested by Dr. Latham. (Cf. Atkinson 1882)

Strachey's methods of collecting information were a coercive yet common form used during the nineteenth century by both high-caste Hindus and British officers. That this officer went to the trouble of meeting Banrajis gives his description more weight, since most such accounts cite second-hand gossip. While they help ascertain that forest dwellers lived in the region, they shed little light on Raute and Raji cultural life itself.

By the mid-nineteenth century, E. Atkinson had collected ethnographic details of Rajis and Rautes, writing:

> Rájis . . . neither cultivate the ground nor live in permanent dwellings. The Rájis are said to have their own peculiar gods, but they also worship those of the Hindús and . . . they bury their dead . . . honesty and chastity they hold in great honour. They hide their women from all strangers, declaring that they are of royal race and must not be seen. They seem to be almost omnivorous and are said to approve especially of the flesh of the great *langúr* monkey. They support themselves chiefly by hunting and fishing and they get what grain they require from the Khasiyas [the Indo-Aryan Khas], giving in return wooden implements of husbandry and vessels which they manufacture with some skill. (Atkinson 1882, 2:367)

We learn from these and other short reports that Rautes and Rajis had established all of their signature cultural practices by this time, or more important, that they had not assimilated to the dominant Indo-Aryan cultural practices by the mid-nineteenth century. They lived dispersed throughout the forests of the west-central Himalayan hilly forests, but their populations had increasingly come into conflict with sedentary agriculturalists. Unfortunately, we are left with no insight into Raute or Raji peoples' own sense of their place in the Himalayan world until the first ethnographic writings (Reinhard 1974).

The first twentieth-century reference to the nomadic Rautes of west-

ern Nepal is found in an astrological and historical treatise of Nepal in
which they are described as wild "ape men," but it reveals nothing else of
significance (Naraharinath 1955/1956; see also Reinhard 1974, 234). The
yogi ascetic and historian who first printed this description, Naraharinath,
was born in Kalikot District, western Nepal, and would have been exposed
to the stories and legends surrounding the forest dwellers in addition to
meeting Rautes himself. Parents tell bogeyman-like stories to their children about Rautes. Some of these legends are terrifying. When children
are running too freely in the forest, parents may scold them, saying, "If
you wander, a Raute will get you. He will put you in a hole in the earth and
bury you up to your neck. When it is time for feasting, he will cut a hole
in your fontanelle and eat your brains. So quit wandering and stay close."
Such stories reflect no knowledge of Raute cultural practices, as Rautes do
not murder or cannibalize villagers. Rather, the scary stories are a way of
instilling obedience and keeping children from straying into the forest at
night. For adults, such stories also reverberate with cultural inversions of
proper behavior. In Jajarkot District, where this story is told, the revered
shamans of rural farming communities are indeed buried in a similar manner. Their bodies are buried sitting in an upright position and their skulls
are pierced at the fontenelle in order to release their spirits to the heavens.
But this mortuary rite performed for shamans is something considered
morally good. In moral inversion, this sacred act becomes profane in the
tale of Rautes kidnapping children. Such folklore about Rautes esssentially
acts as a mirror reflecting the needs and expectations of the surrounding
farm folk.

Aside from folk stories, the first ethnographic field research on the
Rautes was conducted during several weeks in 1968 by researcher Johan
Reinhard in preparation for selecting a Ph.D. dissertation topic. Although
his observations were based on limited research,[7] he nevertheless published
an informative article that contains the first description of the nomadic
Rautes (Reinhard 1974). The information provides material concerning
Raute house types, dress, hunting, dance, and so on, and is useful for comparison with contemporary Rautes. Also in 1968–1969, Peace Corps volunteer Terence Bech made a tape recording of the Rautes performing three of
their songs and dances (Ross 1978). Listening to Bech's recordings, I found
that the musical songs from 1969 constitute almost identical music to that
performed by the nomadic Raute group in 1997. Thus, the work of these
researchers is important, as it provides the first benchmarks for understanding Raute lives in a diachronic perspective.

In the ensuing thirty years, several researchers have contributed toward our understanding of the nomadic and sedentary Rautes living throughout western Nepal (Bandhu 1987; Bista 1978; Fortier 2000, 2001, 2002, 2003; Luintel 1993; Manandhar 1998; Nepali-Yatri 1983; Sahi and Bahadura Ji 2000; Singh 1997). Dor B. Bista, for example, spent only two days with the nomadic Rautes, but he managed to compile and publish a Swadish word list, one of the tools researchers use to compare languages (Bista 1978). The scholar Purna P. Nepali-Yatri, whose family name is actually Nepala, liked to be known as the "religious pilgrim" (*yatri*). Thanks to his nomadic adventures, we became aware of the approximately nine hundred other Rautes scattered throughout western Nepal (Nepala 1983, 1997). The anthropologist Y. Luintel based his writings on about three months of visits, collecting wooden carved objects, including a miniature carving of a Raute traditional wooden canoe. This is important as Rautes rarely carve canoes anymore, being able to cross rivers using modern suspension bridges. The botanist N. Singh interviewed both Banrajis (whom he calls Rautes) and the nomadic Rautes concerning their forest flora and fauna. Singh was the first person to publically advocate on the behalf of Rautes, calling for a forest preserve to be established in one of the national parks to meet their foraging needs (no preserve has been established). N. Manandhar, too, studied the ethnobotany of the sedentary Rautes living along the Mahakali River in Nepal. His findings provide information concerning medicinals of interest to foraging peoples, such as balms for cuts and bruises. Thus, even though most of these researchers spent only a short period of research time with Rautes, pieced together their information helps us to know more about Raute culture, language, and history.

Raute Cultural Geography

Rautes living throughout western Nepal and India are not as homogeneous as one might expect. True, they have many common elements in their language, cultural practices, and religious ideas. Lexical comparisons of Rautes and Banrajis living in the farthest western and eastern regions, for example, continue to share about 80 percent of the same words and almost 100 percent of grammar. But things slowly change, and the various bands of foragers are affected by the different laws and political events of India and Nepal.

One of the notable differences among the bands involves nomadism. At one end of the continuum, the nomadic Rautes with whom I worked move frequently and do not return to a given locale for several years. At the other end of the continuum, sedentary communities of Rautes have taken up farming in the last generation. Most of the approximately twenty-five settlements diffused throughout western Nepal and into India continue to be seminomadic. For example, I asked a woman in a settlement in India where her husband was, and she replied, "He is in Gandora, a dense forest near the hamlet of Charani, and will stay there until the festival time." Her husband had been in the forests for all of October, but he would return come late November. The degree of nomadism among the more sedentary communities of Rautes varies greatly because people tend to relocate for various reasons, such as a death in the family, an upcoming festival, or visiting relatives. The full-time nomadic Rautes, however, move when monkeys are hunted out of a forest, when other resources (water, campgrounds, wild yams) are not up to their standards, when troubles occur, or when they find no villagers who want to take their bowls in exchange for grain. They may reside at one camp for up to six weeks but no longer, and usually something precipitates their migration sooner.

Not only do forms of nomadism among the sedentary and nomadic bands of Rautes differ, but their hunting styles also inform their group identity. Hunting contributes all the protein that Rautes eat (they eat no lentils or dairy), and hunting technologies shape their markedly egalitarian social relations among themselves. But Rautes, Banrajis, and Rajis hunt in different ways; some use nets, dogs, and archery, while others use spears, depending on whether they hunt monkey, deer, or burrowing animals. The nomadic Rautes are the most specialized hunters; they hunt monkeys using solely nets and axes. They do not rely upon broad-spectrum hunting strategies such as hunting a variety of animals. Although Rautes may have practiced broad-spectrum hunting generations ago, today they would face competition with local farmers who also enjoy hunting in the forests for deer, boar, and pheasant. Thus, Rautes have probably adopted their hunting practice of selectively hunting monkeys because Hindus and Buddhists avoid killing them.

While nineteenth-century observers noted that Banrajis enjoyed hunting langur and macaque monkeys, contemporary Banrajis hunt cave-dwelling mammals such as the large Himalayan porcupine (*Hystrix indica*, N. *dumsi*, Rj. *Māshi*), Himalayan leaf-nosed bat (*Hipposideros armiger*, N. *chimkadar*, Rj. *chamrāyo*), and Indian False Vampire bat (*Megaderma lyra*, N. *chimkadar*, Rj. *kilāri*). With their wooden spears, Banraji hunters capture only one to two adults, or at most a mother and her brood of porcupines, during each hunt, rather than the dozen or more monkeys netted during the nomadic Raute hunts. Spear hunting, in turn, has helped to reshape the Banraji social organization. Compared to the monkey-hunting Rautes, Banrajis hunt in smaller groups, they catch less prey per hunt, and they share fewer portions with others. Their hunting and technologies are now associated with an overall social organization that is more individualistic than those of the more communal Rautes.

Raute trading practices also reveal a cultural landscape of similarities and differences. All Rautes and Rajis traditionally make wooden bowls and boxes, and trade them to villagers. However, today this skill is being lost among Banrajis forcibly settled by the Indian and Nepalese governments. Among the more sedentary communities, wooden bowl making is becoming an occupational specialty of a handful of Banraji men. Among the nomadic Rautes, however, all men continue to enjoy carving wood, and some women occasionally carve wood as well.

Some of the most noticeable differences between sedentizing and nomadic communities involves their relationships forged with local farmers. Today, many of the Banraji perform work as rock crushers, farm workers, ditch diggers, wood gatherers, carpenters, honey collectors, and ritual specialists (*dhāmi*, shamans). The full-time nomadic Rautes, on the other hand, eschew all of these dependent activities. They merely create ephemeral fictive kinship ties with farmers during trading sessions. They continue to reject any attempts by farmers to settle them, make them plow, or do other work.

From the nomadic Rautes' point of view, ethnic distinctions among the Rautes, Raji, and Banraji are based on different habits and territories. The nomadic Rautes consider their own band of people to be the only *real* Rautes, whereas others who speak their language are considered different people. For example, elder Man Bahadur remarked about the Rautes living in Dadeldhura District: "The Dadeldhura Rautes' habit is like that of a landowner. They comb their hair just like villagers. Their homes are like this [points to a villager's house]. . . . But they really liked me when they saw me. She [a Raute woman] said her natal family (*māiti ghar*) is Raute. Still, those Raji-Raute are just like villagers. They've become landowners. Before they were Rautes. We call ourselves Raute if people live like us, and all Rautes are just like that."

Like many other small-scale societies, a band's territory represents one of the major criteria in the Rautes' system of social division. As Eric Wolf writes concerning the part-time foraging Yanamamo of the Amazon, "all people are seen as equally benevolent and malevolent and similar in comportment and bodily form; it is their *differential location on a spatial continuum* that identifies them as friends or hostiles" (Wolf 1994, 3 citing fieldwork by Chagnon and Asch 1973; emphasis added). For Rautes, too, this sense of territory is paramount in determining the identity of different Raute bands. For example, Man Bahadur calls the Raute band living in Dadeldhura District of Nepal the "*Dadeldhura* Rautes." Another second criterion involves behavior related to territory—specifically, a band's degree of nomadism. According to Man Bahadur, if Rautes have settled into villages, they are considered "*Raji*-Rautes." A third criterion in the construction of different ethnic identities refers to hair and dress styles. When the settled Rautes start dressing and styling their hair like villagers, the nomadic Rautes do not "see" them as ethnically similar. Conversely, when I showed Banrajis photos of nomadic Raute men, they were taken by surprise. When I asked one Banraji fellow if he thought there was a similarity between himself and the nomadic Rautes, he stared at the photos for a minute, then commented, "These Raute men have facial hair, they have beards, but we can't grow so much facial hair." Whether this is a phenotypic or genotypic difference, the Banraji astutely observed that some Rautes do allow their beards to grow more than do Banraji men.

Statements about appearance and dress play a large part in establishing identity. In addition, layered on top of sartorial expressions of identity, Rautes consider each community distinct because they live in different territories, have become more sedentary, and have a different appearance.

Are the Rautes a Distinct Ethnic Group or a Fringe of the Larger Society?

One of the questions surrounding hunter-gatherer populations worldwide is whether a society of hunter-gatherers can be described as having their own ethnic identity or whether they are part of the linguistic and economic underclass of a larger society. This question involves issues of origins, kinship, and alliance with other social groups. Whether small societies of foragers are indeed distinct or simply groups surviving on the fringes of powerful states has long been debated among South Asian studies scholars. For example, when the Veddas of Sri Lanka were described during early colonial encounters in the 1600s, it was apparent that some bands were "wild" while others were more accustomed to trading with the Sinhalese- and Tamil-speaking farmers (Childers 1876; Parker 1909; Sarasin and Sarasin 1893; Seligmann and Seligmann 1911). While the consensus about most South Asian foraging societies is that they are authentic aboriginal foragers, nevertheless some scholars have argued that the Asian forest foragers are the remnants of "devolution," outcasts from farming caste societes that fled into the forests during periods of war or famine in past centuries (i.e., both Childers 1876 on the Veddas and Dash 1998 on the Birhor support this view).

Our concern as students of contemporary foraging societies is not to consider Raute origins from the dominant society's point of view so much as to look at how Rautes *themselves* consider the nature of their social system. One of the ways we can do this is by examining their kinship and marriage customs. For instance, kinship systems provide us with a cognitive map of the Rautes' ways of thinking about the rules for proper social relations. Looking at the Raute marriage system, we find that the nomadic Rautes marry among each other rather than with local caste Nepalese families. This type of marriage alliance is known as *endogamy*, meaning that Rautes marry within their ethnic group. But of course family members cannot marry each other, and there exist rules of *exogamy*, meaning to marry *outside* of one's family (yet within the ethnic group). Thus, Rautes have their own rules for who is eligible to marry.

A Raute extended family is called a *pā-tsha*, the "father's family"; literally, the two root words together mean "patriclan," a set of kin whose members believe themselves to be descended from a common male ancestor, but the links to that ancestor are not specified (Ember and Ember 2004, 174). Let us imagine who constitutes "family" from the point of view of a Raute boy whom we shall call "Harka" and say that he belongs to the "Raskoti" patriclan. Harka calls his father and paternal uncle *pā-'ksaw* and *pā-mā* respectively. As in other Tibetan languages, in the Raute language there is a root word that may have an accompanying compound root or syllable that modifies the meaning. Thus *pā-* means "father" and the second syllable, *-'ksaw*, signifies that this is the biological father. Since a child might refer to other men as "father" (*pā*) in a loose extended fashion, naming his biological father "*pā-'ksaw*" denotes him as having come from the "loins of this father." Harka's paternal uncle (*pā-mā*) denotes that he is the "nurturing or helping father." Structurally, Harka's social role with both men is one of son to father, and he respects them in the same manner. However, Harka's maternal uncle, *ku-wa* (from *ku* mother's brother + *wa* man, male, person), is given a distinct name since he is outside Harka's patriclan. In fact, he may very well become Harka's father-in-law someday, as Rautes would encourage cross-cousin marriage of Harka with his MBD or his FZS (mother's brother's daughter or father's sister's daughter.)

Harka's mother, grandmothers, mother's sister, and father's sister all act the role of mother (*iya*). The root word *iya* refers to mothers who are filled with the knowledge of child care. Because grandmothers properly have such full knowledge, the term is reserved for Harka's paternal and maternal grandmothers and for older mothers. When Harka refers to his biological mother, he calls her *dzyi-iya* (or *iy-dzya*), adding the root word *dzyi*, which carries a range of basic meanings, including "body," "drink," "suckling," "full." We thus infer that Harka calls his biological mother *dzyi-iya* to signify that she is his real biological mother who nursed him. Harka will call his maternal aunt *tshi-niy* or *tshi-ma*, using the diminutive word *tshi* plus the word *niya* meaning "aunt" or, alternatively, *ma*, a more recently introduced word for mother.[8] In English, Harka would be saying "auntie" or "mommy," depending on which term he selects. Finally, his paternal aunt is *ɲiya*, meaning aunt or "father's female sibling."[9] These women represent Harka's close relatives to whom he can turn for family support.

As Harka becomes a man, he grows more sensitive to which Raute girls are eligible to marry. Harka would not consider marrying his sisters, for example, whom he calls *titi* if they are older than he and *gat-hau* if they are younger. By extension, he would never consider marriage with his "parallel cousins," that is, his father's brother's daughters (FBD) or his mother's sister's daughters (MZD). To reinforce this custom, Rautes also call such cousins "sister." Harka will look for a marriageable girl outside his patriclan, and he will probably find such an ideal bride among his "cross-cousins" who are his father's sister's daughter (FZD) or mother's brother's daughter (MBD); either of these girls would be ideal as they are not in his patriclan.[10]

In patriclans worldwide, the cross-cousins are often considered appropriate marriage partners because they have a different clan identity. If Harka's family is the "Raskoti" clan, then his cross-cousins will belong to the "Kalyal" clan, and Harka may marry these eligible girls because they do not violate incest taboos, and even better, they are girls that Harka already knows. In anthropological terms, the name for the Raute kinship and marriage system is called the "Dravidian kinship system." It is named after South Indian communities in which this inclusive type of kinship and marriage system was originally studied.

While the Rautes' paternal kinship system fits the Dravidian format, the words for maternal relatives (-*iya*-) lump all of the elder mother-like women from both sides of the family together, which is unlike the Dravidian kinship system. Naming all the women using the root word -*iya*- is a feature of a family system called the "Hawaiian kinship system." The Hawaiian system is used among societies that have bilateral kinship reckoning, bilocal residence patterns, and where there are large extended families, and this denomination makes sense because these are all features of Raute society. It explains why Rautes do not have unilineal descent groups like Nepalese families, and also why a child turns to aunts and grandmothers as well as to their own mothers for nurturing. Unlike caste Nepalese families, female relatives from both sides of a Raute child's family are important to a child's development.

We are now in a better position to address our question of whether or not Rautes constitute a distinct ethnic group. By considering the Rautes' kinship and marriage systems, we find that they do have a kinship system that is distinct from that of other social groups in the region. They do not follow the Tibetan systems, nor do they follow the caste Nepalese kinship systems. Their contemporary kinship and marriage systems reflect their own distinct social system, which is marked by the features of bilocal post-marital residence, bilateral kinship reckoning, bilateral cross-cousin marriage preference, patriclans rather than patrilineages, symmetrical and balanced marriage exchanges, and endogamy within their language and social group. These features point toward Rautes as aboriginal and distinct from surrounding social groups. Nevertheless, while Raute family systems are distinct, many Raute communities have been influenced by the encroaching values of other cultures; some patriclans have even settled and assimilated into the underclasses of the dominant majority.

Have Some Raute Communities Already Become Hindu Caste Villagers?

Across western Nepal there are dozens of Hindu caste families with the surname "Raut" and "Rawat." As the British officer Edward Dalton wrote, the name can signify both members of caste families and people from tribal groups. Did Raute tribal peoples become Hindu caste Raut families in previous centuries? Or, in previous centuries did Hindu caste families, during economic or politically difficult periods of their lives, migrate into the forests and take up the hunting-and-gathering lifestyle? In other parts of the world this process is known as "devolution" (Martin 1969; Obayashi 1996) or, more recently, as "cultural reversion" (Oota et al. 2005). Cultural reversions may occur when agricultural households take up a foraging lifestyle during periods of famine, warfare, or other calamity. In such cases, as in the case of the Mlabri, hunter-gatherers of northern Thailand, researchers have found few linguistic or genetic differences between the farming and foraging populations. In this case, "Genetic, linguistic, and cultural data suggest that the Mlabri were recently founded 500–800 years ago from a small group or family that left their hoe-farming community" (Oota et al. 2005, e71). While the Mlabri case is not completely settled, it seems that a contemporary hunting-gathering lifestyle does not necessarily reflect a long-term foraging lifestyle.

As I talked with Rautes, it became clear that, unlike the Mlabri who told of once having lived in farming communities, the nomadic Rautes have never told stories of once having been farmers. Though cultural reversion probably has not occurred, it is still probable that some Raute ancestors splintered away from foraging groups and settled into farming communities on the margins of Hindu society. It is not unlikely that some of the nomadic Rautes' relatives might have married into the families of villagers. As happens with foragers worldwide, as they acculturate into the surrounding farming communities, post-foraging women sometimes marry their sedentary neighbors (Headland 1998). When a woman marries into a farming family, she loses her identity as a forager and her children come to identify with the father's family. In these cases, the children often do not learn their mothers' languages, instead adopting the (fathers') dominant language.

Assimilation through marriage probably has taken place between Rautes and farmers in past generations, although no nomadic Rautes indicated that such marriages had taken place. In Nepal, marriages between Hindu castes and "tribal" women often result in "outcaste" families (Ghimire 1998). Rautes would have more difficulty assimilating, because Hindus are supposed to marry only on their own social level, a process of caste endogamy. As in other parts of South Asia, there is a rule of hypergamy. Hypergamy, as traditionally defined, is the custom of allowing a woman to marry upward in social rank with a husband of a higher social rank. There are two types of hypergamy. In the "free" variety, there are no restrictions on the upward mobility of a woman, and she may marry into a family above her rank by several degrees or even across caste divisions (*varna, varṇašram*). In the parts of Nepal where nomadic Rautes roam, there is a saying among the farmers that "women have no caste" (*āimāi ko jāt hundaina*), which means that free hypergamy is practiced and that a woman can marry a man of a different caste and their children take on the caste of their father. She can even marry below her caste rank and her children assume her husband's lower-caste status. Normally, however, most women practice "restricted hypergamy" and marry a man who is within their caste (*jāt*) and caste order (*varna*) but from a family of greater wealth or reputation. In the case of Rautes, it is possible that some Raute women have run away and married non-Raute men, but their children would enter the father's caste and thus be quickly assimilated into the caste system, leaving no cultural traces of Raute heritage.

A second way in which Rautes may be assimilated into the caste system is for an entire band to settle down and adopt a caste name and identity. For example, when a few Raute bands were forcibly resettled by the government of Nepal in 1979 into Dadeldhura District, they took the surname of Rajwar. And in Jajarkot District there are Raut households settled into villages living alongside, and intermarrying with, Bãdi (drum-maker), Kāmi (iron smith), and Damāi (tailor) caste families. In the case of Raute, then, some Rautes have been absorbed into the Hindu caste system by having entire families settle down in villages. Yet a major obstacle to benign assimilation is that it is hard to overcome villager stereotypes about Rautes. The village women call Rautes *ban mānche*, "forest men," a term loaded with negative connotations. A *ban mānche* is considered to be predatory, dangerous, outside the realm of the domestic and familiar. Consider one description by rural women of the Gurung ethnic groups, a Tibetan society living northeast of Raute territory:

> some vigorous creatures called *ban mānche* (*kyub mi* in Gurung), or forest men, were glimpsed in the woods and in the village itself and were believed to lust for women. About four feet tall with black furry bodies, red faces, and backward-facing feet, these creatures were believed to inhabit the woods and make forays into the village. Gurungs not only mentioned their existence, they spoke of actual encounters with them . . . they were thought to be a different order of natural being inhabiting the periphery of the human community and sometimes encroaching on it. . . . *Ban mānche* were commonly encountered and frequently discussed among villagers. Adolescent girls and young married women reported especially often that they were reluctant to walk alone in the forest for fear of meeting a *ban mānche*. They told of fleeting glimpses of the creatures on wood-cutting trips. Older women, usually those who lived alone, also reported sightings and unsettling encounters with *ban mānche*. (McHugh 2002, 80–83)

Given that village women are reluctant to meet *ban mānche* (and Rautes) and that intercaste marriage is discouraged, I recorded no reports of marriages between the nomadic Rautes and villagers. Nevertheless, Raute families may have settled down together into small satellite communities in rural areas. For example, a development worker described to me how he thought he had heard people from Rautgaun (Raut Village), Jajarkot District, speaking the Raute language with a group of nomadic Rautes as they passed through the area one year. This struck me as intriguing, and I remembered the people of Rautgaun village well, though none of them mentioned being able to speak the Raute language. The people of this village were among the poorest of the poor in Jajarkot, an amalgamation of prostitutes, drummers, fishermen, ferrymen, tailors, cloth dyers, landlords, widows, servants, carpenters, and millers. I enjoyed learning about how these people survived as they regularly portered goods to India and did menial labor for the local high-caste families.

During an interview in Rautgaun village with a centenarian named Gogane Raut, I learned what the area had looked like a hundred years ago when the forests grew almost all the way up to the district capital and wet paddy fields were nonexistent. The son of Biri Raut (a common nomadic Raute name), Gogane claimed to be a hundred and five years old, and looking at his deep wrinkles and knarled hands, I believed him.

I asked Gogane what he had done for a living when he was young. He replied: "In the winter time, I would go to the king's family's home and take them out for hunting. We rode on elephant and hunted deer. We went hunting in Pašaghar and Salakpur, in Bardiya District. We mounted elephants and hunted antelope. There was one elephant driver, and four or five riders who were the Jajarkot Raja and his brothers. We killed the antelope with guns and made dried meat. We also hunted gazelle and wild pig but not tigers. The king did not give us anything for our work, just lodging and food, that's all. Well, sometimes a little money, some clothes, some drink."

In the last century, Raut caste men like Gogane have also earned their living through ferry services. Rauts carve a wooden boat from the *sal* tree (*Shorea robusta*) and take people across the treacherous river waters of the Bheri River, a large tributary of the Karnali River. Nomadic Rautes, too, are locally known for the wooden boats they carve in order to go across rivers (but they only ferry themselves). However, since a suspension bridge in Jajarkot was completed in 1927, there has been little need for ferry services at this key crossing point on the Bheri River.[11] Unfortunately, the first modern development project in Jajarkot wiped out the Rauts' ferry and fishing services.

Since Rauts like Gogane spent so much time at the river, their other work was to catch fish and send it up the hill to the Jajarkot king. Gogane explained, "In the Raja's house we received a *ṭika* [a mark of blessing upon the forehead given by a patron to his servant] and the Raja gave us a goat. For this, each year we brought the king four hundred kilos of fish in baskets. We gave the king's guard the fish and the guard gave the fish to the king. He never gave us money. He said that our service is to kill fish." This sounded strangely reminiscent of when nomadic Rautes received a *ṭika* and a goat for performing their dances for local government officials.

Besides Gogane's work hunting and fishing, I learned that Gogane's father, Biri, worked as a woodcutter for the king. As Gogane said, "My father worked cutting and carrying wood. If the king orders him to contact somebody then he goes and does that . . . just like a *katuwal*, king's messenger, but he wasn't an official messenger."[12] Even today, such messengers are important in Jajarkot since there are no phone lines, motorable roads, or telegraph services for communication. Looking back at this interview, I saw that it resonated with the types of work that recently settled hunter-gatherers would perform, such as working in the forest gathering wood and trotting along forest paths to deliver messages.

Rautes' Social Status in Nepal

It is notable that Rautes say they do not know the origins of their own people. Instead, stories are passed down from generation to generation—not histories, but oral tales that signify bits of Raute experience. For example, when I encouraged people to recall stories about the origins of Raute people, they would remember things their grandparents had told them. Women collecting yams, for example, talked about their origins in relationship to food, noting that God made the water and yams before s/he made humans. As one woman, Dhana Devi, remarked: "God (Sun) gave water and then the yams came. God first made the yams grow and afterwards s/he created humans, so we could have food to eat . . . because what else would we eat?" This snippet of a story highlights Rautes' emphasis upon good water and wild yams as important subsistence staples. In fact, even water is called "food." Water is something consumed, like food, and it is nourishing and can taste either good or bad. When Rautes migrated to a new forest patch during the end of my field research, they told me that they would camp in the the place they called "the place with water that is good food."

In another instance, Raute youth Chandra described an origin story in which, one day long ago, monkeys were born along the Karnali River as the two major clans of nomadic Rautes in his band. He detailed the origins of the two clans, describing the duties and responsibilities of each clan according to who was born upriver and who was born downriver. The Raskoti clan was born upriver, and they were responsible for certain religious paraphernalia, while the Kalyal clan was born downstream and was responsible for other religious items. The story of Rautes being born from monkeys should not be related to Western evolutionary theories, however, but seen in light of their ontological relationships with monkeys. Rautes view themselves and monkeys as siblings among God's children rather than in a social hierarchy of primates. This can be gleaned from other stories about monkeys in which, according to Rautes, monkeys used to be human long ago but lost cultural features such as speech and marriage rituals.

When pressed about their ancestral history by villagers, all Rautes tell a story about how they are ultimately related to the local royalty of the area. They state that they are the *ban ko rājā*, "kings of the forest." Once long ago, Raute elders tell villagers, we stayed in the forest while you made villages and farms. This implies, they stress, that their *jāt* (caste, race) is Thakuri, the social caste of nobility in western Nepal. Most villagers find it a strange contradiction that a noble caste would have remained in the forests, but still largely accept the Rautes' "impression-management" claims.[13]

Claiming a high-caste status is one of the Rautes' ways of dealing with the persistent efforts of villagers to assimilate them. Claiming high-caste status also acts as a camouflaging technique. Rautes do not allow villagers to watch them hunt, cook, carve, or perform other camp activities. At first blush, the explanation for this might seem apparent. As Rautes break so many Hindu rules, they cannot indefinitely maintain the impression of being high-caste Thakuri who "devolved" to the forests long ago. They eat captured langur and macaque almost every day. Such meat is strictly forbidden to Hindus, as they worship the monkey deity, Hanuman. Furthermore, Rautes sometimes eat with their left hands, another taboo. Hindus only eat with their right hands since to eat with the left is considered defiling and polluting. Furthermore, Rautes do not know when major Hindu festivals take place, nor do they know how to perform the simplest of Hindu rituals. For example, Raute men do not wear the high-caste sacred thread which is de rigueur among Thakuri men, and they don't know how to perform the *janāi lagāune* ceremony that bestows the sacred thread upon young men. And these facts of ignorance of Hindu life are compounded by more material differences between Rautes and Hindu villagers. Raute do not own houses, land, livestock, or gold, or know how to take out loans or engage in any number of fundamental practical activities that define what it means to be part of Hindu caste-organized society. Given all these differences, their claim to be "Thakuri" appears to be something of a trick. Villagers, noticing the lack of Thakuri caste behaviors, cannot help but make comparisons and find the Raute lacking in the essentials of high-caste social life. By villagers, then, the Rautes are seen as essentially imperfect Hindus, naive Nepalese citizens, and technologically "backward" people who have lost their property and wander like landless squatters (*sukumbāsi*).

When pressed by villagers to explain their claimed Thakuri caste, Rautes sometimes elaborate upon the following story, as elder Man Bahadur did during a trading session with villagers one morning:

> God comes in the form of Braha,[14] Bisnu, Mahaswor, and Bisokarma. Braha is a Bahun priest, Bisnu is a king, Mahaswor is a Magar, and Bisokarma is a Kami. From the four castes there were seven brothers and you and we are descended from these seven brothers. There were seven brothers eating food at one house. For the seven brothers there were seven plates of rice. All the brothers started to eat. One brother went out to work. All of them were eating their own plates of rice. But Mahila (second-eldest son) ate his own plate of rice and his father's too. Then Father was hungry. Father said to Mahila, the second son, "Why did you eat my rice, didn't you think I'd be hungry?" Mahila said to his father, "Don't thrash me—instead I'll run away from home." After that Mahila went to the jungle and started cutting wood—*twāāk twāāk*—he cut wood. We Rautes are descended from that second son.

In this oral recitation, Man Bahadur begins by showing off his knowledge of a folk classification of caste hierarchy, saying that the Rautes descended from the second of four separate, hierarchically arranged kinds of people: Brahman, Thakuri, Magar, and Kami. The number seven, important in Tibetic and shamanic religious practices (Oppitz 1983), is not explained, but seven is an auspicious number among many people in Jajarkot. Similar versions of origin stories are also told by other Tibeto-Burman ethnic groups in Nepal (Jacobson 1999).

In this story, the Rautes are descended from the second brother, implying that they rank second (as Thakuri) in caste hierarchy. If Rautes claimed to be descended from the first brother, this would be taken as a sign that they were declaring kinship with Brahmans—an impossible claim since they are illiterate, do not control large landholdings, and know little Hindu religious orthodoxy. The Rautes could plausibly claim to be descended from either the third or fourth brothers, making them descendants of Magars or Kamis, but each of these choices would be problematic. Historically, even though Magars were codified in the legal code of Nepal, the Muluki Ain of 1854, as part of the nonenslavable alcohol-drinking castes (*namāsinyā matwāli*; Hofer 1979, 45), Magar living in regions in which Rautes migrate and trade were often enslaved and worked as servants to the high castes. Knowing this, the Rautes would distance themselves from primordial association with Magars. Likewise, if they claimed kinship with the untouchable Kami caste (*pāni nacalyā kāmi*), Rautes would suffer the same cultural ostracism that other low castes have suffered (Parish 1998). This origin story, then, identifies the Raute people as belonging to the high social caste stratum known as *tāgādhāri*, or "wearers of the holy cord," despite their lack of this ritual adornment.

One might think that villagers would disapprove of such claims to high-caste status. However, villagers who heard this story seemed to accept it as authentic. In a local village shop, I listened to the Thakuri shopkeeper named Damodar, his neighbor, Yaggya Karki, and Damodar's aunt, Bhauju, discussing the Rautes' social status. At one point in conversation I asked them, "Are the Raute really Thakuri?" Damodar replied: "I think they're really Magar-like. They're obviously Mongoloid in appearance. And . . . ," at that point Yaggya cut in: "I think they're Thakuri. How else could they know so much about Thakuri rituals? And habits? I think that there were Thakuris a long time ago, and two types developed. One type is developed, they got education. The other type, the Raute, is undeveloped. So I think they're Thakuri." Bhauju just laughed and commented on how Rautes steal from gardens of villagers as they pass through.

While villagers may have various opinions of Raute ethnic origins, many approve of their Thakuri origin story since it allows them to interact with Raute traders and their wooden wares without fear of ritual pollution. The District Forestry Officer also commented that Rautes are "our organs," meaning that he viewed Rautes as an inner, personal reflection of his own ancestry. If Rautes were viewed as another low-caste group, he would never be able to romanticize Rautes in this way as part of his living heritage. In Jajarkot at least, Rautes are treated with visibly more deference than low-caste families. Further, the Raute claim of being "devolved" high castes also accounts for their interest in crafting wooden objects from the forest. Broadly, these origin stories offer villagers a way of connecting as human beings to the people of the forest. Likewise, the Rautes living in Kumaun refer to themselves (when talking with Hindu villagers) as "Banraji" because this carries the meaning "forest princes" for the surrounding farmers. Among themselves, however, they use their own Tibetan language and call themselves Bula or Raute.[15]

Hindu scholars would classify Rautes according to edicts spelled out in the legal code of Nepal. Today, while the constitution of Nepal states that all people are equal, social traditions in Jajarkot continue to apportion castes into status hierarchies arranged according to traditions codified in the traditional legal code. Although recent revisions of the Nepalese legal code have downplayed social caste status, villagers continue to employ caste and ethnic status as a significant facet of social identity. A Nepali aphorism reflects this sentiment, stating, "The low-caste Dom will be rulers after I am dead" (*Āphu mare pachi ḍumai rājā*). This means that all society will turn upside down when its lowest-ranking members reach a state of royalty. Such casteism is not uncommon in contemporary rural Nepal.

Where would Rautes fit into a social system based on ascribed caste status? According to the Muluki Ain, they would fall into the third social ranking, that of "enslavable alcohol-drinkers" (*māsinyā matwāli*), since they are considered to be most closely related genetically and linguistically to neighboring people known as Chepang, who were described as "enslavable alcohol drinkers" (Hofer 1979, 44–45). Ranked above the Rautes and Chepang would be the Thakuri and Chetri caste families, as they are part of the group known as the "wearers of the holy cord" (*tāgādhāri*). The legal code of Nepal recognized five delineated orders (*varṇāśram*) of people in Nepalese society.

1. Wearers of the holy cord (*tāgādhāri*): Brahman, Thakuri, Chetri, highest Newar
2. Nonenslavable alcohol-drinking castes (*namāsinyā matwāli*): Magar, Gurung, Sunuwar, some Newar
3. Enslavable alcohol-drinking castes (*māsinyā matwāli*): Tibetans (Bhote), Chepang, Kumal, Hayu, Tharu, Gharti (Rautes would fall into this category)
4. Castes from whom receiving water is unacceptable or untouchable (*pāni nacalne choi chiṭo hālnu naparnyā*): Newar butchers, musicians, washerwomen, Muslims, Europeans
5. Castes from whom receiving water is unacceptable or untouchable, and whose touch requires purification (*pāni nacalne choi chiṭo hālnu parnyā*): Hindu blacksmiths, tanners, shoemakers, tailors, minstrels, musicians; Newar meat skinners, fishermen, and scavengers

The 1991 constitution declared illegal the practice of treating people from categories four and five as untouchable. However, the law is not enforced at the current time. Today, the people of category five are called "Dalit," with the sympathetic connotation of people who are the downtrodden classes of society. Aware of the caste hierarchies laid out in the legal code, most villagers are open to the possibility that Rautes might historically have belonged to the first social order rather than the third and, for whatever reason, hid like hermits deep in the forests. In addition, most "forest people" and tribals of northern India often claim to hail from royal lineages. This ambiguity of incorporation into the caste system is common among hunter-gatherers, horticulturalists, Tibeto-Burman–speaking peoples, and other peoples (*janāta*) shifting into caste (*jāti*) social systems.

National Identity

Are Rautes citizens of Nepal? What does it mean to be Nepalese? Does it mean speaking Nepali, the national language? That one's father is a Nepalese citizen? Does it mean living within the modern nation-state of Nepal? Carrying an identity card? Does it mean paying taxes to the government of Nepal? Does it involve a primordial feeling of attachment to the homeland of Nepal? Must one have a feeling of loyalty to the government? These are all important questions the answers to which will enable us to understand Raute identity in relationship to their surrounding farming communities.

When the word *Nepali* is uttered, it evokes a host of primordial loyalties concerning national identity (Alavi 1973).[16] Nepalese identity is evoked through speaking the official national language, even though about one hundred other languages are also spoken in Nepal. In terms of geography, Nepalese people identify themselves as born in Nepal or from regions with diasporas of Nepalese communities.[17] Almost all people of Nepal are registered voters and pay taxes,[18] if only a tithe for cutting firewood or registering a gun. But being Nepalese is not simply a matter of voting and having one's name recorded in census, tax, and land records. When I have spoken with Nepalese in Indian borderlands, almost all these migrants mention their sense of patriotism to their homeland. This involves a primordial feeling of belonging to one's home village or town. For some Nepalese, traveling represents an adventurous excursion, but one that eventually brings them back "home." This sense of loyalty to one's place of origin is an especially important marker of identity even though it can shift according to circumstances.

While I was traveling in Kumaun, India, in 1989, I listened to many Nepalese migrants talk about their homes. On one occasion, a group of thirty "Jumli" (men from Jumla District, Nepal) were standing in the rain outside my hotel. As we began to talk, one of the men told me: "We are Raut caste men and we don't own any land. At home, our service is to wade deep into the rivers trapping fish, but it is winter now and we are looking for migrant work. We came here from the district center in Jumla just eight days ago. We have walked for six days and then we took a train for one day and then a bus today. We heard that there would be work thirty kilometers north of here, in the Chākute area. We do not have any work leader (*thekādhār*, "contractor") and we alone just decide where and when to move. Tonight we will sleep in the forest, and, as you see, we have our sleeping blankets and packs with food. We didn't bring any illegal goods with us to trade."

Just then, a bus driver from the nearby town of Ranikhet showed up. He beckoned to the sorry-looking group, standing drenched in the rain. He said: "I can see you have no *met*, work organizer. How will you negotiate a proper deal for your hard work? Listen, I will act as your *met* and ensure you get paid. I will even drive you to Chākute. All my help will only cost you twenty rupees per man." For six hundred rupees, he promised, this was a very good deal. The Rauts looked at each other, and didn't seem to consider the offer very seriously. One of them turned to the bus driver and replied: "We only need a ride. We don't need a work organizer. We can pay you thirty rupees to drive us, but that is all." The Rauts knew that this offer would be rejected, and they turned back to me. "We will return to Jumla in the spring, when the weather is warmer and we can fish." And with that, they walked back up to the forest, braced against the freezing December rains.

Like the migrant Rauts who will return to Jumla, for the nomadic Rautes there is a similar sense of periodic return, as when they return to a camp that they used in previous years. It is then that they point out the trees they remember, the small water wells they dug, and the campgrounds that were used on previous foraging rounds. They love their forested environs, yet nevertheless there exists a certain feeling of ambiguity over their primordial attachments to the Nepalese state. They tell villagers, "We are Raute," but they never say, "We are Nepali." This sense of primordial attachment to ethnicity over nationality stems from their historically tenuous ties to the state. First, their native language is Raute, not Nepali, and many people in the nomadic Raute camp do not speak Nepali. That Rautes speak a Tibetic language rather than a Sanskritic one is a signifier of alterity, of "otherness." They are already marked as different, yet it does not prevent Rautes from ascribing to Nepalese national identity, as many Nepalese speak a Tibetic mother tongue. Even more telling, Rautes resent sedentary and farming lifestyles. As nomads, the Rautes do not register as citizens, do not carry a *nagrikta* (citizen card), do not vote or affiliate as residents of any political district. This is not a simple oversight; the Rautes refuse to register. When asked if they pay taxes on the many types of wood they cut, they say, "No, we are Raute. We do not pay taxes."

Rautes are not proud of being Nepalese nor embarrassed by it. If asked whether they are Nepalese, they say, "Yes, we're Nepalese too," but they add qualifiers. As Mayn Bahadur pointed out, "The king of Nepal is the king of the people of Nepal; the Raute are the kings of the forest." I take this statement to mean that the Rautes want sovereignty over themselves: let them rule their nomadic forest fiefdom and let the government of Nepal control the rest. By asserting the right to control their lives in the forests, it could be construed that they are arguing for the existence of multiple, overlapping, and flexible identifications, and ultimately for an identity that privileges ethnicity over nationality. In other words, they desire a space in which to exist where they may safely claim that they are indeed Rautes above all else but still acknowledge that they live within the Nepalese nation-state and abide by most laws.

Nonetheless, Raute identity is styled to keep party politics at a strategic distance from the everyday politics of their lives. As one elder put it:

> Concerning politics, whichever system comes, we accept it. But we should not make our king of Nepal sad.[19] Whichever party is good in Nepal I am in that party. We don't vote. You can vote but we don't vote. We respect the party that all Nepalese people support. If all people were in the same party, then we could say we are in the party, but otherwise it is better to keep quiet. We respect all the parties. What can we do by saying that we support Rautes? Rautes are so little. This world is very big. Whatever party this world supports, we can all support. If they found out that we are supporting UML communist party and if another system comes along, then they might destroy us. Maybe all the parties are nice. We don't support any parties. But why are some parties bigger than others? Bigger parties look after the smaller parties. If one wins, then other smaller parties should join the big party. . . . I am like a mouse or bird. . . . I don't know anything. I don't care if one side loses or wins. . . . When the forest starts to get thinner, then we have to ask the chairman of the Forest Association to do something.

As political pragmatists, Rautes emphasize that politics is dangerous. It is no wonder that they often refer to themselves as the *milāune mānche*, the ones who get along well with others, because they cannot afford to alienate local political elites. Their strategy is mostly one of avoidance of village politics, while at the same time pursuing their own interests in forest resources through patronage of local elites. They never side with any particular political faction, since the power balance is constantly changing, and in this they demonstrate a certain political sophistication.

Describing themselves as like a bird or a mouse, as utterly ignorant of local politics, is somewhat of a ruse. While it is true that they do not know the names or political affiliations of local politicians, they do know how to lobby and patronize local elites. For example, they will meet with district forestry officers and community forest members in order to obtain support while they are foraging in state-owned forests. Rautes forage in officially designated "noncultivated forest lands" that are the property of the state. With recent decentralization policies, such government-owned lands have been assigned to numerous local "community forest user groups" that have an interest in forest preservation and improvement. Rautes recognize that their livelihood is tied to access to forests, and thus they make an effort to patronize elites who can control access to local state-owned forests.

While Nepalese citizens may not own forests, this doesn't mean that they don't occasionally attempt to steal them. For example, a 1988 Jajarkot District Court case was heard in which the litigant, a Brahman adult male named Pande, paid 1 dam (Rs .05) tax for a parcel of land that he claimed to own. When he attempted to register the land parcel, it was blocked by the Land Survey Office. The head of the office, acting as defendant on behalf of the Nepalese government, demonstrated that the litigant had no *lāl-purja* or *moṭh* (land ownership documents) and that, in fact, the land under question was categorized as "noncultivated forestland." The judge ruled that the litigant could not put forest land under private ownership. This type of case was not uncommon and is particularly revealing of landowners' intentions toward forestland. While Rautes are uninvolved in such machinations, they nevertheless must patronize such landowners, as they camp in nearby forests. Their identity revolves around avoidance of overt politics and tactful social relations with local elites. Such tactful relations have become more important, as communities of Maoists camp in forests as well. Rautes have to negotiate an increasingly dangerous landscape of political intrigue even though they are largely unconcerned about the political machinations of their sedentary neighbors.

The Politics of Identity

Villagers, too, are struggling with questions of identity, for they are often stigmatized as backward, undeveloped, and ignorant by more urbane visitors from Kathmandu (Pigg 1992). After years of being compared with sophisticated urban Nepalese and Indians, rural farmers feel ashamed of their lifestyles and fervently want to "improve" themselves. In their struggle to modernize, rural villagers often feel held back by people like the Rautes, people who don't follow modernist ideologies. Ideologies of social improvement prevent Nepalese elites from being able to appreciate the Rautes' unique history and identity as contemporary hunter-gatherers. Village elites feel that the Rautes must join "modern" society in order for the Nepalese nation as a whole to progress.

Not all, but most villagers whom I met had these ideas of bringing the Rautes, a "primitive" people, into a more advanced or modern society. As Henri Lefebvre (1995, 1) writes, modernism is form of consciousness that successive generations have of themselves that employs triumphalist images

and projections of the social self over previous generations. This form of superior consciousness is composed of many illusions, pretensions, and fanci-
ful projections. Having a belief in one's more "modern" condition over that
of previous generations represents a form of ahistorical and ethnocentric
thinking. Villagers in Jajarkot, similarly, are unaware of their own position
in history and thus believe themselves to be superior to and more modern
than Rautes.[20] This view, unfortunately, would deprive Raute society of any
sense of history, deeming it to be "traditional" and thus lacking in historical
scope.

Although in fact the Rautes are not "behind" anyone, as they have their
own history and obviously are living in contemporary society too, the
convictions of villagers of the Rautes' backwardness are understandable.
Technologically complex societies such as India and the United States have
persuaded technologically simple societies that their methods are backward and inferior. Jajarkoti villagers, too, have experienced this hegemonic
ideological assault ever since the early twentieth century when the first development projects were planned. Currently, even well-educated villagers
find themselves resisting ridicule by citified folk in Kathmandu and other
Nepalese cities. In attempts to model themselves as "modern," villagers
struggle to adopt introduced technologies such as telephones and electricity. Learning from Indian films and magazines, they adopt Hindi phrases,
cooking recipes, hairstyles, and mannerisms. Any unsophisticated practices
are summarily rejected, especially by upwardly mobile village elites. In their
struggle for modernity, many villagers go to extremes in disparaging the
nomadic lifestyle of Rautes. Raute men and women, too, struggle on behalf
of their own identity, but with tremendously different needs and goals. They
need to avoid assimilation into the villagers' cultural life. Preserving Raute
cultural identity takes tremendous effort. Sometimes strategies of accommodation are called for, as when a Raute trader performs Nepalese rhymes
for villagers; at others, cultural resistance is necessary, as when a Raute trading group huddles together speaking their own language, rejecting villager
offers of hospitality.

Yet each generation faces new challenges. The modern Raute challenge
is how to deal with Nepalese villagers in ever more mundane daily interactions. Should Rautes adopt rubber flip-flops? Should they drink *rāksi* rice
alcohol? Should they offer to dance in exchange for goats and rice? Some
Rautes favor adoption of villager material objects, while others prefer to
keep as far distant from villagers as possible. Rautes are thus caught seesaw-
ing between what young Chandra Raute described as a schism between the
old Raute era and the new Raute era. When we discussed a recent Raute

controversy over whether to dance for the villagers or go hunting, Chandra explained:

> On dancing day I really feel like dancing, yeah. But I knew what was in Sher Bahadur's heart [a conservative Raute elder]. If I showed eagerness to dance, he would cancel the dance. So I [cleverly] arranged it so we danced after he moved his camp. I'm a modern man, a modern man (*achelako nāya mānche*). It wouldn't flow in the waters. [This Raute saying implies that you can't get along with others by using a stubborn attitude.] These days there's a new era, separate from the older era. In this new era we should be even more clever. Compared to today, we were pretty naive before.

Chandra's statement is telling in that it highlights a certain attitude of modernity, a belief that Chandra's generation faces the new challenges of a modern era. In situating himself thus, Chandra derives his own political identity as a "modern man" from his opposition to another elder's conservative political position. Chandra's attitude is somewhat different from that of other Rautes, because the range of political behavior in the group is broad and varied. Man Bahadur, for example, adjudicated Raute disputes with amazing skill and was himself a model of fairness. Ain Bahadur adroitly demonstrated the Raute ethos of sharing and accommodation during hunting and camp interactions with other Rautes. Ratna Bahadur organized and led his splinter camp to new hunting grounds just as he had promised, exemplifying leadership and bravery. Some of the most important political behaviors necessary among foraging populations were to be found, not among farming communities, but in the Rautes' decisions concerning hunting, sharing, and getting along with others. This range of political behavior within Raute society itself presented Raute youths with much to consider and learn. In order to make their foraging lifestyle successful, it was these "inner" political behaviors that youths emulated, not the political machinations of surrounding farming communities.

While intragroup political relations are fundamental to the successful continuity of Raute foraging society, intergroup political relations between Rautes and farmers are also important. Rautes know that they must interact with farming communities by extracting promises from local elites and obtaining access to forest resources. They know that they are part of an interconnected political landscape where changes in the dominant society absolutely affect Raute political decisions; they are enfolded within a larger political dynamic that grips Nepalese villagers and nomadic Rautes alike. But the question for Rautes is not one of whether to assimilate and become food producers. As they put it, they would rather "cut their throats" than take up farming. The question of whether or not to identify themselves as Rautes is grounded in everyday matters about whether to adopt Nepalese goods, Hindu ideologies, and other habits that sedentary peoples take for granted. Rautes wish to remain the *bāsisthāne mānche*, indigenous people of western Nepal, and each camp move brings new challenges to maintaining Raute ethnic identity.

4

Forests as Home

Though we see the same world, we see it through different eyes.
—Virginia Woolf, *To the Lighthouse*

"The Forest is where God's children live."
—Mayn Bahadur Raute

Smoking a cigarette, Ain Bahadur Raute walked over to the edge of the Rautes' forest camp and sat down beside me and Prakāsh, a local villager from Jajarkot District. I asked Ain if he knew why I came to do field research with the Rautes living in the forests of western Nepal. "Svādhko lāgi [Because you feel an interest]," he replied, as if that was a natural explanation for my presence. Ain expected that I would ask him the question that all the sedentary villagers ask of him, "Why do you live in the forests instead of in villages?" The question carries much moral weight, for every Hindu knows that living in the forests is primitive, yet also can imbue the forest dweller with moral superiority. Ain proffered, "My heart is in living here, in the forest. . . . Since the time of our ancestors, it has been just like today. The forest is fine . . . the yams are still easy to dig."

But before we got to launch into a longer discussion, a helicopter flew overhead. Ain looked up, obviously vexed, and I thought how very strange. Where did it come from? Kathmandu is hundreds of miles away, and between the Maoists and the monsoon rains, planes fly only rarely in the area. Prakāsh said it probably was routed between Dolpo and Surkhet District, bringing supplies from Surkhet and returning with people from Dolpo. Helicopters represent a newer version of transporting goods, like a complex version of the sheep "trains," where caravans of sheep continue to carry trade salt for groups such as the Humli Khyampa. The sheep trains travel from

*Tibet down to southern Nepal and return again to Tibet with trade goods
from India. These are the same sheep trains that Rautes encounter and with
whom they trade their carved wooden bowls for salt. But it was a helicopter
that raged over the Rautes' camp, not a ragtag line of sheep and humans, not
anyone the Rautes will ever meet in person.*

To Rautes, the forests are not wild places, even though they are filled with
animals and few people. Rather, the forested world is peopled by tigers,
bears, deer, monkeys, birds, small trees, yams, stones, and other sentient
beings. This is where God's children live, according to the Rautes, and it
represents a domestic space. But other humans also live in forests and use
the resources—wood collectors, surveyors, Hindu ascetics, trekkers, forestry officials, forest-user groups. All these groups view the forests through the
prism of their own personal interests and cultural traditions. For these others, forests evoke fundamentally different ideas, usually based upon Hindu
interpretations of the natural environment. The Hindu-based ideologies of
forests as natural/supernatural spaces are interesting because they are so
different from Raute worldviews, and they form a comparative background
for further insight into the forest-foraging Rautes' beliefs. Thus there are
fascinating multiple and overlapping meanings assigned to forested spaces.

The right to define a given locale is not arbitrary; different groups have
vested interests and political power over others and thus have an interest in
asserting the "correctness" of their vision of the landscape (Arnold 1996;
Bhatt 2003; Dove 1994; Humphrey 1995; Jeffery 1998; Parajuli 2001; Skaria
1999). In rural Nepal, particular landscapes, such as community forests,
come to be known by Nepalese villagers through the subjectivity of possession. They are figured as *hāmro ban,* "our forest," and community user
groups aggressively protect their rights to particular parcels of forested land
even though the government of Nepal legally owns most forests. Rautes, on
the other hand, have no vested interest in owning or protecting a particular
forest. Their concern, rather, is in the utilization of its products, in the image of the forest as a nurturing being, and in keeping a sense of gratitude
toward the forest as a parental figure.

Semantic differences concerning forests have fundamentally important
political ramifications, because both foragers and farmers must negotiate
multiple and contrastive claims to ownership and authenticity of forested
domains. As they negotiate not simply the material dimensions of forests
(resources, land mass, biomass quality) but especially sets of meanings, forests become objects of political contention. Are forests to be used as camps,
retreats, preserves, wilderness areas, sustainable growth areas, or ethno-

ecological refuges? In the twenty-first century, forests in Asia are the sites of contested ideologies that face the political pressures exerted by logging companies, government development schemes, and urban sprawl (Guha 1990; Murashko 2000; Peet and Watts 1996). For people everywhere, the forest question looms large as we contemplate the role forests should play in contemporary society and environmental policy making.

For forest foragers, whose subsistence depends on hunting and gathering, forest protection is tantamount to cultural survival. Foragers actually live in the forests and view forested places as their domestic space. They give forest places toponyms that highlight notable natural and utilitarian features. For example, Raute foragers name a forest according to where berries and yams are found, where bears live, or as a place that is the shape of a particular leaf. In their Tibetic language, they can also give forests higher-order names to reference a midland temperate forest (*manāng*), found in Jajarkot District, or a hotter subtropical forest (*damār*), such as is found in Dang District. While Rautes were migrating to a forest patch in Jajarkot District, they told me: "Tomorrow we will be migrating to Cholani. This place means where 'white water that is a good food' is available. Now we will leave Kanchala, the place where tobacco-like chewing leaves are found." Local farmers use none of these names, and, in fact, farmers name the nearby forests according to their own separate toponymic systems.

For millions of forest-based farmers living in the Himalayan hills, gathering wild tubers, berries, and greens is important for supplementing their subsistence diet. N. Manandhar (2002) records an astonishing range of forest plants used by farmers in Nepal, including 1,002 medicinal plants, 651 food plants, and 696 plants used for thatch, fodder, furniture, religious paraphernalia, and so on. While both foragers and farmers share a concept of forests as places to fill subsistence needs, the states of Nepal and India view forests in much more proprietary terms. In Nepal, forests historically have been seen as presenting opportunities for taxation of their saleable products. Farmers in Jajarkot District report that tax collectors often took all edible forest products that exceeded householders' subsistence. The tax collectors even taxed farmers by taking a portion of their wild yam harvests. More recently, however, government officials such as district forestry officers have focused on working with community user groups to reforest and protect endangered forest areas.

How can changing roles and meanings of forested places be negotiated among various interested parties such as foraging farmers, hunter-gatherers, and government officials? Especially between dominant polities and subordinate groups, views of society and nature are often diametrically opposed. Raute foragers, for example, view wild yams as food but also as their own ancestors. Farmers, on the other hand, just see yams as a tasty addition to the evening meal and probably will never adopt a view of them as sentient beings.[1] Some scholars doubt that a posthumanist approach in which society and nature can intertwine can successfully be developed (Howell 1996). Anthropologist Signe Howell is correct in pointing out that most people from agricultural societies will scorn belief in the environment as a sentient being. Other scholars, however, find that humans *must* develop a more integrated understanding of their place in the material world (Hirsch and O'Hanlon 1995). Such a perspective need not incorporate beliefs in a sentient ecology per se, but should acknowledge the ecological role humans play within the physical environment. Ultimately, whether or not environmental policy makers address such ontological issues is important because the perspectives of humans in the "natural" world shape policies that affect forest quality and coverage. Ultimately, it will become necessary for us to revisit cultural attitudes toward forests and to rethink how our beliefs about nature affect forest initiatives such as community forestry projects. Even though paradigms of nature and society are increasingly being ruptured by modern political events and disasters (Blaikie and Brookfield 1987), notions of nature as wild and outside the bounds of the "social" continue to form the basis of modern political policy making in Nepal and India.

In particular, the notion of things as *sanskriti* (cultural) acts as a political tool to enforce a set of hegemonic ideas about forestry use that are employed by the dominant and technologically complex Hindu societies. Villages, fields, orchards, and roads are places where villagers invest time, labor, and money to build and maintain them. Using a policy of social development (*samāj sudhār*) based on the privilege of *sanskriti* social rules, dominant polities control technologically simple societies of forest-dwelling peoples contained within their national borders. Local places, on the other hand, are thought of as *prākriti* (natural) or a local dialect is called *Prākrit*, the natural language of the local people. Things and people deemed *prākriti* will thus be subject to the hegemonies of their more *sanskriti* neighbors so long as there is a political need for it.

The basis for the hegemony of culture over nature ultimately stems from a philosophical balance found within one of the major schools of Indian thought known as the the *Sāṅkhya* tradition. In this religious discourse, *prākriti* elements act as a form of active power, while *puruṣa* lies dormant as a potential, but inert, authority. Broadly, *puruṣa* is activated by *prākriti* and the two metaphorically embrace as equals. In sociological discourse, *prākriti* and *puruṣa* emerge in many significations, with *prākriti* signified as female, powerful, natural, active, uncontrolled, wild, and undirected. The element *puruṣa*, on the other hand, signifies male authority, a kind of seed and carrier of social hierarchy (Doniger 1980, 118). By extension, *puruṣa* signifies control, cultural authority, *sanskriti*, civilized behavior. In the everyday conversations of Nepalese villagers these symbolic distinctions are not consciously evident in folk philosophies of the forest. But these principles are applied in some social situations (weddings, sacred-thread ceremonies), and variations of them ripple away from deeply held Hindu philosophical models of the universe.

In the Himalayan hills, where Hinduism meets shamanism meets Buddhism, concepts of nature and culture are not a duality but are intertwined and play off of historical events. The duality of the notions of culture and nature is transcended, as writers such as McKim Marriott (1976) have demonstrated. For example, while forests are natural places, they are nevertheless the abode of local deities. Further, the social construction of nature as being in opposition to culture is not universal; it is found primarily in technologically complex, agriculturally based societies. Many technologically simple societies have been shown to lack a category of nature altogether (Goodale 1980). As researchers working with horticultural and foraging societies have found, places that more complex societies label as natural, wild, or uncivilized are often culturally constructed in much more complicated ways (Ingold 1986; Rival 1996; Strathern 1980). The end result is a set of mixed messages in which technologically complex societies employ culture-over-nature arguments in order to control simpler societies, while congruently simple societies reject the dualistic culture/nature reasoning in favor of their own autonomous constructions of themselves in the material world.

In South Asia, particularly, there remains a swirling set of polysemic messages, or messages that carry multiple meanings, around things that are *prākriti*. The concept of *prākriti* contains an emergent quality that is contingent on local circumstances and individual experiences, rendering it something pure, local, natural, and uncultivated but also fraught with a negative valence of the *ābikāsi*, an undeveloped state of being. For example, an elderly farmer told me of a legal battle his family won, saying with a certain disappointment: "After we won, the land was full of trees [smacks his lips disapprovingly]. The reason is because the land was never plowed."

This sense of the natural as backward or in need of improvement can also metanymically shift, its meanings can transfer, to people who reside in forests. For example, where I live in southern California there are stories of the "mountain men" of Baja California. These are supposedly hermits, somewhat wild men, who live by hunting and trapping rabbits and deer. They are supposed to eschew civilization and live an undeveloped and primitive life in the rugged Baja hills and mountains. From the perspective of the people living in urban centers such as San Diego or even Kathmandu, rural people who live in forests and mountains are framed as "backward" and "primitive." In western Nepal, years of hegemonic subjugation to urban centers in Kathmandu and India have resulted in rural householders' acquiring a sense of marginalization and backwardness, of feeling they need upliftment and improvement (Pigg 1992). This sense of superiority of the urban over the rural has been found throughout the world and may be a global phenomenon, yet its cultural contours are specific in South Asia to the negative ideals that are associated with *prākriti* spaces.

In rural Nepal, negative connotations of forests as primitive, simple, and undeveloped "rub off" on forest foragers even more as they live within such marginal spaces. In Nepal, the concept of the *banvāsi* (*banmānu, jaṇgyāli*), the Tarzan-like "jungle-man," acts as a metonym for the concept of someone and something primeval. For example, a Kathmandu news reporter interviewed me about the Raute hunter-gatherers and at one point asked, "How many years behind us are the Raute?" As I fumbled to respond that they are not backward or "primitive," he conveyed both concern and pleasure to know of people who could be the target of social upliftment. Farmers, of course, do not view Rautes as Rautes view themselves.

Rautes see themselves as contemporary people who purposely use simple technologies. They consider themselves to be "God's children who live in the forests," as opposed to others who live outside of forested spaces. By situating others as outside of the forests, Rautes are, on a deep level of social ordering, calling into question the humanity of farmers and foreigners. It is precisely these "more complicated ways," involving the heterotopia of forests, that serve as a conveyance for deeper insight into the sociopolitical relations between Rautes and Hindu householders. By a heterotopia, I am referring to places, particularly forests, that have a unique reality for each inhabitant and, more broadly, for each ethnic group or class of people (Owens 2002; Rodman 1992;[2] Foucault 1986; Whatmore 2002). Heterotopias represent other, marginal spaces. But they also represent "jumbled spaces," places that have alternate and contested meanings. And it is in this alterity that the power to know and name a place develops. Thus, while we may state that Rautes live in rural wilderness, such places have entirely different meanings for those moving through the forests themselves. Such heterotopic places are more complex than a mere ethnographic setting; they exist as both a naturalistic object in space and an existential concept. These places have polysemic meanings for different users, since, ultimately, forests are physical entities known to us as symbolic and cultural spaces.

Hindu Householders' Conceptions of Forests

Forests represent many things to different villagers, but several themes run through the literature and my ethnographic field research with household residents in Nepal. Despite the fact that most forests in Nepal are the property of the government, many householders expressed a sense of ownership and control over the forests surrounding their villages. For this reason, community forest-user groups closely watch and control these forests and their resources. Children, for example, are encouraged to roam there and collect items such as fruit, greens, and medicinal plants. Older women will also forage in the forests, especially to harvest available resources such as butter tree nuts (*Bassia butyracea*; N. *ciuri*, to make wine and oil).

The first modern forest management systems in Nepal were put into place circa 1912 under Prime Minister Chandra Shamsher Rana. Over time, the politics of forest use and ownership in Nepal represents a long tale of association between the government, subsistence farmers, pastoralists, and forest foragers (Budhathoki 1987; Chhetri 1994; Gilmour and Fisher 1991; Manandhar 2002; Stevens 1993). Presently six types of forest ownership and control exist in Nepal: private forests, community forests, government-managed forests, religious forests, leasehold forests, and conserved forests. Contemporary government forestry programs in Nepal are based on decentralization policies that have given a remarkable amount of control to community forest-user groups. From 1986 to 1997, for example, Jajarkot District Forestry Officers (DFOs) changed their relationships with local farmers and opened DFO offices to facilitate and negotiate forest-based conflicts. With the increasing control of forests in western Nepal by Maoist groups circa 1998–2008, farmers had to negotiate forest utilization with both the Maoists and the government of Nepal.

The notion of the forest as a source of abundance is also reflected in Nepali poetry and song. Laksmiprasad Devkota, a well-known Nepali poet, associates forest resources with poverty, yet does so with a romantic allusion:

> Purses of gold are like the dirt on your hands,
> What can be done with wealth?
> Better to eat only nettles and greens,

With happiness in your heart.

(Trans. Hutt 1993, 42)

"Nettles and greens" refers to *sisnu* (*Urtica dioica*), the ubiquitous wild food that is emblematic of Nepalese poverty. While many high-caste villagers express shame at having to resort to eating wild food, other householders collect the delicious spinach-like nettles on a regular basis. Thus Devkota's romanticizing of a materially impoverished life enjoins us to believe that those without wealth can nevertheless be happy since the nearby forests are always abundant sources of sustenance. Village women especially have a stake in improving forest resources. Some are hired as *ban herālu*, forest guards, whose duty it is to watch the forests, participate in plantings, and protect forests from unscrupulous overutilization by noncommunity members and poachers. In forest guards a sense of caretaking develops even when their jobs are enmeshed in informal political intrigues involving illicit use of forests. One such forest guard, who was beaten by illegal forest users in the Rāni Khet Ban ("the Queen's Field and Forest"),[3] told how she had confronted the poachers because she was determined to make "her" forest grow thick and lush.

For other men and women, the forest evokes a sense of fear, especially as night falls. Many with whom I spoke were quick to point out that *boksi* (witches) and *bhut* (ghosts) live in the forests and along rivers. Walking through these spaces as night falls or, worse, in the middle of the night can be dangerous as they might be waylaid by a malevolent supernatural being. I remember being woken in the middle of the night on one occasion in which my next-door neighbor was found having a seizure and frothing at the mouth. It was quickly determined that he had wandered home in the middle of the night and a witch had "jumped" down his throat and was eating his stomach. Such an unfortunate event could have been avoided, local Nepalese opined, if only the man had been more careful and avoided walking in the forest at night.[4]

For many Hindu villagers, the entire Nepalese landscape is one in which the social construction of nature is completely interwoven with cosmological ideas of divine grace and wrath. A divine geography enfolds all of the country, like a *māṇḍala* superimposed over the mountains, rivers, and lowlands. The entire natural landscape is conceived as something that can only be revealed by human exegesis: woods, rivers, and mountains are waiting to have their sacred nature revealed by just the right human beholder. The deities reveal themselves through many means, for instance, in the form of sacred sites that contain numerous signs, such as unusual stones (*silā*), sacred river confluences, and other *prākriti* icons. As Lecomte-Tilouine points out (2003), venerated elements in nature are manifest evidence of the divine interventions of the gods and underscore that the whole natural world is their handiwork.

Most Hindu Nepalese also believe that forests are sacred, and even linked with a gendered sense of femininity, nurture, and sexuality. As Linda Iltis notes (1994, 349), the goddess known as Swasthāni, whose name means "one's stopping place," is a goddess of the Himalayas. Not only does Swasthāni act as a protector of Himalayan places and of the state of Nepal, other goddesses regularly are worshipped for their protection of individual homeowners' properties. In Jajarkot, for example, a popular story involves a woman known as Catur Malla (clever ruler) who becomes the goddess Mālikā (head mistress, owner, governess). She is given *pujā* worship each month because she committed suicide (N. *ātmahatya*) in order to become a tutelary deity and protect the land rights of farmers (Fortier 1995, 334–336). As the incarnation known as Mālikā, the tutelary goddess protects the ordered Hindu world of fields, villages, and pastures, while the cosmologically disordered world of the *jaŋgāli* forest is patrolled by witches and more fearsome female supernatural beings.

Goddesses do also protect forested spaces, and these become "cultured spaces" within the uncultured forest ones. For example, pilgrimage sites can be found at forest pools and next to designated trees. Among Tibeto-Nepalese Magars, Marie Lecomte-Tilouine (2000, 137) describes the propitiation of a local goddess, Chābdi Bārāhi (one who appears in the form of greatness), who dwells in a forest pool and demands bloody animal sacrifice. As a female deity, Chābdi Bārāhi represents the earth as a feminine principle (*bhumi*), while the semen/seed that fertilizes earth is represented as the husband of the earth. But in everyday practice, villagers do not worship men or gods in their seminal role, but rather the goddesses at their forested shrines, just as Mālikā and Chābdi Bārāhi are worshipped.

During everyday social interactions between men and women, the notion of the forest also possesses strong sexual connotations. As a sexually charged space, the forest represents a place where covetous liaisons are made, where illicit rape and bride capture occur, and, on a more romantic note, where hopes of love begin. Mohan Koirala, for example, writes in his poem titled "I love your daughter":

> Oh [*sic*] blue reflection on an unstained rock,
> You do not know how I love your daughter
> Who darts behind green shrubs when she sees me

And who is startled when I find her·alone.

(Trans. Hutt 1993, 89)

Yet even as nature and forests are romanticized by villagers, ironically they are also culturally constructed as "uncivilized" and unfit for human habitation in their original condition. The forest may be figured as sacred with respect to its being part of the earth, but it is simultaneously marginalized as a profane space for its lack of "cultureness." Villagers view the forest (*ban* or *jaŋgal*) as a place that is wild, uncivilized, and lacking in culture or a fully developed humanity. It embodies what might be called a marginal place that gives central places definition and legitimacy (Shields 1991). Thus villagers regularly denigrate forest spaces as worthless and inhabitable while at the same time utilizing them for a broad range of products.

Rautes: Forest Dwellers

We may start our efforts to understand Raute cultural views of the forest by learning about their ethnonyms and exonyms, or the names which they use to describe themselves versus the names outsiders use to describe them. Villagers call the nomadic Rautes by the exonyms *jaŋgali* (people of the jungle) and *banmanu* (forest-man) since these names evoke a sense of these people as wild and uncivilized. Farmers view Rautes as uncontrolled, wild, sexually charged, and inhabitants of a place of natural wealth rich in food resources. For example, I asked Maya Khatri, one of my elderly neighbors in Karkigaun village, "How are today's Rautes and the Rautes from before different?" She responded: "They're very different, granddaughter. Back then, we had our ways of getting food and speaking (*lāunu khānu boli bhāśa*) and they were just like deer in the forest." For this reason, the Raute notion that the forest represents a domestic rather than a wild space is difficult for villagers to fathom.

Raute men and women view their forest environs and their place within it in several ways that relate them in more personal ways to other sentient beings that dwell in forests. One of the ways in which Rautes have described themselves is as *Boṭ Prājā*, literally meaning "the political subjects of the trees" (Nepala 1983). This autonym belies a subordinate relationship to the forest, as *prājā* are normally political subjects of a *rājā*, a king. Thus Rautes are saying that the trees are metaphorically not only sentient beings but politically powerful ones—like kings—while they are their dependent subjects. This autonym is interesting for another reason. The neighboring foragers known as Chepang are called the *Prājā* by other Nepalese as an exonym that signals their status as political subjects of the king of Nepal (and also to signal that they are above the social caste status of slave). As an act of defiance, the Rautes called themselves not only *Prājā* in reference to their relation to the Nepalese state, but also *Boṭ Prājā*, indicating their fealty to the forest rather than to the king of Nepal. This represents a significantly different rendering of social space, one that marks the Rautes as fundamentally centered in a political space that includes trees as powerful sentient beings. In this context, the label *Boṭ Prājā* implies that the forest and its trees are one of the most important dimensions of social life for Rautes.

Conversely, I have also heard Rautes more recently describe themselves as "the kings of the forest" (*banko rājā* or *banrājā*). This ethnonym, used by various tribals (*ādivāsi*) in India, portrays Rautes in a politically dominant light within the political world of the forest where all creatures are considered as political beings. A polysemic message, the epithet kings of the forest also implies that if Rautes are indeed that, then their caste status should also be commensurably high, akin to that of the noble Thakuri caste who live throughout the region. Indeed, Rautes, like other foragers who use this autonym, do claim ancient caste affinity with the Thakuri kings and landed nobility. Linguistic evidence, however, points to Rautes as being Tibetic-speaking peoples (and possibly, even earlier, as Austroasiatic or Dravidian speakers) who have been absorbed into the Hindu social caste system.

A third way in which Rautes describe themselves in relation to the forest is as part of the "great family of God." When I asked who is part of this great family, one elder explained that all of God's children live in the forest. For the Raute, the forest is the source of life and sustenance, where reside all of the great family of God. Rautes discussed the various roles of the sun, moon, stars, and other nonhuman supernatural beings that are part of their great family. Man Bahadur, for example, claimed that the sun, known as Berh, represents their father, and the moon, Bairha (Berha), their mother. So when Rautes say that they are the children of God, they are referring to the creation of the world by Berh/Bairha as a creator deity.[5]

Monkeys are especially close to Rautes in their cosmological sense of family and are called "our little brothers." For most Hindu villagers, on the other hand, monkeys are nothing like brethren; rather, they represent creatures of either the natural or the supernatural world. They are either worshipped as the deity Hanuman or treated as wild disruptive scavengers that prey upon the corn crops. In the regions north of Raute territories, primatologists John Bishop and Naomi Bishop emphasize that Buddhist farmers are loath to hunt langurs, since killing other sentient beings is considered immoral (Bishop and Bishop 1978). Farmers will chase the animals when their grain crops are raided, but normally they refuse to kill the animals. In one reported example, however, the Tibetic-speaking Magars of Syangja District, Nepal, occasionally hunt monkeys. The hunters reportedly cut off the heads of their prey because the faces look too human and cannot be eaten (Marie Lecomte-Tilouine, personal communication, Dec. 2005). Thus various castes and ethnic groups in the area may view monkeys variously as deities, as sentient beings, as disruptive scavengers, or as a markedly lower order prey choice that is hunted only on occasion.

To Rautes, however, langur and macaque represent their brethren and one of God's children. As one Raute hunter stated, referring to monkeys: "The people (janāta) are God's sons and daughters. If they are not God's children, we wouldn't speak about them and God would have to create them. God made them for our help [our food] and they're important." The great family of God who lives in the forest is not limited by a geography of temporal and physical constraints. Some of their most important relatives are those who, having died, are now invisible spirits, known by the Raute term horh. The notion of horh is complex, an idea involving the spirits of ancestors. As I understand it, horh refers to the deified human spirit that pervades all forest life.[6] Rautes see the forest as a place of great reverence because it is a location imbued with the horhi atoms of spirit or sentience derived from all the animals, the sentient trees, and their own deceased relatives. As one elder explained: "You are also horh, and God of the forest is also horh and we are also horh. If God does true, then it will be true. If God does false, then the whole forest will be destroyed. All Gods are horhi, because we cannot see them."

In other interviews, horh seemed to have a pervasive quality. Broadly, horh refers in a mass-noun fashion to the Rautes' deceased ancestors, whom they believe exist as spirits, or atoms of sentience, existing all around them as Rautes move, not only through their mundane forest world, but also through a morally distinct domain, a sacred world filled with ancestral spirits. This large family of humans, animals, spirits, and deities may have different duties and characteristics, but all are important within their forest home. As one Raute elder insisted, he is no better or worse than any other of God's children.

Occasionally, Rautes communicate the importance of the forest to villagers by delivering such pithy remarks as "Without the forest, there is no life." Such phrases are heard occasionally in environmental sloganeering in India (Narayan 1997). It certainly is not lost upon Rautes that their sayings may result in benefits to their group, such as protection from political elites like district forestry officers. When Mayn Bahadur Raute said this during a discussion in the Jajarkot bazaar, he wanted to emphasize that Rautes utterly depend on the forest, but so do the villagers, and that both should respect the forest as the source of all life. Regularly, Rautes try to communicate their dependence on the forest as a place of life and not just a place to be utilized by humans. For them, the forest is a source of ultimate sustenance in both the religious and practical sense.

The Rautes' ontological domain of domesticity has clearly drawn boundaries, however. Places that are not part of where "God's family lives" lie outside the forest, in the domain of villages and domestic animals. Villagers are clearly not part of the Rautes' "family" in the cosmological sense, because they do not live in the forest. They represent a "foreign" yet necessary and interdependent realm in which egalitarian familial relationships do not apply.

Living in the Forest: A Raute Camp

For Rautes, forests signify something comforting, familial, and divine. Yet, it is not accurate to say that Rautes live in the forests per se, but rather that they live in huts (*não*) clustered together in camps (*nãola*), and that these camps are just as culturally manufactured and distinct from the surrounding forests as are villages. The camp contains marked boundaries, etched pathways, small drainage ditches, and other physical constructions. Yet because camps and huts are composed of woven leaves and other simple manufactured forest products, villagers gloss Raute camps as "natural" rather than "cultural" edifices. To most villagers, Rautes live "in the forest" rather than in camps, since their camps neither look nor function like villages. This spatial distinction called "camp," imbued as it is with the shaping of materials from nature, marks just one of many important distinctions between Rautes and Nepalese villagers.

Villagers want sturdy, two-story plastered buildings that can house livestock, family, and a front courtyard for entertaining. After adventures in India or Kathmandu, they want to return to an enduring domestic place. Homes represent one's place in the community. Rautes, on the other hand, carry their entire household literally on their backs. They prefer something ephemeral, replaceable, and in fact will burn down their huts at a day's notice before moving on to build their next campsite. One represents an attitude of permanence; the other, of impermanence.

When I visited the Raute camp in Tārāpāni forest, thirty-two huts looked like leafy mounds from a distance. They were set up on the mountain ridge, next to an old abandoned goatherd's shack. As I walked on the winding

footpaths that led toward the camp, I mentally divided the space into several "zones" based on changes in the forest. In "Zone 3," from about two kilometers away from the camp, I began to notice signs of Raute activity. I heard
the ringing *twāāk twāāk* of their axes as they cut trees.[7] I met Raute women
walking in the brush collecting fuel, pine needles, and greens. I walked past
trees that had notches or gouges in them. The trunks of large trees had been
cut to remove material to make bowls and lids. Smaller trees had their inner
bark stripped off. In "Zone 2," just a few hundred meters from the camp, I
came across more numerous signs of activity. Little boys played at cutting
wood with imaginary axes. Little girls built pretend huts, trying to drive
miniature wooden pole stakes into the ground. Thousands of pale wood
chips lay scattered on piles on the ground. Broken wooden bowls lay tossed
on the wayside, and even human feces had to be ignored along the way.
And finally I reached the edges of "Zone 1," the camp itself, where human
activity undulated at a slow pace. Elderly women chatted in small groups,
a woman stirred a cooking pot of roasting grain, children danced about, a
man ambled into camp with his daughter perched on his shoulder. Off to
one side, a young man patiently shaped a wooden breadboard, propping it
up on a wooden stand as the chips piled up around his work station.

As the afternoon approached, I visited elder Man Bahadur's hut nestled
on a bluff five or six thousand feet above a tributary of the Bheri River.
I noticed that the 4 × 8 foot hut was small for a family of four. Later, I
would see at least two other types of huts that varied depending on weather
and length of stay. The huts were surrounded by shallow ditches, which effectively shunted rainwater away from the interior. Man Bahadur's hut led
to others along dirt paths formed naturally by the frequent tread of relatives from hut to hut. Next to him lived his son-in-law and his daughter, in
their own hut. Man Bahadur's hut was roofed with woven *mālu* (*Bauhinia
vahlii*) leaves. Known in English as camel's foot, *mālu* is a gigantic climber
with tendrils that surround trees, eventually choking them to death. Some
rural Nepalese still use *mālu* for making ropes and mats. The new pods
and leaves are cooked as vegetables, while the seeds taste like cashews and
are eaten raw, roasted, or dried and fried (Manandhar 2002, 106). In sun-
ny spots, leafy covers of *mālu* woven into big tarps lay drying in the sun
along the periphery of camp. They were used not only to cover huts, but
to shield the sides of huts from the sun. Shades of these tarps were pitched
next to people working, and one Raute woman wrapped up the *lhāpā* and
stored it in a hunting net (*jābo*). I walked with Man Bahadur's wife over to
a *Bauhinia* vine and stripped some off, noting that it felt as supple as moist
rope. Another woman carried some old pine-litter fencing to the side of

the camp and threw it away. She gathered new ferns, sugar apple leaves (*Annona squamata*; N. *banjhi*), bunches of pine needles and *mālu* leaves and wove them into the side of a hut. As one Raute noted, the *banjhi* leaves keep insects away from the huts, and ferns help keep the monsoon rains from leaking in. "And almost everything is made of *mālu*—covers, plates, baskets, walking sticks, rope, our eating bowls—everything," commented another Raute elder.

Just outside the huts, fermented grain beer was stored in the three-foot-high oval-shaped wooden vessels (*dzhum*). This beer was not for special occasions; it was consumed like cider, for occasional drinking during the day when Rautes returned from working in the forest. The wooden-bowl construction sites were placed next to the huts too. In elder Man Bahadur's work area, a blanket of blond wood chips covered his artisanal arena. A log (N. *achānu*) formed the base on which the wooden items were placed to be carved. The bowls in progress were propped against a wooden stand (N. *kili*) that balanced the bowl as it was chipped and smoothed. Man Bahadur rested against the wooden chest, his arms crossed and legs extended. He noted:

> Right now this forest camp is clean and fine. But soon I think there will be problems with leeches. It is a pretty damp place here, and a few children have already gotten itchy bites. If you have some medicine, let me know. If the leeches are not too bad, we will stay here one or two weeks, then we will be ready to go to the next camp. Except for the leeches, the camp is fine because the women like the nearby stream that comes out of the mountain. We have dug our water tap (*pāni dāda*) very close to camp.

I had hiked into the Rautes' camp, an island of their inner social space, but soon I would walk with them to the nearby village for a barter session. As they move from their camp location to a sedentary village, Rautes will adopt a different persona from that of egalitarian forager. They will don the mask of a high caste, pretending they are long-separated kin of the noble Thakuri elites that rule the region.[8] They will tell the villagers, "Long ago, you were thrown by God into villages while we were thrown into the forest."

Last Camp at Kahanda: The Leaf's Edge

The last camp I visited during the research season was near Luwida and Mājkot, two villages in western Jajarkot District off a route toward the ancient summer palace of Khās Malla kings who reigned in the fifteenth century. To get to the place that villagers called *Tārākhola*, meaning "the distant river," I walked past a small stone temple about four feet wide. It had symbols carved in stone on all four sides, but their meanings and the deities the people worshipped six hundred years ago are largely forgotten.[9] These stone monuments, which rise like fingers stretching out of the ground, are vivid reminders that the forests are not just empty stretches between villages, but part of a constantly changing political landscape.

While villagers call the forest here Tārākhola, Rautes know it as Kahānda. One Raute youth named Mahabiri noted that *Kahānda* refers to the "hilly place of the *mālu*," and he called my attention to the interesting sort of hilly edges of the *mālu* leaf. Again, I was struck by the constant references to *mālu*, and in this case, to a specific part of it, the *edge*. I'd never thought much about the edges of a leaf, except as a diagnostic feature. Looking at a *mālu* leaf, I noticed that its huge leaves are shaped like a camel's footprint. The leaves are as broad as they are long, with a cleft cutting through the middle. Next, Mahabiri pointed to a nearby *āyār* (*Lyonia ovalifolia*, no English name) tree and said, "We camped here last time we came through here. See the *āyār*? It was cut down by us twelve years ago. And next to it can you see the spring coming out of the rock? Its open now, water's flowing where we made our drinking spring. We made the new spring nearby that old spring [pointing], but that old one was made by villagers for their cattle." Mahabiri's observations reminded me that these forests are both new and old for nomadic Rautes. Mahabiri couldn't have remembered this forest more than once in his life, as Rautes had only traveled this route twice in the last twenty years. Yet he came to Kahānda looking for, and finding, physical impressions made by his own people, like symbolic marks giving Rautes the right of usufruct for a short time.

From Threatened Beliefs to Threatened Lives

I have ignored a third point of view, that of government interests in control and use of forests, up to this point, but it deserves our attention while reviewing the broad outline of forest-based interactions between interest groups. State interventions do occur, and these interactions between Rautes and government of Nepal involve power differentials over how to use and view forest spaces. States have interests in forests that affect forest-based peoples, especially in the naming, appropriation of resources, regulation, and taxation of forested areas. Because of the enormous power of governments to influence the lives of their citizens, the state actions concerning forest foragers can lead to faulty results. Recently, for example, Raute elders have expressed concern over Maoist and the state military conflicts. One Raute elder reportly asked the government to be careful during forest aerial bombings. When asked if they had been affected, one elder replied: "The sirs who fly the *gādi* (helicopters) should be careful. What if we Rautes are completely wiped out when they are trying to kill Maoists? However, the CDO [Commanding District Officer] has assured us that our areas won't be bombed. Just to be sure, when a helicopter flies overhead we wave our turbans to notify the sirs that we are not Maoists but Raute and to leave us in peace" (Lawoti 2005, 11).

Rautes do their best to deal with these government actions, meeting with the officials of the districts through which they travel. Yet a district officer may try to persuade Rautes to settle down or take government food rations, or may block the nomads from using forest resources. Their ability to avoid becoming a "criminal tribe," or forest peoples who illegally collect forest resources, is contingent upon the goodwill of elite government officials. This is a precarious situation, and Rautes risk losing the patronage of local elite political figures if they divulge their radically different views and beliefs about the forests.

But to what degree do Rautes live in a "heterotopic," or socially crowded, forest space? In the work of social philosopher Michel Foucault, he discusses heterotopic sites as immersed in contestations of political power over the right to define, to *know*, geographical places (Foucault 1986). The perspective of the dominant society prevails, and marginal groups have to compete to win their favored perspectives of place in the marketplace of competing ideas. In the Rautes' case, this contest over knowing and defining forests is evident. Nepali speakers describe natural places such as forests in their own way, neglecting to listen to how Rautes conceptualize natural spaces. In the United States, we see a similar contestation over natural spaces playing out. For some groups, forests are part of a "wilderness" that needs to be protected. For the National Forest Service, forests represent a natural "heritage" that needs to be managed. For lumber companies, forests are a "resource" to be harvested. And for citizens looking forward to a weekend of camping, forests may be a pleasurable destination. Likewise, Nepalese rural villagers conceive of forests and nature as places constituted by divine Hindu bodies, whereas Rautes see them as a domestic spaces created by God (Berh among Rautes, Bhagwān in front of outsiders).

Observing the Rautes' own topophilia, their own affective ties with their natural surroundings, we discover a crowded and varied world—one inhabited by deities, spirits, humans, and animals-as-relatives. This represents an entirely different form of jumbled space, one containing a dynamic tension ural and natural beings. Here lies an extended family that resembling a busy household. The Rautes desire only to ⟩ a morally good life, hunt monkeys, and migrate to new s Raute elders emphasized, maintaining their cosmo- balance is of prime importance. If individual Rautes were to act immorally, their world would be destroyed. Berh would make the monkeys disappear, and the Rautes would lose their taste for monkey meat. The forested world of "God's children" represents a dynamic heterotopia, one where animals and deities have as much agency as their human counterparts.

In the conflicting views of sedentary and nomadic societies, political issues are paramount. Rautes make their bid for cultural autonomy by asserting themselves as the subjects of the trees, as kings of the forest, and as nomadic forest dwellers. They evoke a familiar political image of people who wish to have their human rights respected. Even though this is a small society, Rautes nevertheless assert their right to maintain their own culture, cosmology, and view of nature and the environment.

5

Monkey's Thigh Is the Shaman's Meat

Monkey's haunch is the shaman's meat,
Having no land, what shall we eat?
—Chandra Raute

Yesterday we spent most of the day with Chandra, a twenty-six-year-old bachelor. We—Bisnu, Chandra, Krishna, and I—ate breakfast together yesterday. My research assistant, Bisnu, and I talked with Chandra while Krishna, my cook, prepared a morning dal-bhat of rice, lentils, chicken, vegetables, and an achār *of pickled tomato. Krishna's cooking is amazingly spicy for Nepalese food, an abundance of coriander and cumin that sometimes tastes wonderful but is occasionally overpowering. Chandra did not eat any of the lentils, and explained that Rautes do not eat this food. It must be true since no Rautes have asked to trade for lentils. Plus, at Regmi's house, when the Raute men and women were served big plates of* dal-bhat, *rice, and lentils, they just left the lentils uneaten. Instead, Chandra explained that Rautes pour beer (*jāḍ*) over their rice or simply eat it plain. Women can pour beer over their rice too, he added, though they generally do not drink as much as the men.*

Then I noticed that Chandra skipped the tomato chutney too. He said, "What's this?" and made a sour face. I mistakenly offered Chandra chutney, forgetting that the Rautes do not grow tomato or citrus trees and so they would not be making any chutneys. Next Chandra looked at the chicken dish. I have to admit, the specimen Krishna got from a local farmer was kind of scrawny and he did not cook it properly—too much spice, too little meat. But Chandra ate some, even though we only had a little bit and it was all bones, terrible in fact. He said that he rarely ate chicken and did not like it much. Raute children are familiar with chicken, however, as they sacrifice

them to propitiate God (Berh) since s/he also controls hunting. If the children
wish, they may eat the sacrificial chicken, but usually they are so small, just
baby chicks, that it would not be worth the effort.

As we continued to eat, I noticed Bisnu mixing her rice and lentils on her
plate in soft squishy clumps between her fingers. The polite way for a young
woman to eat is to mix and mix, pushing the food from one side of the plate
to the other with her fingertips and occasionally bringing up a small evenly
rolled ball of food to her mouth and popping it in with nary a touch of her
fingers on her mouth. When the girls are acting coy, they really turn the food
into mush. I marveled at how differently Chandra ate his food. He seemed
more like some American tourists I have known . . . his plate had the rice,
lentils, chicken, and chutney clearly separated on different parts of the plate.
He proceeded to eat the vegetables, rice, and meat in distinct separate piles
and obviously did not like the idea of mixing anything into the rice. It
remained white and pure, something that I've never seen on a Nepalese
person's plate. Chandra must think we eat like this all the time—sour, spicy
food and very little meat. For monkey hunters, that must seem like a tragedy.

Monkey Hunters

In the Kathmandu newspapers, the Rautes are called "The Monkey Hunters of Nepal." This is true but a scandalous thing to publish given that most
Hindus believe Hanuman, the monkey deity, to be the appropriate object
of prayer rather than prey. In some foraging societies, such as among the
Aché of South America, monkey hunting is a fairly low priority, as deer
and the pig-like peccary provide more calories per time expended hunting
(Hawkes, Hill, and O'Connell 1982). But among Old World foragers such as
the Semang and Batek of Malaysia, langurs and gibbons are larger, providing a better return on energy expended during a hunt. Consequently, larger
monkeys are a preferred food choice. In the Rautes' case, too, the larger
langur is preferred to the smaller rhesus macaque.

In the past, Rautes may have hunted a broad spectrum of other animals,
such as deer and pheasant. One octogenarian villager recalled that when
she was a girl, Rautes wore Kalij (*Lophura leucomelanos*) pheasant feathers
in their clothing. That Rautes might hunt pheasant is not surprising. It is
possible that they pursued a broader foraging strategy in past generations,
when the human population density of the region was much lower. Yet during my walks through abandoned Raute campsites, only goat and monkey
bones turned up, but no pheasant or larger bones that might be from adult
deer. Looking for an explanation, I asked Rautes why they hunt only mon-

key. Their explanation was "God gave monkey for our fodder. Other animals are for others."

Although circular in logic, this assertion does point out a clear "division of forest resources," and this division by sedentary and nomadic groups has certain advantages. For Rautes, it acts as a political buffer in that farmers cannot blame the Rautes for depleting the forests' game resources. Today, much of the game that was plentiful in the past is becoming scarce, and farmers claim authority over their community forests when it comes to game rights. If they thought Rautes competed with them for game, the foragers would be prevented from hunting in the community forests. Also, Rautes do not worry about a "hierarchy of resort," deciding which kinds of game to pursue, as they hunt only two species of monkeys. While other hunter-gatherer groups have to decide what type of animal to track, Rautes know that as soon as a given resource patch has been depleted of monkeys it is time to break camp and move to another area.

Recall that the nomadic Raute foraging migration route is large, about 23,000 square miles (60,000 sq km) in areas that are steep, ranging from about 1,000-foot altitude along river valleys up to 8,500-foot-high mountain ridges. Rautes may relocate their camps merely a few minutes away from the the previous camp or move up to five hours away from a previous camp, and each move takes them slowly across most of western Nepal. Jajarkot District villagers have told me that Rautes move in about a twelve-year migration route, and indeed they did move across Jajarkot District in 1985, and again in 1997. But this rule does not always hold. A more accurate one might be that Rautes only go back into the same forests *in which they hunted* about every twelve years. Thus they might return to Jajarkot after only a few years, but will hunt in forests that they have not visited for a dozen years. This strategy gives local monkey populations a chance to regenerate between hunting forays. Quite mobile, monkeys can move into new forest areas fairly easily after Rautes have passed through. Having a twelve-year cycle of visiting resource patches enables monkey populations to rebound and creates little ecological stress on the region.

Monkey hunting is truly the Rautes' most important subsistence endeavor. It is important not only because it provides them with protein but because it lies at the heart of what it means to be Raute. As one hunter said: "Oh God, I have my share to eat and my death to die. What can I eat now? My work is to catch the monkeys and their babies. . . . We have no agriculture, so what can I eat? I won't leave alone the baby monkeys given by God." What else might the Raute hunt? Prey species in the region actually include many species (see Appendix, Table 1).

Although in fact there are many species available to capture, Rautes and Banrajis leave the larger game to farmers and the endemic tigers of the region. Rautes cannot compete with farmers, as they wield "lawyers, guns, and money." In other words, the hunting farmers are politically powerful, they have more complex hunting technologies, and they hunt for various reasons besides obtaining food. They want to rid their fields of pests and will hunt animals that eat their crops such as rats, squirrels, and boars. I recall one farmer who had a jackal pelt stretched out to dry along the side of his house. When I asked why he had hunted it, he replied, "Because the *syāl* [jackal] might have attacked my goats." Many times farmers will hunt for sport, gathering on weekends for pheasant hunts. At others, they seek medicinals that can be sold in the markets, such as the highly prized musk oil from the scent glands of musk deer, or skins from civets, weasels, and martin.

While there appears to be a relatively wide range of prey species available, Rautes persuasively claim to have always hunted only langur and macaque monkeys, two medium-sized prey species. Though women and children occasionally fish with their hands and skirts, fishing is of little importance to the diet. Further, Rautes do not identify themselves as fisherfolk (*mācha mārne mānche*), whereas other groups of Rawats and Rajis do call themselves fisherfolk. Looking at Raute tool technologies, we see that, while women and men weave nets for monkey hunts, they do not use them for fishing. Previous researchers have searched for evidence of Rautes hunting, fishing, or collecting honey, but have found no evidence of broad-spectrum foraging.

In contrast, neighboring foragers—Rajis, Banrajis, and Chepang—report hunting a wider range of prey. When I interviewed Banraji women, for example, they described their technique for hunting *sambhār* deer. Large and shaggy, resembling the American elk, *sambhār* have a similar height of about five feet at the shoulders and weigh up to 1,200 pounds. They have deadly sharp hooves used to paw the ground around them, marking their territory. *Sambhār* will rear up on their hind legs like a goat sometimes does, and scan the forest glade. While these habits make *sambhār* fairly dangerous to hunt, especially close up, the Banraji women smiled almost ruefully and described their last hunt in Tanakpur, India: "There was one in the forest with her child (*dā māthiya jore-yo manāng-gwi gidale-ka hi-ye*). We hid in the bushes, very quietly. With axes we cut her feet. *Sambhār* are big, but they walk more slowly than other deer. We cannot kill the other kinds of deer because they are very clever and run away. When the *sambhār* does not notice us in the shrubs, we reach out and cut her feet [tendons of

Dhana Devi, a Banraji
woman, forages along
the bluffs overlooking
the Mahakali River in
Dadeldhura District,
Nepal, June 2005.

feet]. She cannot run and then we kill her. Then we have to take the child and kill him soon, because he needs milk."

Large deer are the exception, however, and Banrajis more often hunt their favorite prey, the large Indian porcupine, which may weigh more than sixty pounds as adults. The next most preferred prey species are bats. Bats make an excellent stew, and Raji youngsters often navigate the pitch-black limestone cave networks in search of them. One boy boasted that he could wiggle into a tiny cave opening and climb his way all the way to the top of the mountain ridge, a distance of about two thousand vertical feet. Chepangs, too, hunt bats with great interest. Chepangs living east of Raute territories speak a language related to the Raute language, and they are known for their large spreadnets that are similar to those of Rautes. However, instead of tying their nets to the trees to capture monkeys, Chepang hunters throw their nets over thirty-foot-high butternut trees (*Bassia butyracea*) or fig trees in order to capture sleeping bats.

So why do the Rautes hunt only monkeys? Apparently one of the reasons is that it behooves them to limit their hunting to the largest-size prey (langurs and macaques) that is not hunted by more dominant predators. As already discussed, langur and rhesus macaque are considered to be incarnations of sacred Hindu deities, and are thus not a prey choice for villagers.[1] In addition, tigers prefer to hunt the large ungulates as well, their favorite prey being *chital* deer and *sambhār* deer. Since adult tigers weigh 300 to 600 pounds, deer provide the 25 to 50 pounds of daily meat required to sustain them. Monkeys might be more numerous, but it takes too much energy for the adult tiger to kill and eat one monkey at a time. Encapsulated within such an ecological landscape, it is likely that contemporary Rautes limit their hunting to monkeys and leave the large prey to the other top predators in the region. As Raute hunters put it: "Even if a deer falls into our nets we would throw it out. We only eat all the monkeys that come into our nets."

Just as farmers use numerous hunting technologies (old guns, traps, poisons), Raute hunting also requires certain technologies, namely axes and nets. The nets measure approximately 6 by 3.5 feet and have fairly large loose knots, about one hand-width between knots, and lengths of rope extending from each end of the net. The nets are manufactured from fibrous bushes such as *Girardinia zeylanica*, a local hemp fiber. The fiber is stripped from the bush, boiled, pounded, allowed to soften/rot for a few days, and then twined and woven into the nets, mostly by women. Given the nature of hunting with axes, nets require constant mending. Like other Raute tools, the nets serve multiple purposes. In addition to hunting, they are used to haul goods from camp to camp, to carry children, and to wrap around one's waist (like the Nepali *paṭukā* waist wrap) as a pouch for storage of other small items.

Specialized hunting is uncommon among contemporary hunter-gatherer societies. It occurs in circumstances in which there is steady access to a given prey species during all seasons. The buffalo hunters of the great plains of North America had such access, and mammoth hunters of Paleolithic Eurasia might be another example. In such circumstances, the foragers can use their time and energy more efficiently by learning the behavior of only one or a few prey species rather than the behaviors of many kinds of prey. Further, the Rautes' form of specialized hunting occurs in a warm, wet environment. They can forego complex technologies necessary to northern Asian and North American hunting peoples. Rautes can do without extra clothing, boots, gloves, finely carved harpoons, smartly constructed kayaks, or other relatively complex composite tools. Raute nets are woven of a few types of inner bark. Their axes are made of iron shaped by a local iron-smith caste and fitted into a handle of the Rautes' own making. The

A Raute youth stops to
rest during a camp move.
His possessions include a
wooden alcohol storage
container wrapped within
a spread-net and a long-
faced axe. Axes and nets
represent the Rautes' main
hunting gear.

Banrajis, too, simply carve spears from one long and appropriately straight
bough of *Bauhinia* wood. They don't bother to fit their spears with stone or
metal points and throw the spears away after a hunt. These are very simple,
multifunctional tools.

Finally, the Rautes' specialized hunting results from the population dynamics of the region. In the relatively populous regions of the Himalayan
hills, habitats are decreasing. As the deforestation of Nepal's rugged hills
continues, the prey species have been decimated by shrinking habitats. A
hundred years ago, the forests extended to the tops of most hills in western
Nepal, and deer, boar, pheasant, and wild goats roamed everywhere, but
today most forests have been cleared. The grasslands and forests have been
terraced in order to make fields of corn, millet, wheat, and rice. Today, however, the musk deer have been shot for their prized scented musk; *sambhār*
have been hunted for their generous amounts of meat; and wild goats have
been hunted for sport. The men and women who hunt for sport and food
are known as *shikāri*, a word that connotes wealth, free time, and nobility

in the minds of Hindus. One of my students in America, for example, told me how his father takes him vacation hunting in their home country of Bangladesh. He recalled that they get together with their relatives, have a lot of fun, and donate the meat to the villagers. Men such as these would have been known as village patrons in past generations, and they have been "doing the *shikār*" for many generations. Today, the classic *shikāri* royal hunts, complete with mounted elephants, are being emulated by nouveau riche high-caste Hindu families throughout South Asia. Whether Rautes of centuries ago did or did not hunt other prey species remains unknown; but the fact that they have refused to hunt these species in the last few generations has contributed to the Rautes' cultural survival.

Although they focus upon only two species, Raute are nevertheless prolific hunters; hunting parties search for monkey troops two to four times per week. Hunting parties consist of eight to thirty-five men and boys over twelve years of age, and the hunting party size depends on the camp size. The Raute camp is often split up, with splinter camps of about ten households traveling into adjacent forests. Rautes hunt from either the old base camp, the splinter camp, or the new base camp, since they migrate over a period of several days from an old to a new camp. Each of these camps lies anywhere from five minutes to five hours apart so that each hunting group can forage in a different forest. When Rautes splinter into camps, the number of males available for hunting is lower and so are the number of nets tied together, making animal drives likely to capture less game. During the summer and fall months that I spent with the Rautes, hunters reported netting from ten to twenty-five animals during each successful hunt, and they reported being successful more than half of the time. But larger kills of up to one hundred animals have been reported (Luintel 1993).

The population of rhesus macaques and Hanuman langurs in this part of the Himalayas has not been studied, but according to farmers, populations are fairly dense. In Himachal Pradesh, which has similar mixed oak, coniferous forest, and *sāl* (*Shorea* spp.) forests, monkey populations have been demographically studied. Langurs there reportedly have a population density of fourteen langurs per square kilometer and about the same density for rhesus monkeys (Pirta 1993, 174). But this figure is somewhat misleading, as monkey troops can mass into groups of a hundred monkeys or more. As croplands increase and forest areas decrease, monkeys tend to eat more grain, and their numbers actually increase in disturbed environments with access to nearby forest retreats. The Nepali word for corn, *makai*, reportedly was coined, not from the word "maize," but from the Sanskrit term "*markaṭānna*," meaning "monkey's food" (Turner 1931, 494).

If monkey populations in western Nepal are comparable to neighboring Himachal Pradesh's in India, the Rautes find themselves with an abundant game resource and no competition from farmers.

As already pointed out, while monkeys are obviously a threat to farmers' crops, they are also worshipped as Hindu deities and thus farmers are loath to kill them. When I visited with villagers who had not met the Rautes, such as teenagers, and told them that Rautes hunt monkey, they usually expressed disgust. Villagers regularly worship Hanuman, the monkey god, and the thought of killing a deified incarnation is truly repellent to faithful Hindus. In the epic Vedic text, the *Rāmāyaṇa*, the monkey hero Hanuman is revered for his heroic deeds and for composing the story of the life and deeds of King Rama. In other parts of the *Rāmāyaṇa*, the monkey chief, Vali (Skt. *vāl*, tail), commits dharmic crimes and is eventually killed by King Rama even though he is the son of Hindu gods. As folk heroes in the Hindu tradition, Hanuman, Vali, and other monkey heroes are worshipped by Hindus throughout India.

As people who also know the *Rāmāyaṇa*, farmers in western Nepal share with Indians reverence for the Hanuman langur and the rhesus macaque. The langur mythically embodies the good qualities of Hanuman's friend— bravery, morality, defense of kings and queens, honesty, and faithfulness. For this reason, langurs create a dilemma for Nepalese farmers in that they raid the growing grain crops yet are the incarnation of Hanuman. When the Rautes come to a farming community, farmers are relieved that their di-lemma is resolved. From the villagers' Hindu caste incorporative point of view, the work of the Rautes' *jāti* (caste, social group) is to hunt monkey, and thus the extreme impurity of killing a sacred species devolves upon them, just as the Musahār (rat-killing castes) or the Sarki caste (who dispose of dead cows) play their part in the Hindu caste system.

Preparations for the Hunt

The process of hunting is not linear, with a beginning and an end. Rautes think about hunting, dream about hunting, enact hunts through dance, and prepare for hunting during the times when they are not actually in the process of running and chasing monkeys into the nets. One of the salient aspects of monkey hunting involves properly gifting Berh. The rationale for hunting rituals is that God constantly asks for little gifts like rice and chicks; only then will s/he be satisfied, and only then will the Raute hunts be successful. This rite of exchange is explicitly recognized by Rautes. I asked a hunter named Daracho, "Do you exchange chicks with God? Is it

like you give chicks to God so you may eat His children?" Daracho replied:
"That is true. Actually, for the price of chicks we eat the meat of monkeys.
If we don't give any sacrifice, then God will say monkeys are our children
and we can't kill monkeys. We can't kill langur. What would Daracho eat
then? That is why we bring chicks and give sacrifice to God, and then we
eat the monkeys." When I gave him a baby chick during a barter session,
Daracho explained: "This baby chicken has to be sacrificed on new-moon
day (*sankrānti*). On new-moon day we cut and sacrifice chicks early in the
morning." With an trilling *hurrrraaa*, he added, "Then we go to hunting.
We come back after we take out the monkeys' stomachs."

As the French sociologist Marcel Mauss noted, there are no free gifts.
Gifts to the gods in the form of baby chicks enable Rautes to do several
things. The gift, or sacrifice, enables Rautes to enhance their solidarity with
the supernatural and ensure a closer measure of relatedness to God. Further, these small but difficult-to-obtain sacrifices enable the gift givers to
gain a promise from the receiver. God grants the Rautes successful hunting
in return for the "price" of chicks. As Daracho noted, their gifts influence
the receiver, and thus God grants the petition of the givers. In a small society unburdened by contractual obligations, gifts represent an important
aspect of social exchange. The notion of *fairness* is basic to gift exchange.
In a society where one is obligated to reciprocate, the fairness of gifting is
central to holding Raute society together.

Raute men may sacrifice chicks, but this ritual activity is most often performed by Raute boys. Boys each bring a chick to the ceremony and are
instructed by the ceremony leader (from *nāyak* hero, leader). Rautes see
this process of giving the chicks to God as an act that relates the young boys
and the chicks metaphorically as symbols of life, while the process of hunting and the slaughter of the monkeys represents the inevitable fate of death.
Since Rautes obviously do not raise chickens, they must acquire them from
farmers. This can be a difficult task, given that farmers do not usually like to
part with their chicks. As Man Bahadur anxiously implored during a barter
session:

> . . . you have to find me a hen with chicks. I don't ask for a big cock, I just ask for
> a hen with eight or nine chicks. Just ask for someone to look for it. It is not for
> meat, it is for sacrifice. If it was for meat then I would have asked for a cock. I just
> need a hen with twelve or thirteen chicks. I need those really badly. Just look for
> it everywhere . . . how many days are you going to stay? If you stay for five or six
> days then you can look for five or six days too. If you cannot find twelve chicks
> then eight are also okay. You have to find it. It is okay if you can find between six

to twelve chicks. Actually I have two sons of my own and two of Birka Bahadur's, which makes four. It is our culture to give each boy one chick. Bring up to six chicks, one for myself and four of my sons, that is five of us.[2]

The need for chicks to sacrifice to Berh may have always been part of Raute rituals, given that many regional ethnic groups, such as Raji, Chepang, and Birhor of Jharkhand, also include this element in their hunting rituals. However, since Rautes interact less with villagers than do other regional foragers, chick sacrifice may be a relatively new characteristic of religious practice. Banrajis in Kumaun, for example, pray to their hunting deity, a female goddess named Kaiyyu, by picking forest flowers and sprinkling these over a makeshift alter, such as a nearby boulder, prior to carrying out a hunt. Conceivably, in the past nomadic Rautes might also have used local forest resources such as flowers rather than baby chicks for their sacrifices.

Interestingly, Daracho mentioned that Rautes speak Nepali rather than their own language during the rituals. He noted, "For sacred things (*gajanda*) we cannot use our language. We use the common language to do ritual sacrifice (*puja*)." If true, the fact that Rautes use the "common language" of Nepali rather than their own language indicates that the rituals involving the use of items such as chickens and rice have been introduced into Raute culture.

The Hunt Begins

The hunt itself is reported by Rautes to vary little: "We tie our nets together. We drop our capes. Some people hide in nearby trees and bushes. Some people go out and *hrrrr* . . . call the monkeys to our nets. We chase our little brothers and it's dangerous, somebody always gets hurt. . . ." However, considering that the Rautes migrate through many different ecological conditions, from subtropical lowlands during the winter to mixed deciduous-coniferous highlands in the monsoon season, the hunting strategies are likely more complex, with variations depending on ecological conditions. Respecting nomadic Raute requests to stay away from kill sites, I had to rely on their reports and descriptions of hunts. (With Banrajis, I participated in two hunts.) During my observations of Raute men during their preparations, I noted the relaxed, quiet disposition they assume as they organize for monkey hunts. After one such observation, I wrote:

On the way to the Raute camp at 9 a.m., about fourteen men and two women slowly walked in groups of one to four down the path that we (two assistants and

I) were taking up to the camp. A few had nets with wooden bowls (*koshi*) in them
for sale in Karkigaun village. Most didn't have any bowls with them. Some men
had two nets tied to their waists; most had one net. Later, I was told that they
caught "twelve rhesus and a couple of langur." . . . We proceeded up the road and
met Bhim, Krishna, Gogane, and Nanda as they trickled down the path. Hira and
her friend Tara were also at the tail end of that group of men. They had wooden
bowls with them to trade that they themselves had carved crudely. It is possible
that these women also went to the monkey hunt, though they said they were going trading in the village of Karkigaun.

The closest non-Rautes are allowed to get to a hunt is the path head-
ing into a particular forest. As Chandra explained: "If we kill monkeys today, tomorrow we won't have to do anything. You're the children of other
people. I'm the son of the Raute. If you see our hunting, it'll be spoiled. If
our hunting is ruined my people will blame me." Thus, if Rautes spot a villager in the nearby vicinity, they ask the person not to follow the hunters.
Although villagers have spied on the Rautes before, non-Rautes in the forest will be driven away before a hunt begins. If Rautes come across villagers
before finishing the animal drive, they will abandon the hunt. If villagers
come across Rautes while they are cutting up the meat packages, Rautes will
try to immediately eat as much meat as possible out of view of the villagers
rather than carry it past them toward the camp. Although such extreme
caution seems unusual, recall that Rautes hunt Hanuman monkeys, which
Hindu villagers worship as deities. In addition, animal drives require taking
great care not to disturb the animals until the hunt begins. If villagers, who
are notoriously loud, were to go into the forest hunting patch, this would
cause monkeys to scatter, effectively ruining the Rautes' animal drive. Thus,
for both symbolic and practical reasons, Rautes are loath to be followed by
outsiders during hunts.

During the morning's observation, I saw that two Raute women accom-
panied the men toward the forest hunting patch chosen for the day's hunt.
These women did not have nets or axes with them. Holding their wooden
bowls, they hoped to negotiate successful trades, but I later heard that they
had been unsuccessful in trading their poorly made bowls. Yet, given that
women were there, it appears that Raute women are allowed to accompany
Raute men to a designated hunting patch. It is also possible that they participate in driving game toward the nets, as do Mbuti women in Africa. But
when I asked Raute men and women about this, they said that women do
not hunt because it is too dangerous. Whether this is merely the ideal or is
indeed the real situation remains to be confirmed.

Looking at the question cross-culturally, women's role in hunting raises an interesting issue. Although monkey would be considered medium-sized game, anthropological studies generally find that women participate only sporadically in large game hunting (Harako 1981; Lee and DeVore 1976). Small numbers of women in North America have taken up sport hunting of elk and deer, for example, and there are several examples in the ethnographic record of women hunting deer and other large game (Brightman 1996). For example, Mbuti women of central Africa participate with men in net hunting of elephant (Bailey and Aunger 1989). Baka (Aka) women participate in hunts with their spouses of the antelope-like duikers or burrowing porcupines (Bahuchet 2006, 191). In the Philippines, Agta women hunt the *sambhār* deer and other game with nets and dogs (Goodman et al. 1985). And Paliyan women of Tamil Nadu, India, occasionally hunt *sambhār* as well. Researcher Peter Gardner describes a Paliyan woman saying: "We accompany the men for the hunt. Taking the dogs, the men chase the *milā* [a young deer]. We know in what direction the dogs are chasing the [deer] and sit in hiding when it comes [toward] our side. When it passes us we cut its leg. Then it falls down and, at once, we kill it with big stones" (Gardner 2000, 41). Putting the comparative and ethnographic data together, it seems likely that Raute women mostly perform auxiliary hunting activities such as making/mending nets, accompanying men to the hunting patches, and helping drive game toward the nets. They may conduct spur-of-the-moment hunts of small game, but they do not directly hunt monkey by themselves. Rather than chasing monkeys if they encounter them, Raute women have explained that they go back to camp and tell the men where to carry out their next monkey drive. Carefully planned net hunting is better than opportunistic targeting of one animal. Also, unlike other prey animals, monkeys are fairly easy to relocate after one day. Thus Rautes carry out *planned* monkey hunting, but have no need for *opportunistic* monkey hunting.

Further evidence for women's participation in activities related to hunting comes from clues found in the language. When I asked for the term for "hunted meat," elder Man Bahadur said, "Men say *šyā*. Women say *šywiy*." In the Raute language, men use the word *syā* for game; this is a classic word found among most Tibetan languages to refer to wild game, deer, flesh, or hunted meat. But Raute women use the word *šywiy*, literally "blood." The word choices indicate that women control the semantic domain of "blood" while men control the domain of "flesh." This implies that women are intimately associated with the blood of the animal. In addition, they are said to be in charge of the *bilu*, a word that refers to the flesh after it has been cut up into smaller meat packages. As one Raute noted, *bilu* is "meat from the hunt. It is cut into pieces, for women to cook and share" (*bilu* also connotes sacrificed meat). Thus women are responsible for the meat in the form of blood and meat strips. This is similar to our way of referring to deer as "venison" or "steak" after it has moved from the semantic domain of a live animal to that of meat packages.

Depictions of Monkey Hunting

What does a monkey hunt look like? Drawing is not an indigenous art form of Rautes, but they had seen villagers using pens and wanted to try drawing. Giving them pens, I asked a few Rautes to draw whatever they wanted. They drew pictures of hunts, yams, family members, shelters, and wooden bowls. When I asked Ratna, one of the best hunters, to draw a picture, he drew a large length of net encircling both rhesus and langur monkeys. He explained that the rhesus monkeys were scattered in a long-ish line on the left side of the encircling net. The larger circles on the right-hand side represented langur monkeys. Hunters, the swirling concentric figures in the top left, appear as the largest iconographic circles. Finally,

Ratna's picture of a monkey hunt, drawn in my research notebook, September 9, 1997.

Ratna drew the trees in the top righthand corner, figuring them as circles and loops.

When I asked another elder named Bhakta Bahadur about hunting scenes, he too drew a similar picture. Bhakta Bahadur is a rather shy individual and set apart from the others because of his deformities, a scarred eye and shriveled arm. Yet he was one of the shamans (*dhāmi*) and responsible for the ritual sacrifices to the Rautes' hunting deity. In one of his drawings, Bhakta explained that the straight line represented the net. Then he said that the monkeys were the circular squiggles in the middle of the drawing, while the men were drawn as the connected circles at the far left. He showed me the larger circle at the top right of the drawing. This represented the clothing that the men take off before they hunt because extra clothing would snag on branches as the men race down the hill, driving the game into the nets.

Next Bhakta decided to draw another monkey scene, this time sticking to something more "simple." In the drawings he drew several lines of nets with a jumble of "monkeys" running into them.

Accompanying Bhakta that day was one of his friends, Harka. Harka, too, wanted to draw and made about nine different representations

Bhakta and Harka's monkey-hunting scenes: (1) monkeys running into nets; (2) monkeys; (3) a wood box; (4) a drinking bowl; (5) several depictions of nets with monkeys running into them and humans standing nearby; (6) nets with monkeys running into them; (7) a snake; (8) nets tied to trees, with extra clothes left nearby and monkeys running into a straight-line net.

of wooden wares, monkey hunting, and his "signature." In one drawing
(see number 8 in the figure on p. 89), Harka penned one of the more
elaborate monkey-hunting scenes. His figures are not nearly as circular as Ratna's, but they still retain the loopy quality characteristic of the
Raute drawings. Harka drew a "net" represented by a straight line running along the right-hand side of the drawing and then curved most of
the way around the "monkeys." There were few monkeys in the nets in
this drawing, only the squiggles in the top middle portion of the net. At
the bottom of the drawing, Harka noted that the end of the net was tied to
a tree. The "men" in this drawing are interesting as they are drawn in two
ways. First Harka drew what he said were "men holding nets" on the far
right side of the drawing. Notably, these "men," with their arms extending
like roots, look like the yams that Harka created in another drawing. The
squiggles on the left and bottom left of the drawing represent men beat-
ing the monkeys into the nets. And the jumble at the top, above the net
line, depicts the men's pile of capes that are left aside during the animal
drives. The iconic representations of monkey hunting were remarkably
similar among the six or seven Rautes who sketched images even though
they had never used pens before to render real-life objects into two-
dimensional figures.

Overall, these drawings stand out as signposts of Rautes' world, sig-
nifying real events that have enormous meaning to the hunters. Figured
in swirling concentric circles, they represent the hunt as a relationship of
connectivity between human and monkey. Rautes eschew the arts of more
sedentary peoples, and they have no memory of creating art in places such
as caves. But, like rock art drawn by mesolithic cave artists at Bhimbekta
in India or by Native American hunters, the drawings attribute a meaning to the hunt. These drawings may look like childish scribbles to someone from a literate society, but they represent a means of communication
about hunting. Since ethically we cannot watch a monkey hunt without
the Rautes' permission, the best recourse is to look at how a Raute himself
depicts such an important event. Finally, the fact that Rautes chose to use
circles as a stylistic device rather than squares or hard-edged geometric
lines tells us something significant about the ethos of the hunt and, by
extension, of Raute society itself. This is a highly communal society, in
which Raute ontology encourages notions of sharing and commonality;
circles signify closure, compactness, sharing, and in-group interactions.
Monkeys, as our new artists emphasized, are part of the "in-group," as
men, langurs, rhesus, and even trees were all depicted by their slightly different forms of circles.

Dispatching the Prey

The Raute hunters' conversations, together with descriptions of monkey hunting, allow us to more fully understand the mechanics of a monkey drive. Nets are tied together and the ends are tied to trees in the target hunting area and then camouflaged with leafy branches. Men drop their capes and extra clothing in one pile at the edge of the camouflaged nets and then walk quietly out into the forest hunting patch, spreading out over a wide portion of a given forest. The hunters then begin "calling" the monkeys into the target area. Rautes employ a specific style of communication while hunting, known as "whistle speech." Banrajis and Rautes refer to this as *siṭi māra-ko*, meaning "to whistle kill." Whistling is an important part of the hunt, as it allows the hunters to communicate with each other in a way that does not distract the game. Similar to the Chepang, Rautes perform whistles that shape the rough contours of consonants (Caughley 1976). This enables them to call out to each other while monkeys only hear animal-like whistles rather than human vocalizations. Monkeys do not realize that the hunters are stalking them and positioning themselves in preparation for the animal drive. Rautes noted that, as monkeys begin to sense danger, they initially huddle together rather than fleeing.

With the aid of whistle speech, all hunters are in their places before the animal drive. Some have tied the nets and remain at the bottom of the hill, near the area where the monkeys will be dispatched. Others have positioned themselves as the animal drivers. These hunters will flap their arms and shout rolling "Hrrrr" sounds, essentially stampeding the panicked langur and macaque monkeys downhill toward the camouflaged nets. The stampede itself, however, can be somewhat dangerous, as hunters must rush through forest undergrowth along hillsides with no paths to follow. One hunter, Bir Bahadur, came to me after a hunt with a severe bruise on the instep of his foot. He complained that "somebody usually gets hurt" during the chase and explained that he had hurled himself down the hill, hitting a sharp stone as he ran. He asked me if there was any medicine for such a deep bruise, and I wished I had some arnica for him, but had nothing to ease the pain. My only consolation was that Rautes have several herbal remedies for bruises. For instance, they gather bark from a leafy evergreen tree they call *Indolya* (*Macaranga denticulata*). The bark, ground into a paste, can be applied to a bruise and covered with the heated leaves of this fragrant tree of the Eurphorbiaceae family. One of Bir Bahadur's clan might be willing to walk from their camp, nested in a 7,500-foot elevated forest, down to the 4,000-foot range where *Indolya* trees are located.

While Bir Bahadur nursed his foot during that hunt, the rest of the hunters pursued the monkeys. In a scenario that can at times seem gory and
brutal, the frightened game caught in the nets is quickly dispatched with
axes, which dismember limbs and heads, while the nets get bloody and
ripped. During the actual kill, monkeys scream loudly, and I often could
hear the final moments of the hunt even though I was fifteen minutes' walk
away. Afterwards, if women at the camp have not already heard monkeys
screaming during the hunt, the hunters communicate a successful hunt by
hooting calls across the forest. This enables women in the camp to begin
preparing for the processing and cooking of the meat.

Reviewing the dynamics of the hunt, I am struck by the Rautes' adroit
use of simple tools, the nets and axes. Why do they refuse to use other tools,
such as bows and arrows, deadfall traps, clubs, guns, or other hunting equipment? At first this strategy seems odd, especially given that their neighbors,
the Chepang and Raji, employ a broader range of techniques such as traps,
nets, wooden spears, slingshots, and archery. One contributory reason for
the nomadic Raute's dependence on net hunting may be due to the forest
ecology. Rautes hunt in monsoon rainforests. The forests receive forty to
eighty inches of rainfall, and they are quite dense. Rautes prefer to hunt in
these dense forests partly because these are the areas least frequented by
farmers grazing their herds of buffalo, cattle, sheep, and goats.

As anthropologist Paul Roscoe emphasizes, the vegetational structure of
a hunting range is an important determinant of bow-versus-net technology,
and possibly of any tool kit (1990, 699). Archery, Roscoe postulates, is most
useful in ranges where forests are not very dense and the prey can be spotted and brought down within an arrow's range. He finds that nets can also
be used in these environments, but bows are quicker and more efficient.
With bow hunting, hunters can also harvest the lower density (per area
of forest) of animals found in sparsely covered forest areas. By contrast, in
denser forests nets are more useful. There, it is hard to see animals, making archery difficult but enabling hunters to drive large numbers of game
toward nets. Thus nets can be productively used in denser forests, while
other methods such as archery or blowguns are more efficient in places
with sparse forest, rainforests, or any more open forest floor with a forest
canopy housing birds and monkeys.

Certainly more needs to be learned about the hunting techniques of
Himalayan foragers in general. A few comparative examples can be found
in the ethnographic literature. Rajis of Nepal, for example, hunt in regions
with mixed forests and pastureland. They reportedly use dogs, bow and
arrow, and nets (Reinhard 1976; Valli 1998). A dozen or so remaining for-

agers known as the Kusunda also hunt; but they are archers who shoot deer and other prey with bows and arrows and also trap animals with snares (Nebesky-Wojkowitz 1959; Watters 2005).[3] As mentioned earlier, Chepangs hunt bats with nets, but they also hunt with bow and arrow, deadfall traps, and sticky gummed bamboo sticks that they ingeniously telescope into the trees to catch birds. Chepang ecological ranges are complex, with both dense forests and open pastures (Caughley 1976; Rai 1985). The Banrajis live along the Mahakali River that borders Nepal and India, hunting in forests that are slightly less dense than those of Rautes. During the hunts in which I participated with Banrajis, they hunted porcupines with wooden spears and axes, but no nets. During bat hunts, they used their hands to catch and dispatch the animals, and they sometimes placed a leafy screen across the cave entrance. Thus, we can understand that hunting technologies are influenced by the environmental conditions of a region. With thick forests and a prey species that moves in troops, Rautes find that spread nets and axes are more practical than other options used by neighboring hunters.

The Monkey Hunt Ends

After dispatching the prey in their nets, if there is time and no villagers about, the monkey meat is scorched and cut into larger portions before bringing it back to camp (otherwise it is simply hauled back with no meat preparations). At the kill site, Rautes divide the meat into eight main portions, which are later further divided into much smaller strips. The portions are named (1) *gara* (head); (2) *biya* (neck, upper shoulders, ribs, and back); (3) *ākha* and *bā* (forelimbs and feet); (4) *guŋ-ta* (lower back, lower ribs, and sides); (5) *mhu-ta* (tail); (6) *lākha* (haunch, hindquarters); (7) *bhāra* (liver and heart); (8) *photo* and *guduŋ* (entrails, stomach, offal). Except for the stomach and entrails, no portions are thrown away, and sometimes the offal is also taken back to camp. The monkey head is given to the hunter who struck the first blow on a particular animal, but this is not a firm rule. Some heads may be given to other Raute elders after each hunt. Portions of thigh meat are given to shamans and, as Chandra quipped, "The monkey's thigh is the shaman's meat." This is due to the fact that shamans are instrumental in getting the monkeys to run into the hunters' nets; thus, by extension, they are offered choice pieces of the prey. Subsequently, these portions are given to the Raute shamans' wives, and then women distribute smaller meat packages to their natal family. The tail portion is given to children, while the heart and liver portions are given to Raute widows (along with other meat). One elder said that this is a gesture confirming that elderly women represent the heart of the Raute community. Indeed, widows' huts are located in the center of the camp and elderly women sit together mending nets and chatting in the middle of camp each day.[4] Since women cook, all meat is given to the wife or a close female relative of the hunters. Tara, one of the Raute women, remarked that "If there is a lot of meat, we can make it *karo-tere*, dried. We put it in water, and then cut it in little pieces. After that we dry it in the sun or on the fire. We can eat the blood too. First, you put it in a little [monkey] oil and fry it. But mostly, we eat the meat immediately, even if it takes three days to eat it all." Pregnant females and small baby monkeys are also captured. When asked if any part of the hunt is discarded, Tara said: "Why throw them out? God has given us all the monkeys that come into our nets."

Rautes stressed that, while meat portions are reserved for the categories of persons described above, meat is distributed without any regard to the recipient's social position. For example, when Chandra, often more interested in dancing than hunting, did not go hunting one day, I asked, "Did others give meat to you?" He replied: "Why wouldn't they? My own family went hunting. Four of my brothers went. They gave some meat." If a large number of monkeys, maybe twenty, are snared, portions are sufficient to distribute to all families. If the number is small, only the natal family and some in-laws of the hunters will receive meat portions. Families of men who did not hunt will not be given any meat unless they are close kin. For example, we were visiting camp one afternoon when only three men were present while the others were out foraging or trading in villages before gathering together for a late afternoon hunt. Bhim, one of the most conservative of the Rautes, stayed home to take care of his wife, who felt ill. The next day I asked Chandra whether or not Bhim would receive any monkey meat since he did not attend the hunt. He thought for a moment then said that no one is required to go hunting, but if a man neglects to hunt often, he will be questioned and criticized. He thought that, probably, Bhim would not receive any meat as he was perfectly capable of hunting and they only captured about ten monkeys. He added that if there was enough meat, Bhim's family would also receive a portion. Even though Bhim is considered one of the Rautes' most protective elders, his social position does not entitle him to more resources than other men or women.

Contextualizing Raute Hunting and Sharing Behavior

Hunting and sharing monkey meat constitutes an essential part of Raute economic behavior. Why is sharing meat so important to Rautes? Some researchers think that food reciprocity[5] reduces the risk of people starving because of an ethic in which "One day you feed me, the next day I feed you" (Cashdan 1985; Kaplan and Hill 1985; Winterhalder and Smith 1981). These risk-reduction models suggest that sharing resources is a means of increasing breadth of diet as well as diminishing the risk of food shortages. From my observations of and interviews with Rautes it became apparent that daily food is shared with family members, and that most meals are eaten at the hearths of a close female relative. However, large amounts of monkey meat are shared with the entire group, and feasts of goat and sheep (acquired through trade of wooden wares) occur monthly. In addition, men and women drink grain beer throughout the day. The beer is made from grain obtained from villagers and is an important source of carbohydrates. The mildly alcoholic drink is stored in large wood containers (*dzhum*) from which anyone may drink. Greens are not shared quite as much, but large amounts of gathered greens are a favorite accompaniment to monkey meat. However, not all men hunt, and people who cannot obtain meat from hunting (women, children, and elderly) do receive shares.

Ritualized gift exchange has also been hypothesized as a strategy for reducing insecurity about food (Wiessner 1977). Among the !Kung San (Ju/'hoansi) of southern Africa, for example, people participate in trade networks (*hxaro*) that allow them to visit their trading partners when food resources become difficult to find. But this particular external form of sharing is not found among the Rautes. They do form "bond friendships" or "fictive kinship ties" with villagers, however, which are called *mit*. These *mit* friendships with elite villagers enable the Rautes to obtain vegetables, tobacco, fruit, cloth, goats, and political protection from villagers who may perceive Rautes as competitors for forest resources. In that these friendships facilitate access to food, they can be seen as a strategy for reducing food insecurity; but they are not a form of sharing. As practiced by the Raute, *mit* relationships are more like a form of begging or negative reciprocity than sharing. Rautes only interact with a partner for the duration of their camp stay near a villager's home; they give nothing freely to their new "friend."

Another explanation for the primacy of sharing, based on research among South American foraging horticulturalists known as the Ache of Paraguay, is that large food packages are shared in order to gain social status, to demonstrate that a man can be a "breadwinner" and increase males' mating chances. Some sociobiologists even assert that men hunt in order to exchange meat for sex (Kaplan and Hill 1985). Based on conversations with Rautes about their courting, marriage, and sexual behavior, they strongly stress monogamy and disapprove of infidelity. The only time a man has two wives is "when his first wife has died." Further, boys do not instigate sexual interest; girls do. Unmarried girls are expected to indicate whom they wish to marry by flirting, cooking for the man, and foraging with the man's sisters. After marriage, however, women do not joke sexually or flirt with other men. Even widows are barred from remarriage, and this cultural rule may function as a means of limiting population or may simply be a practice that emulates the Hindu custom of disallowing widows to remarry. Unlike the Ache of South America, the Rautes exert no sexual claims over each other. Illicit sexual behavior may occur—as one youthful hunter growled, "I don't know what others do in the forest, but they better not do it with *my* sisters"—a response that indicates strong disapproval of such behavior. Thus, far from gaining social status, Raute hunters would lose social status by trying to provide meat in exchange for increased mating chances.

Another explanation for sharing, based on observation of the Nayaka (Jenu Kurumba) of South India, is that "the natural environment is seen [by foragers] to be peopled by human-like relatives who share food with its human inhabitants" (Bird-David 1992). According to anthropologist Nurit Bird-David, foragers feel a "cosmic unity of sharing" due to their nature-bound social existence. During interviews, Rautes often stressed the human-like characteristics of animals or, in reverse, the animal-like qualities the Rautes share. For example, birds were sometimes referred to as the "fathers of the heart," implying that they have a close, paternal understanding of the feelings in one's heart. Yet the idea that animals can choose to share themselves with the Rautes was not noticeable during interviews. For example, when asked if monkeys "share themselves," people responded by saying that it is not exactly like that, but that "*God* gives us all the monkeys that come into our nets." Thus, it appears that Raute foragers do indeed feel a "cosmic unity of sharing," but one in which supernatural agency plays a more important role than that of either humans or monkeys.

It has been hypothesized that sharing results simply from people badgering each other for food, demanding it from each other, or even just taking it without asking. Indeed, reluctant sharing behaviors do occur among the Rautes, and these are delineated by anthropologists as "demand sharing" and "tolerated theft."[6] In these cases, sharing is based on the fear that not giving will create more hard feelings than agreeing to the demand. Among the Rautes, reluctantly sharing food and materials probably is a mechanism for redistributing resources and may indirectly contribute to ideologies of sharing.

In research on the elderly in foraging societies, it has been noted that the elderly may provide valuable services by passing on knowledge, providing child care, and serving as storytellers, shamans, drummers, traders, adjudicators, rhetoricians, and political leaders. In another related theory of the utility of post-childbearing age, dubbed "the grandmother hypothesis," anthropologist Kristen Hawkes suggests that there may be an evolutionary advantage to foragers who can preserve knowledge of resources and the environment in the longer lifetimes of their elder members. In Raute society, abilities to adjudicate disputes, express compassionate love, cook, carve and trade wooden wares, hunt, drum and dance, and heal were often praised as useful qualities. As social reproductive strategies, these skills contribute essential services to the survival of Raute society, and they are not skills that can be mastered by every person. It seems reasonable, then, that division of skills has developed based not only on age and sex, as is often described in introductory textbooks, but also on individual skill and ability, and that members do exchange these skills with each other.

While many skills are important to Rautes, two in particular were cited as important to Rautes: the ability to adjudicate disputes tactfully and the ability to express compassionate love. Fine rhetorical skills and compassion may not be recognized as important in our own societies, as we have written laws to help judge disputes and rules of etiquette that govern our everyday interactions. But imagine living in a society of only a hundred and fifty people—people who invariably get on each others' nerves! Because the nomadic Rautes are a small society, disputes in camp threaten band integrity. For example, several times I witnessed Rautes expressing anger at each other. Sometimes people disagreed about where to go hunting; at others they disagreed about whether to perform dances. Decisions about when to relocate camp, where to obtain water, when to hunt or trade are all open to dispute. Unlike our own society in which there is a leader who makes decisions for others (a city mayor, a school principal, etc.), Rautes engage in evening conversations about these issues. People are free to choose one of two or three options, and thus fine rhetorical skills are necessary. Disputes were resolved by the measured adjudications of elder men and women through gentle suggestions of resolutions and giving attention to each disputant's opinion. For example, even though young men are the main providers of meat, that does not entitle them to more political influence over others. Most villagers are unaware that Raute women influence decisions about where to trade, seek monkeys, or relocate camps. One of the Raute men explained this to me by way a short rhyme, singing:

> My sheep shed collapsed, o father,
> leaving the buffalo shelter,

My wife is a leader, father,
I must nowadays follow her.

(*beḍi goṭha laḍe bãbāi,*
bhaisi goṭha bhara //
meri jahãnwa nāyki [nāyak, naike] bãbu,
ājā kaichha bharna)

To sing involves releasing words to "fly out" (*bwā gite gā'hāre*), a kind of verbal art that teaches listeners important messages. The first message in the lyrics acknowledges a great deal of empathy for the hard life of a farmer, a life in which there are constantly troubles with maintaining livestock. But the second part of the rhyme delivers the punch line and the main message. Raute men have a great deal of respect for their wives, and they obey them as often as they obey other adults. The rhyme calls the woman a leader (*nāyak*), which invokes the image of a village headman, one who adjudicates disputes and makes important political decisions for the community. The take-home message for us is that, among the Raute members themselves, decision making is largely a process of consensus building among all adults in their community.

Another quality the Rautes feel is compassionate love for each other, and this helps people to share without hard feelings. For example, as we talked about the importance of Raute friendships with villagers, one elder explained that "Yes, our fictive brothers [villagers] are important, but our love (*hit*) for relatives is greater than friendship (*mit*) with others."[7] In another conversation, an elder described his love for his spouse, "We should drink a little, not a lot. . . . if I drink and hang out with my pals (*istā*, clan relatives), my wife will question why. . . . I feel such deep kindness for her. I don't know what you do, but we feel much caring. We care if someone cries. I love my wife." Thus feelings of love enable Rautes to share with each other without feeling undue resentment over giving away meat, sandals, and other resources. Sharing monkey meat, then, is not the result of an intrinsic altruism, but the outcome of many social and economic factors.

The reasons for sharing so far presented are general explanations that have been observed among Rautes and in other hunter-gatherer societies. Yet cross-cultural generalizations may not be the best explanations for why Rautes share meat and other valuables with each other. As the archaeologist Robert Kelly points out, "We should not expect to find one explanation for sharing" (Kelly 1995, 180). In reviewing the Rautes' way of life, there appears to be a multicausal explanation for their particularly intensive sharing practices. In functionalist terms, Raute sharing behaviors stem from their particular circumstances. They share resources such as meat in order to (1) increase diet breadth; (2) reduce risks of food shortages; (3) accommodate food requests; (4) facilitate social networks between natal family and in-laws; (5) exchange individual skills with each other; (6) give meat to loved ones; and (7) avoid spoilage of large amounts of hunted meat. One hunt, for example, may net twenty monkeys, yielding about 275 pounds of edible food (or about 350,000 calories). Yet Rautes practice very limited meat drying. Who wants to haul dried meat from one camp to another when there are more monkeys in the next forest? Thus, their nomadic net-hunting lifestyle ensures that meat is shared widely among themselves.

6

Let's Go to the Forest and Eat Fruit

Tasty mustard greens in a field, delicious tubers reflected by
  the moon.
Kind-hearted people are important, and salty vegetables taste
  good too.
—Raute saying

*One little farm boy commented upon the dandelion greens that a Raute girl
was chewing on raw. Raw! Farmers rarely eat greens raw. Ratna Bahadur
had a bag full of greens with him tonight too. In fact, I have noticed that
almost every time I meet Rautes, they have a little or more of some food
items stored in folds of their shawls. Sometimes I've seen salt, potatoes, or
tobacco gifted from farmers. Most other times I've noticed wild greens and
roots in little tied clumps. So, while I have assumed that women are primarily responsible for collecting greens, the men also do a great deal of opportunistic collecting as they amble through forests and nearby villages.*

Because Rautes cultivate no crops and raise no animals, wild plants are
particularly important for food, materials, and medicines. Rautes enjoy
stewing, roasting, and boiling wild spinach-like greens and wild yams and
other tubers. Forest greens represent one of their most important edibles,
as they are a calorie-rich, indispensable accompaniment to monkey meat.
They nibble on raw greens as they forage through the forests. In the warm
rainy season, Raute women and men search for greens and fruit. In the dry
season, they find wild yams and other tubers. In this chapter, I shall focus
on their plant-based diet, while in the next chapter I'll explore how culturally significant plants are used for trade, manufacturing, and construction
materials.

A Complex Diet

The nomadic Rautes forage for about ninety types of wild greens, fruits, vegetables, nuts, tubers, mushrooms, and spices. While a wide variety of edible plants exist, Rautes take advantage of the seasonal fluctuations of flowering and fruiting edible plants. Berries ripen in the summer just as the monsoon rains arrive; larger fruits ripen in late summer; and tubers grow large in the dry season, although a couple others are dug up in the summer. Rautes sometimes do not differentiate a food by whether it is eaten as a food or as a medicine, so the following list will include some medicinal foods. For example, the plant known in English as ice vine or velvet leaf (*Cissampelos pareira*) is eaten because the roots taste good, like the anise root available in American food stores, but it can also be eaten to alleviate constipation. Note that while many of these edibles are important food sources for Rautes, farmers disparagingly call them "famine foods." Farmers obviously have a different viewpoint as they grow crops and downplay any reliance on wild foods. But to Rautes, these are not so-called famine foods; they are their subsistence (see Appendix, Tables 2–4).

As Tables 2–4 demonstrate, Rautes gather from a wide range of plant species. Excluding cultivated plants, these include about a dozen types of edible roots, forty types of leafy greens, and fifty types of fruits. The root crops are particularly important, as they provide Rautes with a source of carbohydrates, giving them a diet distinctive from than that of surrounding farmers.

For vegetable protein, other foragers may rely upon nuts, such as *piñon* nut mashes and pine-nut dishes eaten by California foraging peoples, or mongongo nuts eaten by Kalahari Bushmen. In Nepal, there are several nut trees available for harvesting (pines, oaks, and walnuts) and the butternut tree (*Bassia butyracea*). Yet, butternut is the only one that provides a large amount of edible meal in a manageable processing time, as wild walnuts and pine nuts yield relatively little for the effort required. However, butternuts (*ciuri*) are coveted by farm families, while Rautes mostly eat the flowers and fruit of the trees. The lack of nut proteins in the Raute diet coincides with the fact that they are not territorial. Foraging societies that rely upon nut proteins usually claim use rights over the rich resources, making nut trees a sort of property; thus nut-based subsistence is characteristic of more territorial foraging societies. In addition, Rautes do not grow or eat lentils, which represent a staple protein for farmers. Perhaps the Rautes' most important nut protein derives from orchid tree (*Bauhinia*) shrubs. Though there are not a lot per tree, these have tasty cashew-like pods. But Rautes really don't need nuts for protein because they are dependent on animal proteins. So there is an economic division of protein resources in which farmers consume lentils, nuts, dairy, and animal meat. In turn, Rautes depend upon monkey meat and vegetable proteins, with occasional goats and sheep obtained from farmers.

In addition, leafy shoots and leaves provide necessary vitamins, minerals, and roughage, while fruits provide calories, vitamins, minerals, and sugar. As one of the Rautes sang one day, "*bindadā ban basnu / kanda phal khānu*" (We'll keep within the woodland / We shall eat the forest fruit). In this rhyme that has been repeated to myself and several other researchers over the years, Rautes sing of a nearby forest where they sate themselves with berries. They even performed a dance for another researcher and told him it was called "Let's go to the forest and eat wild fruit" (Ross 1978). The text of the song mentions many kinds of forest flora and beseeches one to enjoy the fruit and the beautiful flowers of the forest. It ends with a few verses that beseech the listener to "bring some forest greens, because bread from villagers is not available."

Forest foods, as the song and dance show, represent not simply edibles but something more. They represent a destination of enjoyment and a place filled with other creatures and flowers. Forests are a source of beauty as well as of sustenance, and the song reveals and conveys to us the Rautes as people who enjoy, and rely on, the fruits of the forest. As the song concludes, one is told to fill her/his bamboo carrying basket (*nigāla ko buntho ḍokiya*) with different kinds of edible leaves.

Fruits and seeds represent an important source of nutrition to Rautes, particularly berries that ripen in the early summer when many other food sources are unavailable. They provide a significant source of vitamins and minerals and represent a high order of food choice. Forest fruit trees also have multiple purposes, such as providing flowers for decoration, medicine for wounds, and inner bark for making rope. Forest resources that can be used in multiple ways tend to be favored over other single-purpose trees. Witchberry (*Rubus paniculatus*), for example, is not only edible, but its bark paste can be applied to scabies and rashes, while leaf paste is applied to sprains. Witchberry represents a useful fruit in that it is ubiquitous, easy to obtain, and has medicinal value. Another important fruit, fig (*Ficus* spp.), can be eaten even when immature, and the inner bark of the tree can be used to fashion rope. Ficus trees, of which there are at least seventeen species in Nepal, represent an important "keystone" genus because they provide food and homes to various birds, bat colonies, and farmers. The *peepal* tree (*Ficus religiosa*), for example, is considered sacred by both Hindus and Buddhists and is planted at temples.

To complement vitamin-rich greens and fruits, Raute foragers must obtain enough carbohydrates to fuel their energy-intensive activities. Women are especially adept at digging wild yams, their most calorie-rich food. In Nepali, yams are called *tārul* with a modifier that describes different varieties. *Ghār tārul*, for example, are "house yams" and are grown in kitchen gardens, while *ban tārul* are "forest yams" and are gathered from forest glades. Rautes call yams by several different names as well—*nyuhri*, "main/mother tuber," *dzyāhra*, "edible tuber," and *koi*, "tuberous root"—and they dig other edible tubers belonging to the genera *Arisaema*, *Cirsium*, *Cissampelos*, *Gonostegia*, and *Phoeni*. The neighboring Chepang, too, have fully fifty-one names for tubers.[1] Banrajis distinguish a yam's lower root area (*lwā*), a branching segment (*indālye*), a stem near the bulb (*lwā-kui yu'u*), the bulbous nodules (*ghā-tyu*), and the stem segment above the bulb (*narwa'a*). The obvious lesson is that Nepal's forest foragers know their tubers well, just as potato farmers in the Peruvian Andes know their potato varieties well. During my first visit to the Raute camp, the elder Ain Bahadur emphasized the fundamental importance of yams for their nomadic foraging lifestyle, saying, "*dil bascha* . . . our hearts live here, in the forest. Since the time of our ancestors, it has been just like today. The forest is fine for us. The wild yams are still easy to dig." As Ain Bahadur emphasized, it is really yams that matter for subsistence.

Digging for yams involves a different form of human social organization than planting potatoes or other agricultural crops, however. Foraging for them demands that people spread out into small groups of two or three, which encourages more individual autonomy. When I asked a Raute youth named Harka Bahadur whether they perform ceremonies (*puja*) before yam foraging as they do for hunting, he scoffed at the idea, saying, "We don't have to." He drew a picture of a his family collecting some wild yams, and continued: "We have to dig yams to eat. If we have to really spread out for this work, *how* [his emphasis] could we do *puja*? No, we don't do *puja* in the forest then." But, he added, Rautes do honor a yam deity and occasionally carve yam roots into likenesses of this supernatural being. In a drawing, Harka drew his father as a line and squiggle mark. He drew himself next to his father, as the middle squiggly line; and he drew his mother digging the yam. The yam was drawn in a realistic manner, complete with roots extending in different directions. Harka described how the yam was part of their family, like their mother or one who feeds them.

Tubers represent a great subsistence food, but are they also valuable for trading to villagers? One might think that Rautes would trade forest products such as wild yams for desired commodities such as rice or tobacco. In India, other foragers are renowned for their trading practices (Fox 1969; Morris 1982; Morrison and Junker 2002). In other places, from Africa to New Guinea, yams have been a staple commodity that has been used for economic exchange (Bohannan 1955; Godelier 1977). So could Rautes use yams as a limited form of monetary exchange? For example, Rautes need local iron smiths to make and sharpen their axes, chisels, and scrapers. Why not use wild yams to pay them for their services? In this part of Nepal, at least, farmers have used wild yams as a form of money. As one farmer living in Butternut Village (Ciurigaun) explained, government officials used to take "even wild yams that we collected in the forest" as part of local taxes (Fortier 1995, 176). But unlike farmers, Rautes do not exchange yams for goods, services, or even social prestige, preferring to avoid social interactions with farmers.[2] They also eschew trade in honey, spices, rope, or other forest products, trading only wooden wares to villagers.

Could Rautes exchange yams for personal merit or to gain social status? Among many horticulturalists of New Guinea, for example, yams are a form of money, and their trade is part of exchange networks with other peoples of the region. But Rautes explained that they do not need to create exchange networks with each other because they simply share their daily yam collection with family members at a kinswoman's morning cooking pot. Yams, then, are not commodities that form the basis of prestige networks, nor are they tax payments. During internal barter sessions with farmers, wild yams have no exchange value. When a Raute barters for an iron smith's goods and services, for example, payment is made only in wooden bowls and boxes. Rautes will *take* garden yams from farmers, but they will not give them to farmers.

As a broader picture of Raute forest foraging develops, we see that while Rautes forage for yams as well as a variety of forest edibles, they consume only negligible amounts of fish, mushrooms, honey, nuts, seeds, spices, or teas; these represent "low-order" food choices. For example, Raute elder Mayn Bahadur stated that women and children catch fish with their bare hands in the pools and eddies of rivers, and while washing dishes at the river "go fishing" by looking under rocks for hiding fish and crustaceans. But the Rautes ignore fishing weirs, spears, or fish nets. Their lack of interest in honey hunting, fishing, and nut collecting differs from the practices of most of their regional neighbors, however. Similarly, Banrajis living in Kumaun also fish only with their hands and take relatively little interest in fishing. But Rajis living in southwestern Nepal are known for their daring honey-hunting expeditions (Valli 1998) and for their interest in fishing as well. And Chepangs, living to the east of Rautes, are recognized as adept at the use of fish poisons during fishing (Caughley 1976; Gurung 1989).

We can describe Raute foraging strategies, then, as relatively focused, while their hunter-gatherer neighbors pursue more broad-spectrum foraging strategies. One explanation for the Rautes' emphasis on yams and monkey involves their need to find an ecological niche that does not compete with other ethnic and social groups, particularly with rural villagers. In Jajarkot, for example, farmers are keen to describe their favorite fish, of which there are about twelve species fished frequently out of about a hundred available species in local rivers. Another reason for Rautes' disinterest in fishing may lie in the fact that they rely so heavily upon monkey meat, so it may not be necessary for them to resort to procuring another high-protein source. For them, fish represents a lower-level food choice than monkey meat.

Not only nomadic Rautes but farmers, too, rely on the forests for numerous needs, including fruit, vegetables, meat, fish, fuel, fodder, timber, compost, rope, spices, vegetable fat, soap, dye, religious trees, honey, and mushrooms (Fortier 1993, 14; Manandhar 2002). These products may be consumed in the home but can also be sold on the market. Wild mushrooms, such as highly prized morel mushrooms, are eaten in homemade vegetable dishes but are also traded to middlemen who market them to India and abroad. A luxury item, morel mushrooms currently cost about US$30.00 per dry ounce in the United States.

Even though farmers often rely on forest products to make ends meet, the foraging lifestyle is not a dominant form of food procurement, as it is among the Raute hunter-gatherers. Foraging, for farmers, is linked to more complex social divisions and to particular cultivation rights to wild resources such as cinnamon and butternut trees (Fortier 1993). Farmers will even cultivate some forest products, such as medicinals, with the sole intent of portering them to India for commercial sale. In Jajarkot, foraging farmers enjoy collecting and selling the roots of *bhulte* (var. *jaṭāmansi*, *Nardostachys jatamansi*). In the United States this plant is pressed into perfume oil known as "Spikenard Oil" which currently sells on the Internet for US$50.00 per ounce. Spikenard is valuable partly because it is described in the Bible's Song of Solomon, when Mary Magdalene anointed Jesus' feet before the Last Supper. It is written that "Mary took a pound of ointment of spikenard and anointed the feet of Jesus, and wiped his feet with her hair; and the house was filled with the odor of the ointment" (John 12:3).

Although they consume many forest edibles, Rautes also acquire domestic cereals during barter sessions with farmers. In fact, Rautes adore rice. Perhaps their wanting to eat domestic grains may seem odd, but in fact contemporary foraging populations worldwide have been trading for grain and other desired objects for centuries, and probably since the origins of food production began millennia ago.

The Myth of the Full-Time Hunter-Gatherer

Many books about contemporary hunter-gatherers would have the reader believe that foragers live in fairly isolated circumstances and rely fairly little, if at all, on agricultural foods and products. For example, Robert Kelly's book, *The Foraging Spectrum*, includes a chapter on foraging and subsistence. Information is supplied on the percentage of foragers' diets in 126 foraging societies from various parts of the world (1995, 67–69). But the information is presented in terms of categories that do not include information on how many candy bars, cups of rice, or tablespoons of sugar are consumed, only on percentages of the forager diet derived from hunting, fishing, and gathering. An Ojibwa Indian's diet, according to Kelly (1995, 67), is supposedly made up of 40 percent hunting, 30 percent gathering, and 30 percent fishing. Yet common sense indicates that Ojibwa (Chippewa, Anishinabe) groups would also have traded with nearby sedentary farming communities. Even if the data in Kelly's analyses of hunter-gatherer societies represent a European early contact period,[3] they fail to show that hunter-gatherers historically and globally have relied on barter with agricultural societies for many products. In precolonial periods, Ojibwa peoples traded with Algonkin peoples, their nearest neighbors, who practiced corn farming. These communities raised corn, tobacco, squash, gourds, pumpkins, sunflower, and beans. Nearby, communities of Ho-chunk (Winnebago), who carried out lead mining, also traded with Ojibwa hunter-gatherers.

The forager–farmer relationship is created because foragers want to obtain agricultural products but don't want to grow them. The forest foragers of the Ituri Forest in central Africa also engage in intensive hunting and trading for grain from villagers.[4] The Ituri forest foragers represent a good comparative example with Rautes since both groups practice net hunting and trade with villagers for agricultural produce (Ichikawa 2006). In a dietary study, Robert Bailey and Nadine Peacock found that their Bambuti study group had a diet that consisted of 8.5 percent hunted meat, 0.5 percent fish, and 14 percent wild plants. Including an important 13.5 percent of calories from wild honey, their total "foraging" diet amounted to about 37 percent of their total calories. The remainder of their diet came from maize, sorghum, and other cultivated food brought into camps (Bailey and Peacock 1988, 101). Yet the agricultural base of the foragers' diet may be ignored by or eliminated from scientific studies that try to focus too much on foraging and too little on foragers' overall diet. Looking at the cross-cultural table of forager diets in Robert Kelly (1995, 69), we see that the Bambuti have a diet that is reportedly made up of 60 percent hunting, 30 percent gathering, and 10 percent fishing. How can we explain this difference between the statistics reported by Kelly and the research data recorded by Bailey and Peacock? *The difference lies in Kelly's exclusion of agricultural products from reporting on forager diets.* Only by *excluding* the agricultural products consumed by Pygmies does the ratio of hunting/gathering/fishing reported by Kelly become consistent with that reported by Bailey and Peacock. In trying to reconstruct a "pure" forager diet, Kelly's figures obscure the important fact that agricultural foods provide about 65 percent of the Pygmy diet. An accurate rendering of Pygmy diet would list it as composed of 22 percent hunting, 9 percent gathering, 1 percent fishing, *and* 64 percent cultivated foods.

By erasing the real relationships forged between hunter-gatherers and agriculturalists, we lose sight of the importance of the forager–farmer relationship and their mutual interdependence. Researcher John Hart sees this as a balanced mutual dependency, in which foragers obtain carbohydrate-rich foods while villagers obtain protein-rich forest meat from the Mbuti. This relationship is not one in which one side wins and the other loses, for they are locked in a relationship of mutual interdependence. In fact, even though the various forager groups in this area are considered classic examples of the hunting-gathering lifestyle, the fact remains that none of the Ituri Forest foragers have ever been known to live for more than a month without consuming some sort of agricultural produce (Bailey and Peacock 1988, 92). The lesson to be learned from this case is that foragers worldwide forge viable trade relations with agriculturalists and have done so for a long time. Among southern African Bushmen foragers, for example, archaeological evidence exists for over a thousand years of trade with agriculturalists. And in South Asia, the earliest city-states have border communities, such as the city of Lothal, in which forest-based resources appear to have come from trade with forest foragers (Possehl 2002).

If the Rautes' subsistence activities are calculated in a manner similar to that used comparing foragers worldwide in Kelly 1995 (without agricultural products included in the analysis), then their estimated diet would seem to consist of mainly hunted meat, namely 80 percent, with 18 percent gathering, and 2 percent fishing. Such a diet would match those in Kelly's tables of the Blackfoot (Siksika), Crow (Apsáalooke), Cheyenne, Kiowa, and Apache—all of whom relied heavily on highly communal group-oriented hunting techniques involving animal drives, though of buffalo rather than monkeys. Interestingly, the Rautes' monkey hunting can also be described as a highly communal group-oriented hunting technique involving animal drives. There are differences, however, involving the ecology of the prey, the environmental conditions, and the weapon technology. In terms of weaponry, for example, the Rautes drive the animals into nets and kill with axes. Native American high plains buffalo hunters, on the other hand, used a variety of animal capture techniques including torch fire, brush corrals, axes, bow and arrow, driving the animals over cliffs, and, in postcolonial times, horses and guns.

However, presenting information on only hunting, gathering, and fishing would not give a complete picture of Raute subsistence activities. Like other contemporary foraging societies, the Rautes have a relationship of mutual interdependence with neighboring farmers. A more detailed estimate of Raute diet indicates that it is composed of a large percentage of grain (see Appendix, Table 5).

With this fuller picture of Raute diet and dependence on agricultural products, it appears that in the summer/monsoon season, wild plant foods, meat, and fish account for about 50 percent of their calorific needs. And wild plants, though low in calories, are important nutritional supplements to their diet. As Rautes underscore, monkey meat tastes best with greens. When discussing their food, Man Bahadur sang:

> Fields are good filled with greens.
> Yams look good by the light of the moon.
> Good people have a kind heart.
> Vegetables taste good with salt.[5]

He explained that "You should have a kind heart and people should have good things to eat," and went on to describe how monkey meat is delicious when eaten with greens. Greens, while important nutritionally, nevertheless must be paired with high-calorie foods. During the fall, grain represents a consistently acquired high caloric food, being delivered into camp almost every day after successful barter sessions with villagers. In the winter, wild yams are abundant, while in the summer, fruits and greens are readily abundant and thus the amount of grains acquired is reduced. Broadly, grains supply roughly 30 percent of Raute calorific consumption, depending on the season and availability. When farmers experience famines, which happens about once every seven years, Rautes obtain far less grain. Rautes trade their bowls for grain, and they also ask farmers to "top off" their trades with such garden items as pumpkin, squash, gourds, tobacco, potatoes, corn, and so on. Grain, especially rice, is one of the Rautes' favorite foods, but they nevertheless refuse to grow it themselves. Why grow rice when you can get it from the millions of surrounding farmers?

Could Rautes Become Farmers?

Although Rautes refuse to settle down and take up farming, some villagers have suggested that they learn farming. They argue that the Rautes would be better off and that they could experience a more "developed" way of life. However, most farmers do not recognize the problems associated with the transition from a foraging to a farming livelihood. As the Raji can attest, when recently settled foragers are given land, inevitably they lose it to more sophisticated and clever farmers. When this happens, beginner farmers like the Raji become landless laborers, the tenants of high-caste farmers, and their quality of life diminishes.

One would think that subsistence farming of rice and other grains is uncomplicated, and that social relationships involved in such farming are simple. But the process is complex, partly because farming involves the exchange of labor obligations and financing of grain loans. These loans and labor exchanges have to be reckoned and remembered between households, sometimes for generations. Our own capitalist social relations are based on payments using money or credit cards. These transactions are less personal, and they can be completed without further obligations between two parties.

One of the common labor relations in Jajarkot involves tenant sharecropping in which households either lease or rent land. Commonly, high-caste families lease out their land if they work in government offices and no have time for farming. Low-caste families rarely have enough land to farm, so they either rent or occasionally lease their land if they are full-time artisans with no time for farming. The tenants who rent land to farm may be high- or low-caste, but they are always "land hungry." In Jajarkot, the sharecropping system is called adhiyā, meaning "halves." In this system, the sharecropper farms the owner's land and gives half of the harvest to the owner, keeping half for him/herself. While this system sounds simple, farming the land and getting a harvest big enough to share can be difficult. For this reason, the owner (sāu) and the tenant (mohi) discuss the expected harvest in relation to the quality of the land and agree to divide a percentage of harvest yield based on past harvests.

In one interview, I brought together a wealthy landlord named Khadga Regmi, who runs a development program, and his sharecropper, a man named Narjit Khatri. Narjit works hard, sharecropping for three or four different high-caste landlords in addition to farming his own land. I asked Narjit to tell me about his sharecropping situation. He said, "Well, I bought land for myself, but it is unirrigated and does not produce much of a harvest. My father too has land, but I have not asked to inherit my share of the family land yet. So I have been working as a sharecropper for the last twenty-three years. I have gotten *adhiyā* parcels from three or four people. Of them, one piece belongs to the wife of the government court officer in Maide Village and another belongs to one Bāmni [Brahman woman]. Another parcel belonged to Khadga Regmi's wife's father and now Regmi has bought it. In total the land equals about 55 *ropani* [2.8 hectares]. I get about 50 *muri* [3.5 tons/6,885 lb./ 3,123 kg.] of unhusked rice and 10 *muri* [0.7 ton/1,378 lb./ 625 kg.] of wheat. I give about 50 percent of the rice to the landowners and about 40 percent of the wheat to the landowners."

I wondered how he could farm so much land by himself, so I asked him if he hired people to help him. But before he could answer, the landlord, Regmi, jumped in and asked him, "Why do you consume your grain so quickly?"

To this, Narjit responded, "Well, I guess we eat too much. If we can eat about seven or eight pieces of *roṭi* bread, then we will consume up to two pounds of grain each day." I noted that this was actually the local standard estimate of grain a farmworker eats per day. Responding to his landlord, Narjit politely but firmly defended his right to eat enough food.

Then, turning to me, he replied, "I need to get help to do all the farming. In the past, I got help through labor exchange (*parma*) with my neighbors. But this year I couldn't get any help this way. Everyone was too busy. So I had to hire help. I say here truly, I had Rs 1000 before the planting season in June but afterwards, I found I only had Rs 300 left."

Regmi found this interesting and asked, "How did you call the *roparni*, the women who planted our rice land?" But before Narjit could answer, Regmi's business partner chimed in, asking "Who paid the planters?"

Regmi responded to his partner, saying, "We paid the women Rs 10 per day plus a tip (*hilāuri*)." This obviously was another contentious point, and I wondered if Regmi or Narjit had paid the field hands.

Narjit followed up with, "We agreed to pay cash. We paid each woman at least 10 rupees [equal to US$0.38/day][6] plus provided one morning meal and a tip at the end of the day."

"A tip?" I asked. "What kind of tip do you give the planters?"

"Well, it is difficult to define strictly, but it's the old tendency that was derived from the very beginning. *Hilāuri* comes from the word for 'mud,' and it implies that the women get a little something extra for working so hard in the muddy paddy fields. We can give them a little grain, or money, or these days, the planters want alcohol. But I simply can't afford that kind of a tip. That's very expensive and the expense can't be met."

After thinking for a minute, Narjit concluded: "Even though I haven't got enough land compared to others, I have no problems of food security because I practice sharecropping. I have some dryland in which I grow the dryland rice and a bit of maize. Now I have got a stock of 4 *muri* [0.28 ton/550 lb./250 kg.] wheat, which will last up to the next two to three months . . . by that time the maize will be ready to harvest. In this way I am bringing up all my family." Narjit was obviously proud of his ability to make ends meet, and we continued our talk about subsistence farming and the problems it entails.

This relationship between Narjit and Regmi was not uncommon, with the tenant and landlord having to negotiate many details about what type of grain to plant, any fertilizers or pesticides to purchase, how to divide the harvest, pay extra laborers, and so on. This represents the type of tenancy arrangement that the Rautes would experience if they were to give up their nomadic hunting way of life. More likely, however, Rautes would not be able to negotiate the intricate sharecropping deals and would lose any land granted to them. Further, Rautes, with their completely egalitarian social organization, would disapprove of the necessary social hierarchy in which the landlord dominates the economic relationship. Like the Raji, the nomadic Rautes would soon quit or lose their land and become landless daily laborers, scraping to meet their subsistence needs. Another problem that would arise would involve storing any grain harvest for the future. In other foraging societies such as that of the Hadza of Tanzania, when foragers do try to grow and harvest crops, their relatives all come at harvest time and feast on the harvest! This common "demand sharing" behavior effectively eliminates the harvest and leaves the incipient farmers with nothing to eat in the months to come (Woodburn 1982). For all of these reasons, it would be impossible for Rautes to become farmers. In any case, they do not wish to do so. As one Raute affirmed, "I'll not farm in my lifetime."

Yet almost all farmers believe that the Rautes should become subsistence farmers. They consider the farming lifestyle moral, simple, and proper, not realizing that farmers have to know an incredible amount about how to grow corn, rice, wheat, and other crops. Even more important, they have to know how to exchange labor with their neighbors, call daily laborers to their fields, negotiate fair tenancy agreements, and even make arrangements for tipping field hands. Even if the Rautes agreed to settle down, it would take a long time to learn the social intricacies of farming.

Food Choices

I am sitting here, thinking about the food choices of farmers and foragers. While thinking, I munch on a rice cake, dipping it in honey. This food nourishes me, but it is also a choice; I could have chosen to eat many other things (I wanted black licorice but had none available). If marketing and advertising execs were to survey my eating habits, they might place me into a natural-foods-consumer category. This would position me in a certain social category within American consumptive behavior. Likewise, among every social group, food choices represent a marker of what Pierre Bourdieu called "habitus," a distinctive position in social space. In common parlance, Americans say, "You are what you eat," meaning that identity is reflected in one's food choices.

Among Nepalese, also, food choices mark one's distinctive position in social space, for their ranking is an important aspect of caste status. Does the Nepalese farmer eat *dāl-bhāt* (rice and lentils) every day? Or *roṭi* (bread) more often? Does she eat *ḍhiḍo* corn porridge for the morning meal? And does she eat *sisnu* (stinging nettles) when the vegetable garden is barren? Each of these food choices reveals information about wealth and social status in Nepal. Rice and lentils are more expensive than wheat flour. Wheat flour is more expensive than corn meal. Stinging nettles are free for the pinching from any nearby scrub forest.

I recently talked to Niraj Giri, a Nepalese friend whose grandfather follows the Brahmanic food rules. Niraj said that his grandfather quit eating meat at about age thirty-five, for "religious reasons." (In their quest for spirituality, Brahmans avoid eating other sentient beings.) Inquiring further, I asked what meats Niraj's grandfather gave up, and he explained that his grandfather had previously eaten only goat meat. A hierarchy of meats, then, is in place, in which goat meat is considered ritually purer than other meats, such as chicken, pig, or water buffalo. Although there are exceptions, wild meats such as deer, pheasant, or boar were already considered too impure to eat. And meats of important religious significance, beef and monkey meat, are of course strictly taboo to Niraj's grandfather.

When a Nepalese farmer meets a Raute hunter-gatherer, the question of appropriate Hindu Nepalese food choices often enters the conversation. The farmer knows the social rules for food consumption and he can rank the Raute's social status by his food choices. Like most people, farmers have ethnocentric ideas about which foods are good and bad, based on their own culture's food proscriptions. For the farmer, wild foods are socially inferior to domestic crops. It is a sign of family food insecurity if food has to be foraged in the forest. Therefore, since the Rautes eat primarily wild foods, their social status is questionable. How can they claim to be Thakuri, a high caste, when they eat *jaŋgali* forest foods?

In Jajarkot, the issue of food ranking is actually more complex than a simple hierarchy. Some high-caste and wealthy families do not mind eating wild foods occasionally. They consider it healthy and frugal. Part of the dilemma over how often and how much *jaŋgali* food to consume involves a deep ambiguity about wild foods. I found this ambiguity in many interviews. When I interviewed a woman named Radha Chetri who lives near Machaina Village where the Rautes hunt monkey, she voiced some of these mixed feelings about *jaŋgali* foods.

I met Radha in Khalanga, Jajarkot District's capital, when she came to have an ear infection treated. Although she was about sixty-five years old, she had walked for seven hours to reach the district capital. I asked, "Radha, do you have a garden?" and she smiled ruefully, "We had one last year but not this year." "So what do you normally eat?" I asked. "We just gather and eat (*lyāiyo khāiyo*) . . . just enough for ourselves but nothing to sell," she responded. This implied that she gathered wild edibles from the forest and, hearing this, the listening crowd at the health clinic laughed.

Then her son broke in, worried that I might have gotten the wrong impression. He wanted me to know that their family is not as destitute as his mother makes them out to be. He interjected: "We eat bread, greens, lentils, and cooked rice [*roṭi, sāg, dāl bhāt*] and we eat nettles (*sisnu*) from the forest too. But we don't eat other wild food. We know nothing about other wild food. We own more than five *ropani* [0.25 hectares] of land."

Continuing, Radha first denigrated her vegetable garden as a "weedy patch" (*jhāraka*) and a bit later in the conversation exaggerated it, calling it her "estate" (*kamat*) rather than simply a garden (*bāri*). She admitted she grew radishes for making chutney, but she described them as "stubby little things" (*chota*), which again caused the gathered crowd to laugh, as Nepalese radishes are the long white variety.

From my conversations with Radha and other villagers, I remembered that "You are what you eat." I learned that to eat *jaŋgali* foods is a stigmatizing sign of poverty. And to be seen as eating jungle foods like *jaŋgali* people do would be humiliating to subsistence farmers—a sign that they themselves were wild and poor.

7

Economy and Society
A Complex Mix

Those men who make the jute umbrellas and portering baskets,
They don't make the woven grain bins.
Those who make the grain bins, they can't make the wooden
    koshi bowls.
Those who make *koshi*, they don't read and write.
Those who read and write, they don't plow.
Why is this so?
The cow can give milk, but the bull can't give milk.
If this is a lie, then the bull should give milk.
    —Mayn Bahadur

Villagers often express amazement over the Rautes' skill at carving bowls. And it is true; their bowls are simple and elegant masterpieces. Rautes are proud of their carving skills; they are expert at carving a number of different wooden articles. As the Raute leader Chandra remarked, "Others do not know about our bowls, they don't even know if they are made of mud or wood." By this, Chandra meant that villagers receive the wooden bowls plastered in red ochre mud, and often they wrongly assume that the objects are made of clay. A few young men even prefer to spend the day trading with villagers rather than hunting monkeys. One of the best traders, Chandra, noted that "Hunting is hard, you have to walk on the sloping hillsides. Selling a bowl is much easier, all you have to do is walk on paths for one whole day." But Rautes emphasize that they are not wood-carvers by occupation. Indeed, they strongly resist farmers' suggestions that they become carpenters or wood-carving specialists.

To Mayn Bahadur and Chandra, there is a world of difference between "carving wood" and being a "wood-carver." Artisans must spend years learning specialized skills to make jute baskets, umbrellas, grain bins, and other crafted objects. They must learn how to find the materials in the forest and how to prepare them for craft manufacturing. Mayn Bahadur knows that the people who can weave jute, geranium, wild cotton, birch, cannibis, yucca, and other fibrous materials into household wares have acquired special skills that mark them as basket makers, mat makers, rope makers, and other craft specialists. Likewise, Mayn Bahadur points out that such craft artisans normally do not read and write, for this is the province of the elite Brahman families. Mayn's explanation even suggests that work activities are deeply engrained in the identities of people and, whether through learned ability or caste position, crafts and skills become practically immutable aspects of identity. In this way, he urges us to understand that the Rautes' ability to carve wooden wares is an integral aspect of their identity, but this skill never takes privilege over hunting. Rautes always resist the suggestion that they settle down into villages as a caste of wood-carvers.

A villager of Karkigaun in Jajarkot District displays two of the Raute bowls that he received in exchange for enough grain to fill them. The bowls are tied tightly for a few weeks to prevent them from warping or cracking.

In previous generations, Rautes traded differently than they do today. Villagers recall that two generations ago Rautes did not speak with them during exchange sessions but practiced silent trade, sometimes known as "dumb barter." Kumauni villagers in India even referred to the Banrajis as "invisible traders," while local villagers in Jajarkot use similar descriptions. Jajarkot villagers recall how, without actually meeting the householder, the Rautes used to carry out trade by depositing a bowl and head wrap on a villager's courtyard floor at night. The householder was expected to put some grain and garden produce in the head wrap and take the wooden bowl. If the transaction occurred successfully, the Raute would reclaim the head wrap with its bartered goods the following night. When I asked an elderly village woman, Maya Khatri, about the Rautes' bowls from fifty years ago, she said: "The *koshi* from before were also different. They used to crack. Today's bowls seem much better." This may be an indication that Rautes have not been carving wooden bowls for trade for many generations. While they would have always carved eating bowls and utilitarian objects for themselves, they have had to change their carving practices to accommodate new trade relations.

Internal and External Exchange

While we use the term "sharing" in a general sense, a more specific term used by social researchers is "exchange." Anthropologists analyze "spheres of exchange" found in marriage, ritual, gift, language, and economic exchanges. For example, friends may exchange gifts as part of a circle of gift exchange. In this chapter, I shall focus on material exchanges, such as grain, shop goods, money, and commodities. Material items can be exchanged either among people one knows and trusts, or with strangers/outsiders. These two forms can be called (1) internal (intracultural) exchange; and (2) external (intercultural) exchange. Internal exchange refers to exchanges between members within Raute society only, while external exchange refers to barter and trade between Rautes and non-Rautes (with farmers, myself, administrators, etc.).[1]

Rautes spend most of their time with each other, and thus it is understandable that most material exchanges are internal, occurring among Rautes themselves. Sitting in Raute camp one day, I watched as people quietly went about weaving, chatting, chipping wood, carrying a child. Since Ain Bahadur was working nearby, I asked him about his tools. "Is this your axe, Ain?" I asked. "Well," he replied, "I am using this ax, but if someone else needs it for hunting, they can take it." As it turned out, shared ownership of tools was normal. As I looked around camp, I noticed that all of the tools appeared to be set up for shared use. The grain huskers consisted of two sunken wooden platforms with several eight-foot-long wooden poles. Men and women would slam a pole down onto the rice-filled platform, effectively separating the rice husks from the rice kernals. The rice huskers were a shared tool that people took turns using, and no one had priority rights to them. Around the huts, small bowl-making stands (*kili*) were scattered about for anyone to use. I only noticed men using these stands, but several women told me they were also learning to carve bowls using the stands. The women's bowls, however, were shaped in a noticeably cruder style than those carved by men. A third communal item of use were sewing needles. Women congregated in small groups in the middle of camp with sewing tools. Raute women sat together with their sewing needles, stitching torn clothing or mending nets. When a new woman joined them, she often borrowed a sewing needle. I asked Ain whether people were buried with their favorite tools? But he explained that people are not buried with tools.

Shared tool use is one of the characteristics of an "egalitarian society,"[2] and one might say that an enforced ethos of equality permeates every aspect of Raute culture. They not only share tools, but also other things of value, including labor time. When Mayn came to trade a large wooden box with me one day in July, I asked him about the time it had taken to carve. "Did you make this yourself?" I asked. He responded: "Five of my relatives helped me. It took us two days to cut and carve the wood." And then I wondered aloud: "So will you pay them for their help? I have given you 500 rupees [equal to about US$8] and your relatives might want some of that money." But no, he wouldn't share the money. He demurred: "If they need help, I will help them. If we are supposed to make our work equal then we would have to measure it on a scale and that is impossible. We don't complain about working hard. If one has a lot to do one day, then I go over to him and help him all day. We don't worry about more or less work. If we get a chance, then we will relax."

Mayn's reply reverberated with several interesting points. First, he emphasized that Rautes help each other and try not to "measure work on a scale," meaning that they don't quantify work like weighing a bag of grain on a scale or punching in on a time clock. Significantly, this means that Rautes don't estimate workdays owed to each other. In later interviews, I did find that, if someone often doesn't go hunting or do their work, they will be criticized and possibly won't receive a share of the meat and other foods brought into camp. Thus, Rautes do keep a sense of general reciprocity of labor contributions from each of the adult camp members, but these are not measured in workdays.

The other interesting facet of Mayn's remarks is that he was not going to share the 500 rupees he received in exchange for the wooden box. At the time, I thought this would be a good example of hidden exchange in which Mayn would hide his money and spend it surreptitiously on tobacco or other consumables. But in a later interview I found out that, instead, he used the money to purchase rice in Khalanga bazaar. The rice then would go to feed the entire group, as rice is always given to the various women who regularly cook for their families. But in a strange twist of fate, Mayn entrusted the money to another Raute youth, who in turn gave the money to a farmer on his way into the bazaar. Instead of bringing back sackfuls of rice, the farmer never returned to the path outside of Khalanga. So Mayn lost his money and later ruefully asked me if I would give him another 500 rupees to cover his loss.

Even if Rautes don't want to share something, petitioners sometimes resort to "tolerated theft" or "demand sharing." In tolerated theft, the person who gives something does so to avoid too much conflict if he/she refuses. For example, when you are eating at a cafeteria a friend might reach over and eat some french fries from your plate without asking. Does that bother you? Was the gesture annoying but you tolerated it because it would be useless to put up a stink about it? Or perhaps you remember a friend who asked for your pen on their way to class and never returned it. Maybe you liked the pen and wanted it back but felt petty to ask for it back later. These are ordinary examples of demand sharing that occur in our own round of daily interactions and social exchanges. The provider gives something away but often knows that, in turn, he/she may demand something in return at a later time. In my observations of Raute transactions among themselves, I often witnessed a variation of these types of pressures to give. Instead of outright demands, however, they seemed to me more to resemble "request sharing" or simply "requesting." In request sharing, a Raute would ask for, and immediately receive without any noticeable hesitation, an item from his/her Raute relative. For example, before a dance performance, Chandra talked about whether or not I would bring him some shoes, saying that his brother would be wearing the shoes I had given him earlier. In other words, Chandra's brother had asked to wear the shoes for the dance and Chandra had readily agreed, even though he himself fervently wished to wear shoes too. In a similar example, Raute youth Harka Bahadur collected several pairs of shoes yet continued to ask for more from his village trade partners. His village trade partner complained to me that Harka seemed greedy for always pressing for a deal that included relatively expensive shoes. When I asked Harka why he kept bartering for shoes, he said that whenever his relatives asked for his shoes he would give them away, so he still had none of his own to wear! I rarely noticed any resentment on the part of Rautes in their sharing of shoes and other store goods.

In a third example, two Raute women and a Raute man named Hari Bahadur were negotiating with me for a piece of red cloth in exchange for a *dāro*, a drinking bowl with a handle that doubles as a pouring spout. The moment I gave Hari Bahadur the red cloth, since he was the one who carved the item, a Raute woman looked at him in that "expectant" way, and he handed it over to her. The women had agreed to visit with me that day because they were curious about me, not because they knew Hari was going to get red cloth. If the request sharing had been planned earlier, it would have been difficult to carry out as our exchange was not prearranged. Thus "request sharing" appears to be something that is fairly spontaneous and does not appear, on the surface at least, to involve any emotions of resentment on the part of the giver.

It is not that Rautes are more altruistic than the rest of us, but that the ethic of sharing is deeply engrained in them. Rautes do not feel animosity when their relatives request food or shop goods. They know that they can depend on their relatives to share with them in the future. Resentment can be aroused, however, when there is an unbalanced meting out of resources that will result in complaints. Once Moti, a recent Raute widow, complained that she had not gotten her fair share of greens to eat with her meat. But since she was a noticeably chubby woman, we wondered if perhaps she just wanted more greens than most others. On another occasion, Raute women were bickering with each other about carrying water. The water supply for one camp was located about a half an hour's walk away and the women didn't like having to carry three or four pots of water back and forth from the riverside water source.[3] Women may pool their labor resources, but they ensure that each person does her fair share.

Labor time, food, and bartered goods may be shared without too much evaluation, but Rautes are ambivalent about sharing money. When trading wooden wares, Rautes receive grain, not money, and thus money is a rare and precious form of exchange. As Chandra, one of the best traders, said: "All Raute will ask for money, they don't get money from anywhere. They all ask for it, but even I don't get money from anywhere. I am also the man who does not get money." Nevertheless, a few times per year, district officials give the Raute money for their wooden wares and dance performances. This low flow of money is used to purchase cloth, tobacco, beaded necklaces, sandals, and other store-bought goods. Goods are shared through demand sharing but do not flow as fluidly through households as grain and meat. For example, Gogane complained: "My mother-in-law sent me with some money. She sent me with this money to buy her some tobacco from Machaina village. My in-law can get tobacco, but since I don't have money I can't have any. It would be so nice to have tobacco of my own."

It may help to understand that, in the western Nepalese countryside in which grain is essential for survival, the barter of labor and grain is often more important than spending money. A common saying in Jajarkot is "Can't get a piece of bread even for twenty rupees" (*bis rupiyā ek roṭi pāudāina*). Thus, even if you do have plenty of money, if there's no grain to make bread you cannot buy a meal. On countryside walkabouts, I brought along grain and other food so that I was an easy guest for my village hosts. If I had offered money, it might have been accepted, but still there might have been no food available or I would have been putting a strain on the family grain reserves. Further, paying for meals would distort social relationships, making people into strangers rather than friends.

For the Rautes, too, grain is more important to their survival than money. They preferred to barter for grain over money because it may be stolen, as in the example above, or there may be no place to buy grain. Money is surprisingly hard to use, given that there are few shops in the Jajarkot countryside and rural farmers do not pay cash for wooden wares. Money thus represents a difficult yet valuable commodity. It is amenable to hidden exchange, as when Mayn received 500 rupees from me for a wooden box but didn't tell his relatives how much he had earned. But money is vulnerable to demands and request sharing, since Mayn eventually has to buy something with his money that will be shared with all of his relatives. Money is thus qualitatively different from the other commodities that Rautes exchange among themselves.[4]

Perhaps the only other items of exchange between Rautes that were not freely shared with others were recently carved wooden wares. If a person had carved a bowl or box, it was his to trade in whatever manner and whenever he wished. He would receive the benefit of the trade but would probably share his payment, especially if it was a payment of grain or goats. The only time I heard of wooden bowls being given to other Rautes was when someone was sick and a shaman spent a great deal of time curing them. When Mahabiri, a teenager who could make nice wooden chests, was bitten by a snake, his foot swelled up, huge and puffy. The elder Krishna spent a few days blowing and sucking out the poison and received a small wooden chest from Mahabiri in gratitude.

Whether hunting, gathering, or working, Raute intragroup social relations are marked by an ethic of symmetry and sharing. Sharing, however, does not extend to Raute relations with outsiders. With strangers, Raute resort to an entirely different set of economic exchange strategies, including patronage, barter, begging, and petty theft.

The Value of a Wooden Bowl

During the day, a few Raute men can be found at camp chipping away at wooden bowls and boxes. This led me to wonder how much energy was devoted to hunting versus trading. I had hoped to do a time allocation study combined with in-depth interviews in order to address this question, but Rautes would not allow me to make a quantitative assessment of their activities. They said, "We don't count things." But I did notice that Rautes *measure* things, and measure them carefully. When Rautes exchange their bowls for grain, they are particularly adept negotiators, often getting the farmers to give them an "extra" bit of grain or vegetables for their wares. External trade was completely open for me to assess, and I could estimate how much grain Rautes obtained during trades with reasonable accuracy. I was thus better able to understand the role of trade among these nomadic foragers.

Rautes take great care in measuring the amount of grain they receive while bartering. Normally, a wooden bowl is filled with unhusked grain to an 80–100 percent capacity in exchange for the wooden bowl itself. If the transaction is successful, the Raute trader takes the grain and then the farmer takes the bowl. In this act of simple barter, there is no further commitment and the deal is complete. During the trades that I observed, Rautes traded for rice (*dhān*), wheat (*gāhun*), or barley (*jaun*). From the garden, they received potato, taro, corn, radish, pumpkin, bitter gourd, sponge gourd, snake gourd, and garden yam. From the orchard, Raute foraged for peaches, apricots, and apples.

Raute grain trading depends upon a number of factors, such as their camp location relative to nearby villages. During the four months when I conducted field research, Rautes were based near three distinct locations: (1) Khalanga district bazaar; (2) Machaina, a small mountain hilltop village; and (3) Karkigaun, a large village of about a hundred houses that is prosperous by Nepalese standards (they also passed by a few tiny hamlets). In each of these locations, Rautes had slightly different trading patterns. In Khalanga, they traded their wares mostly to the local elites, people who wanted a Raute bowl as a keepsake to complement their other kitchen wares.

Many of these people were large landlords who had ample supplies of grain. Others were administrators working in the Forestry Office, Agricultural Office, District Political Office, and so on, who paid rupees (or bought grain and gave it to the Rautes). These people wanted an example of the exotic Rautes' wood carving but they didn't really need the wooden bowls for everyday use or storage. In addition to providing grain and money, the government officials could be relied upon to provide a few goats and about a hundred kilograms of rice in exchange for a day of dancing for the entertainment of villagers. Most people in the district bazaar believed that the Rautes' wares could not compete with other market goods made of plastic and copper, and thus had only artistic or intrinsic value. Most of these bazaar householders opined that Rautes needed to assimilate and become farmers or wood-carvers who would make plows, furniture, and other wooden crafts that they desired.

In rural areas like Karkigaun, farmers held the opposite opinion. Rural farmers appreciated the durability of the wooden bowls and usually wanted to acquire one for its utilitarian value. In villages without easy access to plastic, metal, and clay vessels, Rautes could peddle their bowls in most households. Thus, I saw a continuum of value for the bowls based on village location and competition from other kinds of storage vessels. If Rautes wanted grain, they sought out the more rural villages with less access to imported containers. If they wanted a large amount of grain for a monthly feast, they traded in the district capitals.

Athough Rautes do have grain storage bins, they limit their grain surplus to what people can carry on their backs to the next camp location. For comparison, the sharecropping tenant described earlier kept about 600 pounds of stored grain for his family of five, enough to last two or three months. As relatively little grain was stored for the Raute camp's needs, this made it is possible for me to estimate how much grain is consumed on a daily and weekly basis. In the summer and fall, Rautes preferred rice and wheat to other available grains. Their order of grain preference is (1) unhusked rice; (2) husked rice; (3) wheat; (4) wheat flour; (5) barley.[5] First, unhusked grain is preferred because, according to Rautes, it will not soak and rot during the rainy season. Second, Raute women can use their ten-foot-long *dhiki* grain pestles to thresh daily amounts of grain. But if they get a large amount of unhusked grain, such as after a dance performance, they have a problem processing all of it. They don't like going to the farmers' community grain mills but will do so if necessary. For example, I went with a group of seven Raute women to a grain mill near Karkigaun, where they found themselves waiting in line behind six groups of farmers. The anxious Raute women immediately demanded to be moved to the head of the line, claiming that Rautes can't congregate with farmers. Nonplussed, the mill operator refused to accommodate their demand. The Raute women angrily stormed out of the mill with their unhusked grain, carrying about a hundred kilos of grain back to their camp located one hour's walk away.

Grain may seem like an awkward and limited form of money, but it makes an effective exchange medium that has a number of advantages over cash. For my part, I bought husked rice from the stores in the bazaar and unhusked rice and wheat from area farmers and used this grain for everyday trades with Rautes. When my grain supplies ran low, I bought bowls with rupees (about 20 percent of the time), which is more like the behavior of Nepalese administrators and bazaar householders. By the end of the field season, I had accumulated a total of fifty-three wooden-ware items, far more than the one or two items each farming household would collect. In some ways, my trading collection resembled that of an entire village; I had what a typical large village with some administrative elites might collect from the Raute in a single month.[6] In retrospect, I found that both the range of items that I'd collected and the fact that I had traded with twenty different Raute trading partners would be similar to Raute trading patterns in Karkigaun and other neighboring villages. Bartered trades were conducted with many Rautes, including three trades with women (Hira, Sahra, and Moti). The trading partners' names with the number of trades in parentheses include: Bhadra (1), Bhakta (2), Bir (2), Birka (1), "Child" (1), Chandra (10), Dhan (2), Hari (6), Harka (1), Hira (1), Karna (2), Mayn (5), Man Bahadur (10), Manjubiri (1), Moti (1), Nar Bahadur (1), Ratna (2), Sahra (1), Sher (1), Surendra (1), and Tularam (1).

This set of trading partners reflects both some typical and atypical aspects of Raute trade partnerships. The trades are typical in that four men —Chandra, Man Bahadur, Mayn, and Hari—do the most frequent trade entrepreneur work among the Rautes. Chandra was good at trading because he enjoyed carving and trading sessions, having natural talents at both carving and conversation. Man Bahadur, on the other hand, wasn't so good at carving anymore, but worked as a "point man," in that he obtained pieces carved by others and brought them to villagers for exchange.

Each of these traders had their unique aspects as well, in that trading was contingent upon many circumstances that enter into the exchange process. In some cases, individuals' trade skills were minimal. Dhan, for example, didn't know how to use rhetorical flourishes such as rhymes or blessings. In two cases (Sher and Moti), the traders did not actually have *koshimāl* to trade but instead wanted to give me their own eating dishes. In Moti's case, she gave me her eating bowl and asked me if I had any cloth for her (I did). This "unnegotiated gift exchange" style of trade was unique among the trades. It reminded me of how Kusunda foragers had reportedly conducted exchange in the past (Nebesky-Wojkowitz 1959). In the case of Sher, he brought me his own drinking cup as thanks for helping his wife when she was ill.[7] These two trades are special in that normally the Rautes' own eating utensils are not bartered to farmers.

With the exception of the Raute eating dishes, the items collected during my research represent a profile that fits what one farming community might obtain in a month of trade with Rautes. I received fifteen bowls with lids (*koshi ra birko*); nine unlidded bowls (*koshi*); nine breadboards (*coki*); six chests (*mādush*); five of the Rautes' own drinking cups and bowls (*dǎro, dzhākure,* and *yaybā māna*); four small bowls (they hold one kilogram of grain and are called a *pāthi koshi*); two boxes made with special dual compartments (*piṭṭi*); one low-rimmed bowl (*tala koshi*); a stirring spoon used to stir rice water (*āniya,* also known as *puniyǎ*); and a sitting stool about the size of a step stool (*pirka*). I collected no bed-sized chests (*kāt*), although they were lovely and practical for the villagers.

Note that these items do not include the Rautes' full repertoire of carving. Their own wooden items, such as eating utensils, walking sticks, axe handles, boats, and so on, are not carved for exchange with villagers. What they do carve represents a specialization in that they make storage items useful to farmers. Most villagers wanted to obtain the lidded bowls, because grain or clarified butter can be stored in these airtight containers for long periods of time. Rodents cannot get into these items and they are lightweight and transportable. Village women sometimes showed me bowls that were heirlooms or wedding gifts from their grandmothers. Bowls harden over time and become very durable, making them highly desirable. The second most desired items were wooden chests that multifunction as storage for bedding and novelty chairs. Rautes tried to trade the chests to village elites who could afford to part with a goat, sheep, or enough grain to fill a wooden chest. Villagers also collected breadboards because they were relatively cheap.

Twenty-nine of my trades involved the exchange of grain for wooden wares, while twenty-two trades involved other commodities. My grain payments for wooden wares thus brought in 116.2 kilograms of edible cereal for the Rautes over four months. The trade payments, with weights in parentheses, included six trade payments of unhusked rice (23.5 kg.); ten trade payments of husked rice (31.5 kg.); eleven trade payments of wheatberries (58.2 kg.); two trade payments of wheat flour (3 kg.); one payment of husked rice for dancing (70 kg.). Since a loss of 30 percent weight occurs during the husking and milling process (B. Bishop 1990, 238), the total edible grain payments amounted to 186.2 kilograms, although the total amount of grain (unhusked as well as husked grain) equaled 231 kilograms.

In addition to grain payments, I traded various commodities to Rautes in exchange for wooden bowls and chests. The total of these trades amounted to about US$100 (Rs 5,330), including the occasional cash payments for bowls. Rautes were interested in obtaining the following items: cloth, tennis shoes, tobacco, chickens for sacrifice, goats, and biscuits. These are also the most common items that Rautes purchase in local stores. To place this amount in perspective, an average day's agricultural wages in the area in 1997 equaled about 35 rupees, or about fifty cents per day in US dollars.[8] Although this amount seems incredibly low by our own standards, keep in mind that cash is not a terribly common form of income. Agricultural laborers often earn fifty cents a day but also will enjoy a portion of each harvest from the landlord. These other payments are called *khalo*, payment from "from the threshing floor." And together, the payment in cash plus the grain payments tide the subsistence tenants over until the next harvest season.

From a labor time perspective, the sum commodity and cash exchanges that I paid Rautes in exchange for wooden wares equaled the wages of one farm laborer for six months. My total contributions of grain (231 kilograms) over the four months of research time provided the Raute group of 150 people with an average of about two kilograms of cereal per day, or about a hundred calories per day per adult. Since Rautes traded with many other villagers during the research period, the overall effect of my trades was merely supplemental.

Looking at the trade data, the main point is that Rautes would have to do a great deal of wooden-ware exchange in order to feed their entire population grains on a regular basis. If Rautes' caloric needs are about the same as those of Ituri Forest foragers of central Africa, they need to consume about 2,680 calories per day (2,509 for women, 2,848 for men; Bailey and Peacock 1988). If Rautes derive about 45 percent of their total calories from grain, goats, and garden vegetables, they would need to trade enough wooden wares in order to acquire about 1,200 calories per day from villagers. If indeed Rautes do obtain 45 percent of their calories from grain and goats, they would need to trade with villagers a total of about 130–140 wooden items per month in order to meet their subsistence needs. Is this a lot of carving? With a camp of about seventy-five adults, each man would have to carve about three to four items (women currently carve few wooden-ware objects) each month. This level of carving activity seemed to me, as an observer, to be the *uppermost* limit that Rautes spent in carving wooden items; and probably they carve less than three to four bowls per month per carver. The activity that I observed, together with my trade experiences, indicates that Raute men spend about eight to ten workdays per month on carving, with a few women carving one to two workdays per month.

The take-home message here is that *Rautes remain forest foragers who supplement their diet with agricultural foods.* They would have a hard time becoming more reliant upon grain for several reasons. First, it would be difficult for them to find enough wood in the forests in order to carve enough bowls to become full-time wood-carvers. Second, even if they did carve full-time, it is doubtful that they could find enough farmers able to part with precious grain reserves. If Rautes were to become full-time wood-carving artisans, they would have to supplement their work with farming themselves in order to subsist. Third, it would require a lot of traded bowls to feed the entire camp. If Rautes were to rely solely on wood carving as their occupation, they would soon saturate their markets, as villagers can only acquire one or two bowls in each trade. Fourth, Rautes would run into trouble with villagers over cutting down trees in community forests. Bowls ultimately derive from forest trees, and villagers covet both useful trees and their use rights to their community forests. Thus, if Rautes concentrated only on carving wooden wares for farmers, they would soon have to diversify their subsistence strategies, possibly learning to carve agricultural implements such as plows, and to supplement this activity with carpentry, portering, migrant work, and tenant farming for high-caste households. This might work, but they would be unhappy.

The Rautes' Gold

Some of the villagers referred to the wooden wares "the Rautes' gold." They envy Rautes, saying, "The Rautes are lucky; they can get grain whenever they want it. They only have to carve a bowl and bring it to a farmer to get their rice." Although this is the farmers' perception, Raute wooden-ware production actually is a fairly complex activity.

One of the Raute men named Daracho asked that I meet him in Kalṭhākura forest,[9] near a Raute campsite perched high on a mountain ridge. Daracho told me that he didn't want other Rautes to know about our meeting, so he would leave branches as signs (Raute: *śyāola*) for me to follow. And sure enough, on a flat saddle that connected two mountain ridges lay a small tree branch with a small stone resting on top of it. Daracho had told me, "Follow the *šyāola* in the direction it points." My assistant Bisnu, my cook Krishna, who persuaded me to let him come, and I followed the signs, walking along a small goat path winding along the side of the mountain. Soon we found another tree branch sign, and then another, then another. Along the way we spotted trees that were roughly cut and shaped by Rautes for transportation back to camp. One pine had been shaved of its bark and cut in the rough shape of a mainstay pole for their huts. Other trees had chunks missing the size of a wooden bowl. But we must have made a wrong turn, or Daracho decided not to meet us after all. We couldn't find any more signs and we couldn't find Daracho.

Dejected, we wandered along the path. But the view was breathtaking, and we continued walking until the path ended at a huge flat boulder jutting out into space. We sat on the giant pedestal and looked out at the river 5,500 feet below.

Turning to Bisnu, I asked "Do you hear people?" Creeping to the edge of the boulder, we looked down and saw Raute men gathered at the foot of trees growing on the mountainside below. Listening to the woodcutting for a few minutes, we wondered what to do next. I knew that I had not been invited to this particular daily event. I hadn't planned on eavesdropping, but I did want to rest before turning back to look for Daracho again. The four men did their chopping, *"twāāk twāāk"* as Rautes say, and cut some of the logs into smaller, more manageable pieces that each man could carry on his back. I noticed that only the part of the tree that was necessary was carefully cut away from the rest. For a breadboard, for example, only a thin slice was removed from the side of the tree. In these cases, the trees survived the woodcutting.

Hearing a rustle in the trees, I spotted a group of Raute women farther off in the forest. I imagined that they would join the men to help carry back materials, but I didn't get the chance to rest and observe very long. My cook, Krishna, seeing the wide valley, let out an ear-piercing whoop that echoed across the valley and laughed to hear his echo. Irritated, I thought about Krishna, loud as a barking dog, compared to the quiet Rautes. The Raute men came bounding up to our overhang in irritation. No doubt remembering similar encounters with villagers, one said, *"Luki luki*—peeking, peeking—why are you here?" I couldn't let them know that I had an appointment to meet Daracho, as I suspected they would be upset with him. Instead I told them we were out looking for forest medicinals and were sorry that we had accidentally come upon them. I assured them that I would never go *luki luki* again, and they said they would invite me for a tree cutting someday soon.

The Meaning of a Tree

Selecting tree species to cut is not a random act; it depends upon two symbolic distinctions in Raute arboreal classifications. Trees are generally divided according to underlying principles of ethnic and gendered distinctions. In ethnic terms, Raute crafts exhibit a distinction between trade items destined for others and products made for their own use. For themselves, Rautes carve items mostly from orchid trees (*Bauhinia variegata*), pines, and trees of medium density. In carving goods for villagers, they use alder, magnolia, and other relatively soft woods. During my field research, Rautes reported that they carved 50 percent of trade items from magnolia, 25 percent from "stinkwood" (*Persea odoratissima*), 20 percent from alder, and 5 percent from other woods (see Appendix, Table 6). However, in other political districts, Rautes have been observed carving other local woods as well, and some of these are included in the table (cf. also Singh 1997).

From the list in Table 6 one can see that Rautes use a wide range of woods, from soft ones for trade bowls to hard ones used for their own articles. For villagers, Rautes fashion items such as (1) large bowls (*cār pāth koshi*, volume about 12.5 kg./27.5 lb.); (2) small bowls (*pāthi*, 3.125 kg./ 6.8 lb.); (3) large chest/beds (*kāt*, approx. 4' high × 3' wide × 5.5' long); (4) medium-size chests or boxes (*madush, sandush*, approx. 20" high × 15" wide × 22" long); (5) bread-making boards (*choki*); and occasionally other items such as stirring spoons (*paniya*) and low seats (*pirka*). These items have either a little decorative carving, such as on the edges of boxes, or no decoration at all. Rautes report that carving each of these objects takes one to two days. Villagers recognize that little labor is involved compared to farming tasks, which is why they refer to their wooden wares as "the Rautes' gold."

Most important, Raute wares accommodate the cuisine and culture of sedentary farmers. In the rural countryside, where no potters, few coppersmiths, and few goods shops exist, storage vessels are hard to come by. Since the Kumhāle caste potters live three days' walk from Karkigaun, there are few clay pots in the village. Likewise, the Tamata (Tamaute) caste of coppersmiths seldom come through the villages to fix and sell metal containers. Raute wares thus are valuable and are just the right size for storing grain, lentils, potatoes, butter, and other goods. Bowls with lids are perfect for storing clarified butter (*ghiu*), and their round shape can fit comfortably in a porter's basket (*ḍoko*). Raute breadboards make a simple but useful addition to the stone mortarboards of most women's kitchens. In addition, villagers have very little furniture, so buying the Raute wares represents a significant investment in a household. I was surprised to see that a bed-sized wooden chest (*kāt*), for example, enables a family to securely store numerous blankets, rugs, and valuables, and then can even function as a bed for one or two people to sleep on at night. Villagers joked that, by making it possible to sleep on top of one's precious family treasures, a Raute *kāt* is the safest way to protect their valuables!

While Rautes sometimes use wooden wares designed for villagers before they trade them, they themselves generally use significantly different bowls, known as *māna*. Food is served in small eating bowls (*yaybā-māna*); drinks are served in cups and bowls with a handle/pour spout (*dāro* and *dzhākure*); and mothers serve meat on small cutting boards (*coki*). Rautes also carve large containers for alcohol (*dzhum*), kegs really, that hold eighteen gallons of brew, and they occasionally carve canoe-like boats for crossing rivers. These items used by Rautes are not traded to villagers. For storing their own blankets and clothing, Rautes use a *piṭṭi*, a box with a divider inside. One half is for each of two family members, such as two sisters or two brothers. Even villagers know about the *piṭṭi* box that held the religious icons for two of the patriclans. Unfortunately, this ritual object was stolen by villagers a few years ago.

Because of their nomadic lifestyle, Rautes' household wares must be portable. Small and lightweight, most items require a good deal of carving skill and are not disposable. They include grain-storage bowls, serving bowls (*tala koshi*), water jugs of wood (plus brass and iron bowls obtained through trade), eating bowls, cups, storage hooks (*dzyu-ke-la*), and grain threshing poles/pestles (*ḍhikur, ḍhiki*) that can serve as carrying poles during camp moves, and grain winnowers (*supo*). The only heavy wooden items are the alcohol containers (*dzhum*) and grain-grinding platforms (*musal*). Grain bins are emptied and burned before each move. Using a large net and basket (*ḍokiya*), Rautes strap heavier objects onto their backs during moves. When they arrive at a new camp, the grinding platform is nestled into the ground near their huts. When someone is ready to prepare grain, the unhusked grain is poured in handfuls into the center of the wooden platform and pounded with a five-to-ten-foot-tall pestle, releasing the husk from the grain.

Other household items can be thrown away and refashioned at each camp location. Items awkward to transport, such as tent poles (*dhuri balo*), woodworking stands (*kili*), and dried leaf-woven screens (*lhāpa*) are burned rather than being transported. As one of the Raute men remarked, "We don't want villagers to scavenge through our camps. We burn everything before moving on to the next camp." In the abandoned camps that I visited, within a couple of weeks green plants had reemerged, village dogs scavenged bits of monkey bone, and the rains had washed away the fire soot; one could not tell that a group of over a hundred people had lived there. Although Rautes do not grow crops, their burning habits enhance the new growth of forest plants. From the ashes of the burned camps, young shoots of ferns, berries, willows, and sages were already beginning to shoot up after a few weeks. Such controlled burning of dead materials promotes growth through the recycling of nutrients and decreased plant competition, thus maintaining the plant community for deer and other animals.

For their own utensils, Rautes carve items from the orchid tree (*Bauhinia*), which is durable, smooth to the touch, and of medium density. They need meat-chopping plates, food bowls, and drinking cups. The eating bowl that a young widow named Moti gave me is about six inches in diameter and holds exactly sixteen ounces. The drinking cup I received from Sher Bahadur holds exactly eight ounces of beer and has a spout for pouring or sipping. This measurement size is standard, and Rautes use their hand or forearm to measure the diameter of bowls as they carve them. Of all the wood species available, orchid tree signifies the Rautes' sense of ethnic identity, occupying a special place as an important all-purpose wood: as they say, "We make all our things from orchid tree (*mālu*)," and indeed they use varieties of it for eating bowls, drinking cups, leafy tarps, windscreens, roofing, and net hunting gear. The flowers and buds are eaten as vegetables; the flowers are tucked behind the ear as a hair decoration.

However, for Rautes, wood is not simply a utilitarian object but has a set of meanings that reflect their social ideals. Ideas about men and women are integrated into their understanding of trees and tree parts. During a conversation with a villager, for example, a Raute commented, "I'm not just the bark of a tree you know." This metaphor meant that he was not worthless or unimportant. Specifically, men remarked that wood, especially core wood, is like men—strong, valuable, central, and inside. On the other hand, men said that women are like a tree's bark, inner bark, and vines. Although women do not agree with the tropes created by men, they were aware that bark is considered unimportant.

Raute men use such metaphors because of their intimate contact with trees. The symbolic classification of tree parts into male/female, core/bark, inside/outside also has a basis in Raute gendered divisions of labor. Normally, men work with wood, carving the core wood into bowls and boxes for trade. Women, on the other hand, do the work of weaving leaves, bark, and inner bark into nets, windscreens, and other household objects. Nonetheless, tasks are gender *specific* but not gender *exclusive*. Men may also weave nets and women sometimes carve wood as well, but I seldom observed men weaving or women carving. As the Raute hunter Ratna explained, "The nets are made from nettles [*Girardinia diversifolia*]. We use the bark of the plant. First we scald [it] in hot water, and then dry it in the sun. When it has started to become *kuhiyo* [to fall apart], we pull it apart and make thread from the dried pulp. With this prepared thread, we weave nets. We need nets to hunt and also for carrying packs. We need to carry small children. Nets are prepared by men. When we are not hunting, at nighttime, we can store things in the nets."

Wooden-Ware Production

The process of wooden-ware production begins with the delivery of wood packages into camp. After cutting magnolia, alder, and other species in the forest, men and women load up their nets and tie these with cloth shawls onto their backs. Walking back to camp and dropping the chunks of wood at the woodworking sites, Raute carvers begin shaping bowls using a curved

Raute wooden wares. *Clockwise from bottom left:* small *pitti* box (14 × 9 × 4"), large wooden chest, low eating bowl *(tala koshi)*, large drinking bowl with handle, rice ladle (in drinking bowl), three large bowls with lids, an adze (sitting on bowl), a villager's sickle in its scabbard, a wooden chest, a legless wood seat *(pirka)*, two lidless serving bowls, a Raute family drinking cup with handle, four bowls with lids, a wooden chest on which the author is leaning, two woven corn-straw cushions *(cakati)*, and a wooden food preparation board with small feet on which the author sits.

adze (R. *thow-raya*, N. *basulo*) and chisel (R. *kuniya*, N. *chinu*) to chop out the inside of the bowls. This process of hand shaping wooden bowls is different from that of other wooden bowl producers in the Himalayas. Among Tibetans, for example, a wooden bowl (or cup) usually is turned on a lathe, a spinning machine that produces a finely carved object with rounded grooves inside and out. Being nomadic, however, Rautes do not use lathe technology, instead hand carving the objects.

At the sites where wooden bowls are carved, a layer of wood chips blankets the ground. Here, the carver sets the block of wood, readying it for shaping. Raute carvers are extremely skilled in the fine chiseling technique necessary to carve a lightweight bowl. The bowl's diameter must be perfectly round, and the carver uses either his forearm or a walking stick to measure the diameter at various times in order to shape the bowl perfectly. Further, the thickness of the bowls is important. If the bowl is too thick, it will be heavy/cumbersome, may not cure well, and may crack. If the bowl is too thin, it may develop a hole during the chiseling process. Occasionally the carver does break a hole in the side of the bowl or hits a wood knot that doesn't carve neatly. In these cases, he may either throw the bowl away or apply a bit of mud in the hope that it will smooth the appearance and keep the bowl in tradable condition. After carving, small bumps are shaped with a flat-head chisel. The final step is to cure the newly carved wood.

Curing the wooden objects is of critical importance in the process of wooden-ware production since Rautes want to avoid having their objects crack or warp. For the drying process, Rautes employ four methods to prevent warping and cracking. The object may be (1) soaked, (2) buried, (3) mud-plastered, or (4) mustard-oiled. During the soaking process, groups of bowls are tied together with nets and submerged in a stream, using stone weights to keep the bowls in place. If a stream is not nearby, wooden bowls can be slathered with mud from a wet rice field and then pushed back into the field. Rautes do this for bowls that are freshly carved and in danger of drying out too fast. In the burial method of curing, bowls are put into a pit and covered with earth. For example, a group of elderly women were mending clothing and chatting in camp one day. One of them ambled over to a tree located nearby and, using an adze, dug a hole next to the tree. She then deposited a bowl inside, explaining that it needed to cure some more. Chandra later explained that the soil acts to protect the bowls from drying. He added that carvers don't have time to go through all the curing steps for every item, but that buried bowls cure well. He also noted that carvers both bury and soak their bowls not only after carving but during the carving stage too. When they take a break to leave camp during hunting or other work, partially carved bowls are buried, covered with river mud, or submerged in water. This hides bowls from the sight of strangers, keeps the camp uncluttered, and protects the bowls at the same time. Although I did not correlate the curing methods with the types of bowls produced, Rautes note that the bowls of most importance to them, such as those made for their own use, are given more curing time.

A third curing step involves the application of red-mud plaster. Like the other curing methods, this is an optional measure. Red mud is applied just before bringing bowls to villagers for trade sessions, giving the items a colorful appearance. Many traders will stop and collect some red mud to plaster on the bowls as they walk toward the villages, taking advantage of resources that are encountered along the way. Red mud was smeared on thirty-six of the items that I received while seventeen remained unplastered. When I asked traders why they applied the red-mud plaster, they said that it was not in their best interest if a bowl cracked after an exchange, for when it does, villagers feel they have been duped and word spreads to neighboring villages of bad trades. Therefore, traders will put a layer of mud on bowls to slow the drying process and also to give the bowls some color. In addition to its curing properties, the ochre-colored mud also acts as makeup to hide imperfections. As for the Rautes' own eating bowls, they also apply mud to these, but they offered no suggestions that red is a sacred color as is common in some other small-scale societies in Africa and Australia.

The last curing method is actually done by farmers as Rautes have no vegetable oil in their own camps. After a trade, Rautes show farmers how to polish the bowl with the oil of ground mustard seeds (*karuwa tel*). Just as when we apply linseed oil to furniture, the oil in the ground mustard kernels soaks into the fresh wood. This not only keeps the wooden bowls and boxes from cracking but gives them a polished surface and protects food against insects. A bowl plastered with mustard oil/kernels and tied tightly with *dubo* ritual grass will guarantee that a freshly carved bowl stays true to form.

Exchange Encounters

When wooden bowls are ready to trade, small groups of Rautes set out for the nearest village. Raute men often split up and go to homes by themselves or travel in pairs. Raute women travel in groups of seven or eight and then split into pairs of two women per home as they try to win the confidence and grain of the local farmers. Usually they try a "cold call," which involves

Raute girl carrying recently washed eating dishes in 1968. Photo courtesy of the Terence R. Bech Nepal Research Collection, Archives of Traditional Music, Folklore Institute, Indiana University. Photo taken by T. Bech in 1968.

approaching a household of prospective customers who were not expecting peddlers. If they are lucky, the women successfully persuade the householder to accept one of their bowls in exchange for grain. If a farmer asks for a small bowl but the women have only large ones, they will take "an order" and tailor the bowl to the farmer's needs. Their encounters with villagers represent an important point of cultural contact, since this is almost the only time villagers get to visit with Raute women. For Raute women especially, trade encounters are stressful because they are the only means the foragers have to obtain grain and other food products from farmers. Successful trades vary according to the personalities of the traders, their experience, and the quality of their wares. Many of the encounters are tinged with fear that the villagers will hurt the Raute women.

During my first trade with Raute women, Man Bahadur's wife, Hira, and niece Sahra met me in my rented room in Khalanga and proceeded to examine my things. Sahra did not speak Nepali, but spoke quietly in Raute, saying things such as "This [photo] must be her husband" and "This scarf is what I want to trade for." Hira carried out the transactions, and they eventually traded a bowl and breadboard to me in exchange for a sackful of husked rice and the scarf that Sahra admired. Man Bahadur latter scolded all of us. He said that I had not given them enough! I apologized and sent them a chicken to "top off" our exchange. During a later trade and interview session with the Raute leader, Man Bahadur met with me in Karkigaun one afternoon and negotiated a trade of a wooden chest that he promised to deliver a few days later. Meeting with me in my study room, Man Bahadur said: "My wife returned to camp today with a bowl that she couldn't barter and we can't get rice or wheat here. Yesterday, you called me to come today, so I can't lie, I had to come. The people in this society don't like to take our big bowls. You also requested a small one-kilo bowl (pāthi-koshi). But I can't do this. I can trade another's bowl to you and repay him, maybe. But my hands are too weak to make a small bowl. Today, I can't lie to you, so I came here empty handed and I feel embarrassed. Others can make small bowls . . . my daughter and niece, my other people can make small bowls for you."

Since I couldn't afford to take any more large bowls, I replied, "That's good to hear that your relatives will make small bowls. Please send them to us." I actually didn't want to take any bowls, but since Man Bahadur had promised to work on his life history interview with me, I knew that I would have to repay him by making a generous exchange for his bowls.

He continued: "But I have made one wooden box. If others make a small bowl, then I'll send them to you. I'm an old man. I've told my grandchildren to make one bowl for you. How can my grandchildren eat if I ask them to make only a small bowl? Do you say that you'll take a big bowl or a *madush* box?"

"Well," I replied, "not a small one, or a big one, one that's just right." My assistant Bishnu added, "How many quarts of grain will it take?"

Man Bahadur responded: "It could take up to four *pāthi* [1 *pāthi* = 4.75 quarts]. I'm an old man, I can't make bowls. There's no grain, no rice, what can an old man eat? If you don't take my bowl, what can I do, my niece? If you hate me, then other boys can make bowls for you. Why did you call me?"

Bishnu tactfully replied: "We don't hate you! We don't have any unhusked rice, but we have husked rice and we can compromise and give that. We have respect for you. How much husked rice do you want to take for a bowl?"

Man Bahadur then pressed us to take both his box and his bowl, which would cost a significant sum of rice that we did not have on hand. He replied, "I've become an old man. I can earn some food (eat your payment, *ājena khānu*) if you take both my bowl and chest."

I sighed, thinking that I would have to try to purchase some rice from local farmers, but I didn't want to inconvenience my neighbors. I said to Man Bahadur: "We can fix the price to equal a bowl full of husked rice. Husked rice would equal twice the price of a bowl of unhusked rice." But Man Bahadur preferred to negotiate for a better deal, and replied: "You asked for a small, small bowl, so I came here. Unless you respect me as you would your parents, we can't make a deal."

As the discussion continued, Man Bahadur held to his rigid negotiating position, since he was hoping we would take both a wooden box and a bowl. I felt loath to take a box as I already had six and couldn't afford another. Wooden boxes were relatively expensive and I was near the end of my budget. Later in the week, we did negotiate a trade, and I took a wooden bowl and a wooden box. I had no way of paying grain for the wooden box, however, and had to offer Man Bahadur money. In this closing transaction, he expressed his preference for grain and was upset that we could only come up with money. He scolded us: "I wanted to take rice for this exchange but you can't buy rice here. I was hoping for rice . . . but you said that wasn't possible. I asked you to look for rice. So how much money can you give? I've had a hard life so give me five hundred rupees [approx. US$8.00] for the box. I wanted to exchange for rice so I made the box from the core of the tree. Give me five hundred rupees and some wheat flour. I had other people help with making it. I was in the jungle when you came to camp yesterday. Since yesterday, it took five men to make this box. If all these people hadn't worked on it, we wouldn't have been able to finish it."

In the end, I did pay 500 rupees, but we agreed that the box was only worth about 250–350 rupees and the other money was for time spent interviewing.

During exchange encounters, all Rautes use this pressuring method of negotiation with farmers. But they conduct their trades in their own personal styles. Chandra, for example, tends to joke around with his trade partners. Ratna, his half-brother, chooses to act earnestly and patiently. Mayn Bahadur quietly smiles a lot, while Bhakta stutters and doesn't speak smoothly. Chandra explained that to trade wooden bowls for rice, you must be smart rather than strong: "Use your brawn and get unhusked rice. Use your brains and get husked rice" (*kām bhayo dhān bhayo buddhi bhayo cāmal*). Although most Rautes prefer unhusked rice, we had to smile at Chandra's deft saying. His words reminded me of how important it is to charm the customer with blessings, proverbs, and sweet speech.

Barter, Blessings, and Begging

The barter sessions involve trade and include certain rhetorical strategies such as patronizing the farmer, giving formal blessings, and begging for more grain. One begging strategy involves having a villager "top off" their grain payment with something "extra" such as yams from the garden. Rarely did villagers decline to offer at least a token gift when beseeched with praise, songs, and entertaining rhymes. For the Hindu villager, gifting represents an opportunity to earn religious merit, and they will bestow a little extra if they can afford it.

Performance of blessings represents a Raute strategy to obtain the maximum in goods during trade sessions. Mayn Bahadur, one of the most skilled traders, was adept at giving blessings. His method of obtaining extra garden vegetables and tobacco was to tightly bind the newly carved *koshimāl*, to place ritual grass (N. *dubo*; *Cynodon dactylon*, Bermuda grass) on the lid of the bowl or box, and to sing a blessing over it in praise of the new owner. The use of Bermuda grass symbolizes several things during the exchange encounter. The Hindu villagers make Bermuda grass necklaces (*dubo ko malla*) to bless the wearer with a long life. Bermuda grass does not die because it is a hardy perennial that lives in almost any climate or condition. By analogy, Rautes ritually bless the boxes with Bermuda grass, imbuing them with an aura of durable longevity. This is done by first tightly tying shut a box or bowl with lid. Next, the trader sticks ritual grass in the knot and recites a blessing. The ritual grass symbolically transfers its essence of longevity, not only to the wooden object, but by extension to the farmers who receive the blessings over their wooden bowls.

As Rautes move through villages, they need to project an aura of legitimacy about themselves. Note that they are always strangers to a village and the issue of economic trust is one of the most difficult problems they have to surmount during a transaction. Thus Rautes don a guise of Hindu legitimacy by using a few of the paraphernalia and techniques of Brahman priests and professional beggars. Specifically, they mimic Brahmanic rituals by tightly wrapping the bowls with Bermuda grass, smearing the boxes with cow dung (*gobar*), and chanting blessings (*āšik*) over bowls. These Hindu practices have been adopted by Rautes because Hindus believe that dung, Bermuda grass, and chanted blessings will impart ritual purity and holiness to both performer and receiver. The best Raute traders incorporate Hindu rituals to signify that a box has become pure, along with the new owner. In return, the Raute "officiant," by analogy, becomes like a priest—the highest, purest social caste.

The trade encounter culminates with the Raute "officiant" reciting a ritual blessing on the owner and his/her wooden box or bowl. During a trade between Raute elder Mayn Bahadur and a village elder named Karki-ji,[10] Mayn tied ritual grass into the ropes of a box Karki-ji had obtained. Mayn next smeared *gobar* on a box as if he were plastering a wall for a religious ceremony. Finally, after negotiating and receiving three hundred rupees from Karki-ji, Mayn Bahadur Mukhiya intoned the following blessing:

> May you always have food to eat and cloth to wear.
> May this box be filled with spices.
> May you raise cattle and buffalo,
> May you raise twelve sons and eighteen grandsons.
> May you have lots of yogurt, honey, ghee, and spices in your home.
> May you always be bright and grow.
> When you go to Bombay may you be able to buy white and
>   red clothes to keep in this wooden box.
> May you fill your box with wealth, gold, and silver.
> Whatever you think to do, may you be successful.
> May the blessings given by Mayn Bahadur Mukhiya come true.
> And may all your family be happy.
> May you have your own clothes to wear, your own food to eat.
> May you be able to travel, may you prosper.
> For my blessing, may all the gods be on your side.
> May you three people [Y. Karki's family] live a long life.

Mayn's chant closed with a sweep of his hand and a falling tone. Karki-ji and his family clearly enjoyed the performance and the feeling of being supplicated as benefactors. As a person who is deeply religious, Karki-ji also appreciated receiving the blessing with its many hopes for a bright and prosperous future. Afterwards, Karki-ji thanked Mayn Bahadur Mukhiya and discussed with his wife what kind of tip to give for the blessing. They settled on a plateful of unhusked rice topped with a few potatoes and chunks of salt from the storage room. In the rural villages, Rautes often receive garden vegetables and tobacco leaves, while in the towns they get more grain and stored foods. But not all Raute blessings are successful. Rautes perform blessings differently depending on their skills and experience. Some perform short, poorly recited blessings and thus receive little for their efforts.

In addition to blessings, Raute men sometimes use playful poetic speech in order to win the confidence of villagers during barter sessions. During a barter session with a village woman, the Raute named Ratna couldn't get her to fix a fair barter; she was undervaluing the Raute bowl and offering too little grain. At one point, she dashed his wooden bowl onto the courtyard floor. Those of us watching were frightened by this outburst. Rather than reacting violently, however, Ratna said flirtatiously, "*mānche herda rāmro byābahār herda cāmro*" (She appeared to be a good woman, but now it seems she's a hard woman). In his backhanded flattery, Ratna adroitly managed to be diplomatic even when arguing with an angry farm woman. She had to smile and compose herself, and the trade of grain for wooden ware eventually occurred.

In barter sessions, one can see, it is important to have a repertoire of blessings, songs, and other poetic speech. These can mitigate moments of confrontation and conflict. They can help Rautes avoid saying anything blatantly immoral or wrong by Hindu standards. And they can ease relationships so that villagers end up giving Rautes more during a trade. Their words, then, represent a technique that the hunter-gatherers employ as a trading skill.

In addition to blessings and rhymes, Raute men seek out elite villagers with whom to form a fictive (feigned) kinship bond. During my stay, for example, Raute men became fictive kin with at least four village men in different villages. I also became a fictive daughter to three Raute male elders while carrying out my interviews. The fictive kinship ceremonies occur during meaningful experiences between a Raute and a villager, such as an important trade or a dance festival. During a dance festival in which Rautes performed for villagers, Raute elders Bir Bahadur and Man Bahadur brought me several wooden items. Bir Bahadur gave me a bowl and breadboard while reciting:

> May you have enough to eat,
> May you have wealth,
> May you have clothes, spices, greens, rice, cows,
>   and water buffaloes.
> May your name be everywhere and may my name
>   be everywhere.
> May the breadboard that I have given you remain
>   with your grandchildren, great-grandchildren,
>   and great-great-grandchildren.

I noticed that Bir Bahadur framed the blessing in such a way that it was bestowed upon both of us, including his wish that both of us benefit from the sacred words. And with this more mutual blessing, he then took my hands in the Raute fashion of greeting. He gently held both my hands in his while looking at me quietly and announcing: "From now on we have be-come ritual kin (*mit*). Today you are my daughter." Bir Bahadur then placed a *ṭika* mark on my forehead and raised his hands to give me a ceremonial *namaste* greeting. In turn, we performed this blessing to each other[11] and gave each of the elders *ṭika* marks and saluted them with *namaste*. As my gifts to them, I gave the men what they had requested: worm medicine, a large piece of plastic tarp, two dollars,[12] and a small rooster. From this time on, I had to give certain concessions to my fictive kin during trade. Lest I get too chummy with my new "fathers," however, Man Bahadur would sometimes remind me that "family is more important than friends" (*mit bhanda, hit ṭhulo chā*). This was his way of telling me that his loved ones, his blood relatives, are more important than his fictive kin or friends. This was a reminder that I shouldn't expect too much from our new relationship. In other fictive relationships between Rautes and villagers,[13] Rautes expressed deeper friendship, but they did not fulfill any of the customary Nepalese obligations associated with ritual relationships. For their fictive brothers, Rautes did not do agricultural work, thresh grain, lend money, or indulge in other common practices among farmers who form fictive friendship and kin relations with other farmers.

Foragers in the Larger Social Landscape

From this chapter's examination of the Rautes' exchange system, several conclusions can be drawn. First, we cannot define hunter-gatherers in isola-tion from their social surroundings. Studies of hunter-gatherers that exam-ine only their internal exchanges often produce a false sense of holism, as if a foraging community exists without influence from neighboring farmers. Foragers are people who engage in internal exchange and egalitarian shar-ing but also in external asymmetrical exchange. This is not to say that a particular foraging society is no more than a disenfranchised peripatetic fringe of its surrounding agricultural societies, as has been argued on occa-sion (Hoffman 1986; Wilmsen 1989; Wilmsen and Denbow 1990). Rather, foragers represent a node within a larger socioeconomic landscape. They are shaped by the dominant system, but they also continue to hunt, gather, and trade. Paradoxically, it is only through the accommodation of hierarchy among agriculturists that these contemporary foragers are able to maintain an egalitarian sociality.

Second, "simple egalitarian societies" like the Raute are not all that sim-ple. Rautes practice a variety of forms of sharing and trade among themselves, such as hidden exchange, demand sharing, tolerated theft, and general reciprocity. These types of exchange operate as leveling mechanisms that redistribute accumulated wealth. Rautes value equality and reproach any member of their society who tries to hoard wealth or influence others by accumulating wealth. Thus their internal economic system is actively managed and maintained by enforcing egalitarian social relationships; we can think of it as rather more like a form of structured simplicity. In their dealings with villagers, on the other hand, Rautes practice more asymmetrical forms of exchange. In particular, they employ barter, patronage, fictive kinship, and other strategies to facilitate trade relations. In fact, even their manufacture of wooden wares highlights this difference between internal and external exchange. Large wooden bowls and boxes are produced for marketing to villagers, who need them for storage of grain, pulses, butter, and so on. Contrarily, Rautes fashion mostly smaller wooden cups, eating bowls, and other utensils for themselves. This dichotomy of wooden wares echoes the perceptions and expectations that Rautes have of how villagers behave as farmers who value large storage vessels versus hunter-gatherers who value small portable vessels.

Room exists for various intricate patterns and rules within each of the Rautes' systems of exchange, but Rautes generally recognize a dualistic pattern of trade and exchange. They practice an egalitarian set of exchange rules among themselves and conversely adopt strategies of asymmetrical social exchange with farmers. One of the most important reasons for this remarkable schism in economic strategies is the fact that Rautes live inside the forests of Nepal, while others live outside of them. Highlighting this distinction, Rautes define their landscape as a large familial domain. As they say, "We are the children of God. All of God's children live in the forest."

8

The Children of God

Stones break, earth quakes,
Trees tumble down,
But the sun always stays the same.
  —Chandra

We are God's livestock.
  —Raute elder

In conversations, I noticed that Rautes often talk about the "children of God,"
and that these offspring live in one of two realms. One is ethereal. In this
realm live the distant gods such as the Sun, Moon, Clouds, and Stars. The
second realm is one of substance, of the earth, which is itself a relative.
During one conversation, Chandra explained, "Even I, Chandra, need my
father. My father is the forest and he is the most important thing for Nepal.
You see, forests are our parents because we live in them, they're the source
of life."

The nomadic Raute lifestyle is founded upon religious ideologies that
deify natural resources. Like other foragers in South Asia, such as the
Birhor who live in Jharkhand and the Jenu Kurumba (Naiken, Nayaka)
of South India, Rautes create a personal relationship with other beings in
their environment. Some of these beings are celestial bodies, forest creatures, deceased ancestors, and weather events like thunderstorms. For Rautes, the "children of God" refers not only to people, but also to animals,
stones, yams, trees, and other living, sentient entities. These beings are
supernaturally living "nonhuman persons," though we see them only as
natural objects.

Anthropologists have historically described hunter-gatherer belief systems as based upon "animism." This term derives from the nineteenth-century writings of Sir Edward Tylor, who thought that the belief in souls was the earliest form of religion (Tylor 1871; Bird-David 1999; Ingold 1987). In animistic systems, animals and natural phenomena represent social others who have "souls" or are in some way animated and alive. Rautes do ,indeed animate many of the forest beings, often referring to them as family relatives. This represents a subjective rather than objective relationship with others, resembling the English term "persons." Thus, Rautes speak of animal-persons, rock-persons, and other nonhuman persons in addition to human persons. In an extension of this relational worldview, Rautes create relationships with other-than-human persons. About an animal, a Raute asks not "What is it?" but rather "Who is it?" and "What relationship does she or he have to me?" A bird, for example, is called not just "bird" but "elder brother bird" (*maŋko bwā*). In other words, the ontological relationship between Rautes and social others involves degrees of *relatedness* to others, even if they happen to be rocks, trees, or animals. Thus, it is only natural for Rautes to utter such statements as "We who live in the forest are all the children of God." It conveys the fact that rocks, trees, and animals are also part of their ontological family.

Relations to these other social beings are also evident in metaphors and other figures of speech that are based upon family relationships. The stars in the sky are designated as "sisters-in-law," monkeys are "little brothers," and "King Bear" rules the forest, as no Rautes believe they can confront the predator at the top of the food chain. Even a simple yam is honored as a mother, and its main tuber designated as the "mother root" (*nyu-hri*). These social others are what we, raised in a complex society, think of as objects and animals. But to Rautes they are important "other-than-human" relatives.

The belief in "other-than-human" persons has been documented for many hunting-and-gathering societies. For example, when discussing the worldview of Anishinabe (Ojibwa) hunter-gatherers living in Manitoba, Canada, one scholar stressed that "the metaphysics of . . . persons provides the major key to their world view. . . . The more deeply we penetrate the world view of the Ojibwa the more apparent it is that social relations between human beings (*anicinābek*) and other-than-human persons are of cardinal significance" (Hallowell 1975, 143–145). Likewise, in his studies of the Rock Cree Indians of Manitoba, anthropologist Robert Brightman emphasizes that "Cree conceptions of the social and sacred animal are maximally visible to outsiders when embedded in practices conventionally labeled 'religious . . .' but the animal figures also in more technical contexts.

Some Rock Crees experience animals as social others not only when they sing and burn offerings to them but also when they search for them, kill them with weapons, butcher their remains, and eat them. Cree discourse itself represents animals concurrently as use values and as *social others* in all the contexts in which people understand themselves to be interacting with them" (Brightman 1993, 2–3).

It is clear, then, that when foraging peoples subsist by directly utilizing natural resources in their environments, they develop worldviews that personalize and deify those resources that are crucial to their survival. The ontological shift recognizing animal-persons and other nonhuman persons shapes the way in which they perceive hunting others who are crucial to their survival. If we wish to deeply understand Raute hunting, we must admit both the material and the ideological sides of things. As anthropologist Richard Lee noted: "Patterns [of hunting-and-gathering] work are embedded in a distinctive social and economic organization and are buttressed by a characteristic cosmology and world view. All three sets of criteria set foraging apart from the industrialized wage labor that dominates the world economy today" (Lee 1999, 11). To fathom the power and complexity of hunting and gathering as a way of life, not just a way to make a living, provides us with an opportunity to understand how food collection shapes other meaningful aspects of societies.

This seems the appropriate point at which to survey the major supernatural deities of the Rautes. During interviews with Rautes and with neighboring Banrajis, people occasionally talked about the organization of their various supernatural beings. Rautes acknowledge different classes, or kinds, of beings, including (1) major divinities; (2) ancestral divinities; (3) supernatural animals; (4) supernatural forces; and (5) "borrowed gods," meaning deities that are borrowed from surrounding agrarian traditions of Hinduism and Buddhism.[1] Many of these beings have both a natural and a supernatural manifestation, such that there is a natural object, such as the sun, an animal, stones, stars, and there is the supernatural manifestation of these objects or beings.

Major deities: (1) Sun, known as Gwāhiŋ, Dāmu, and Berh; (2) Moon,
    known as Berh, Bayrha
Supernatural forces: (1) stars (*twi-twi*); (2) weather (*ha'wa*); (3) stones
    (*dholiya*); (4) clouds (*dewa*)
Deified plants and animals: (1) yam being (*dzhya-hra*); (2) animals,
    including bear (*rāj-bhālu*), tiger (*bāgh, gurau*), langur (*guna, gudu*),
    macaque (*māta*), snake (*mābu*)

Supernatural humans: (1) human ancestors (*Horh, Doulikānato*); (2) ghosts (*šyiya, masān*)

Raute Solar and Lunar Deities

When I asked about who created the great family of God, Rautes emphasized that they did not know; but they did offer comments about some of the beings in their universe. I asked elder Man Bahadur how he imagined that the sun and moon were related to each other. He began by noting a contemporary piece of information—that he knew that men had been to the moon—and continued: "Well, sun and moon; sun is male and moon is female. This is because people can't go to the sun because it will burn them, that is why it is greater. People have gone to moon, that is why moon is female. That is what I know. I don't know how sun and moon got married. If you know it, can you explain it to me? I don't know who their child is, either. Maybe stars are their children. This is what I think. Maybe their children are forests. They might have made us too."

After this statement, which obviously blended some "impression management" with some Raute authentic beliefs, we came to understand that Man Bahadur wanted us first to know that he was aware of something important, that people had traveled to the moon. In later conversations, it emerged that the solar deity is unisexual: it does not really personify a male or female personality. Rautes used three names for their solar deity—Gwāhiŋ, Dāmu, and Berh. They only split the celestial deity into gendered parts when we, as interviewers, pushed them, and then they preferred that the lunar deity could be called "Bayrha" as a female counterpart to Berh. But in our conversations, the lunar deity was never mentioned as having roles in hunting, foraging, healing, or other activities.

When talking about the sun as a deity, Rautes use the name Gwāhiŋ as one of deity's avatars or deified forms. Chandra, who had visited one day and stayed for lunch, pointed to the sky and said: "Stones have broken, earth has fallen apart, trees have fall down, but the sun is always like this. Sun is just like fire, they can both burn people. We call Surya 'Surjya' when speaking with villagers and Gwāhiŋ among ourselves."

Rautes share the term Gwāhiŋ with the neighboring Kusunda hunter-gatherers; both groups associate Gwāhiŋ with giving them the power to hunt successfully (Kusunda: Gwang). The meaning associated with Gwāhiŋ may derive from a shared history of belief in a supreme solar hunting deity and may provide insight into an early, unwritten cultural landscape of indigenous sacred names. Not accidently, the name for the sun as Gawang also has been used by the Konyak Nagas living near the India–Myanmar border. The Konyak Nagas are recorded as saying that Gawang "lives somewhere in the sky and that long ago he made the firmament. Gawang made also the earth and man . . . but how he made man, we do not know. But we say that we are his children. When we become rich or poor, it comes from Gawang; when we have plenty to eat, it comes from Gawang; when we have fever, it too comes from Gawang." Researcher C. von Fürer-Haimendorf interviewed the Konyak Naga people of Assam in the 1930s, asking them, "Does Gawang live quite alone in the sky? Has he no wife and no children?" And they replied, "We do not know anything of a wife of Gawang . . . and his children, these are we ourselves!" (Fürer-Haimendorf 1976, 176).

Further, like Rautes and Kusunda foragers, the Konyak Nagas profess that Gawang must be propitiated before hunting can begin. In C. von Fürer-Haimendorf's 1938 diaries, he reported, "For a hunt a *genna* (ritual sacrifice) is performed. Before we go hunting we say 'Gawang make [it] that we meet boars and wild pigs on our way'; in addition a man can sacrifice a chicken and in his house sprinkle the blood on the skulls of previously caught pigs . . . . But if the hunter injures an animal and it gets away he believes that Gawang is angry with him and he goes home and sacrifices a chicken and says 'Gawang let me have it tomorrow.'"[2]

Incarnations and alternate names of deities occur in all religions. In Judeo-Christian traditions, God has been called Yahweh, Elohim, Jesus, and other names as well. Another Raute name for the sun deity is Dāmu. The name Dāmu seems to be widely used in northern South Asia; Austroasiatic-speaking ethnic groups such as the Hor, Santal, Mundari, and Korwa, and Dravidian-speaking groups such as the Kurukh (Oraon) and Kharia, all have similar terms for the solar deity. Mundari and Kurukh peoples call the sun Darha; Kharia people say Darom; Korwa peoples say Dulha; and Hor say Dharam. The neighboring Chepang peoples call some of their deities Dhare, and the Banraji say Diho, emphasizing that "Diho caused the earth to be created (*diho-ya dharti panawa*)."[3]

While the Rautes' solar deity is often called Gwahing and Dhamu during conversations, the most frequent name given was Berh. When I asked "What does Berh do?" Raute elders often replied, "Berh is the one who makes it possible to hunt." When speaking of Berh, Rautes also say things such as, "We like to dance because Berh will see us and be happy," or "Berh is the main god and the stars are his temple," or "Berh needs baby chicks to make our hunt successful." Similar to the other names for God, Berh may be tied to a larger regional belief system concerning the sun, as a few other former hunting societies, such as the Hill Kharia of northern India, also call the sun/supreme deity Bero (and Darom).[4]

For Rautes, Berh is associated not only with hunting and the sun, but also with dancing, shamans, blood sacrifice of baby chicks, death, and illness. I remember watching a Raute dance one misty afternoon. I was videotaping and listening to elder Mayn Bahadur say a few words about the dance called *Pāyśyāri*, meaning the "surround the animals" dance. As Mayn Bahadur talked, his eyes filled with a sort of rapture, and he said softly, "Dancing is not of men, it is of God." This important emotional contour played out against the background of a larger emotional setting described in Nepali as *manko thulo lagyo*, meaning that his heart felt large with emotion, or in Sanskrit as *perinandam* (awesome bliss). Mayn Bahadur's heart was filled with the sacredness of the dance for God (Berh), and the people love to dance for the one who watches, protects, and helps them. Rautes sacrifice baby chicks to Berh and avoid offending him/her so that their hunting will go well. While they generally do not express excessive fear of their deities, they did sometimes express anxiety that Berh might be angry, take away the monkeys, and otherwise punish them if they commited wrong actions.

The Solar Deity's Children

As I got to know the Rautes better, they explained that the solar deity created the forest long ago, and that s/he also made the first foods grow. The very basis of Raute subsistence, the first foods God created were yams and water. Naturally, Rautes explained, God created yams and water first because Dāmu knew that people would need something to eat after being created. Dāmu has other children too; s/he created all the creatures of the forests, such as birds, insects, monkeys, tigers, snakes, trees, the forest herself, and even the stars resting in the cerulean blue sky.

As you can imagine, looking at the stars at night in the Himalayan hills is quite a beautiful experience. With no electricity in the region and hilltops thousands of feet above sea level, the millions of stars appear like jewels against black velvet. Even star groups such as the Pleiades, which are difficult to see in urban areas, stand out so clearly that one can see not just the seven "sisters" recorded in Greek mythology, but eight or more stars in the cluster. For the Rautes and Banrajis, the Pleiades represent Dāmu's children. In particular, Banrajis called the Pleiades "the seven sisters-in-law and one brother-in-law," saying that when they came up over the mountain to the east each night, they felt reassured to see their ancient kin and, on a more practical note, they knew it was about eight o'clock by local time standards.[5]

The Pleiades star formation has, of course, been an important nighttime entity in many world societies. Among the Soren, an Austroasiatic society in northern India, the Pleiades represents a totem clan deity of star-persons. Greek mythology refers to the seven most visible stars as the daughters of Atlas and Pleione and the half-sisters of Hyades, whose mother was Ethra, a goddess of the sky. The Pleiades were also half-sisters to the Hesperides, who were the daughters of Night.

The morning star, which is actually the planet Venus, represents another major astronomical figure in many cultures throughout the world. It is called Bin Tārā (Bright Star) by Rajis and Dā Twi (One Star) by Rautes. Rautes noted that the One Star can be seen from about four till eight o'clock in the morning. Thus the two celestial bodies we know as the Pleiades and the Morning Star enable Rautes and Banrajis to mark time in a simple fashion, as the beginnings of each day and each evening. One further point is that the sister-in-law/brother-in-law relationship is particularly important among Rautes. In familial situations, Raute seek to join each clan groups' children in marriage, since they only marry within their own society and not with Hindu villagers. The exchange of siblings between two families represents a valorized form of marriage and is iconically represented in their cosmology of the stars.

Another set of God's children includes a group of supernatural females named Doulikanato, Hunemithu, and Dudhemithu.[6] It is unclear whether these females should be called deities or human spirits. Doulikanato (da'li-ka-na'to) literally means "the living spirit of us"; she represents a deified ancestral spirit worshipped in a way similar to a Hindu devi goddess. Raute speakers have described Doulikanato as a deity who is responsible for actions related to life, childbirth, and sustenance, such as successfully finding wild yams in the forest. Rautes propitiate Doulikanato when women are ill, in childbirth, or in need of help in other ways. One Raute speaker nervously said that a shaman will collect some tobacco, pumpkin, an ear of corn, some garlic, a handful of grain, salt, and red pepper. He or she will sit and shake, going into trance to communicate with Doulikanato. Then the helpers nearby the shaman will sacrifice a nearly full-grown goat (bakrako paṭhār), performing their version of the common Nepali goat sacrifice (pāṭho puja). Finally, the shaman will massage the person until the poison or illness leaves her body. Rautes obtain a few goats each month during their trading sessions, and these would be the animals they use for the sacrifice to Doulikanato. Rautes don't like to raise goats or keep them for more than a few weeks because they require food and water.

Another female deity propitiated by Banrajis during hunting is known as Kayu (alt. Qāyu). Placing a small offering of flowers on a large rock near the hunting area, the hunters ask Kayu for her help by protecting them and helping them find animals to be hunted. While Kayu has a female gender, she is not conceived of as human or ancestral. Kayu may have derived from a belief in a hunting deity that was shared over the region by other hunter-gatherers in the past, as the Kusunda foragers of western Nepal also worship Qaoli as a hunting deity (Watters 2005). Looking at the meanings of the Raute deities, we see that they possess both creative and destructive aspects. Although some are female and others unisexual, their major deities provide food and protection, and nurture them like parents.

Both Berh and Doulikanato are part of the Rautes' manifest world, their world "here and now," as opposed to an afterlife, heaven, or netherworld as found in Western cosmologies of complex societies. In this regard, the sky represents both a supernatural and a natural place; it is everywhere. Doulikanato and Berh literally surround Raute people, as part of their invisible but personified supernatural surroundings—part of the very air they breathe. And direct communication with these deities occurs during dance and ritual shamanic performances. As Ratna explained, during shamanic healing, Doulikanaato and Berh are propitiated by Raute shamans. He noted, "the shamans, they heal. They have to give benediction (N. *achita*) for Doulikanato and Berh. They have to sacrifice a chicken in the forest. Seven times they'll do the healing."[7]

Another category of deified beings who are an important part of the Rautes' family consists of their ancestor spirits, known as collectively as Horh, who pervade all the spaces around Rautes. Thus, at the same time as they move through their secular world, their spirit world fills the air around them. As one elder explained, "All gods are Horhi, because we cannot see them. If we sit here and if God sits there, right in front of us, then we could see him."

Horh refers to "spirit," one that is invisible yet omnipresent, powerful, and found in both natural and supernatural realms. The only way to see Horh is to sit like a shaman, shaking in a trance, and call the spirit. But even then, Horh would not exactly appear, as s/he has a pervasive quality, like atoms of spirit or sentience that pervade and surround all beings. At times Rautes explained that Horh is a form of their deceased ancestors, whom they believe exist as spirits, or sentient atoms, around them as they move through the secular world. But the journey from the mundane world to the

Raute ancestral spirits inhabit the forests around them, like the mists moving purposefully through the trees during the monsoon.

spiritual world also entails travel into the sky. As Ratna opined, after people die they don't just decompose: "Wood deteriorates, but humans don't just deteriorate—they go into the sky."

Ancestors are not seen as malevolent or evil but rather continue to dwell in the earthly ether, invisible yet omnipresent, as part of the Rautes' extended family in their forested home where all of God's children dwell. Rautes did not elaborate on any distinctions among the spirits of the ancestors, but another group of monkey-hunting foragers, the Birhor of north India, make a cosmological distinction between ancestors remembered by name and those not known by name (Adhikary 1999). Somewhat similarly, Banrajis have borrowed the local Nepali notion of spirits of the dead, known as *pichā* or *pichāsa* (from N. *pitra*, forefathers), but their generic term for the ancestors is *seda*. The *seda* can make one "shake" or go into a shamanic state of altered consciousness.

Another salient point about the ancestral spirits is that they are associated with human foods and ailments. As Raute elder Daracho notes, "Horh is also a god. Whenever hair hurts or head aches, then at that time Horh blows and drops. . . . If any part of my bones hurts, the shaman (*dhāmi*) has to heal it with Horh's help [in the form of the ancestral spirit, shamans use techniques of blowing and dropping malevolent entities out of and away from the sick person]. Healing is for head. It is also for stomach. Even for cut hand or legs, it is for everything. . . . If a person's head, stomach, or hand gets hurt or cut, if their foot gets cut, Horh is the one to propitiate. . . . Horh is the shaman's god. Horh is the one that the shamans beseech when people are sick." When I asked, "Which is more effective when people are sick, medicine or the shamans?" Daracho responded, "Recovering from illness by means of God or by drinking fresh water [as medicine] are the same (*deuta ko sānco ra pāniko kāco ekāi ho*). If God does right then it is all right; if He does not do right, well then, no one can do anything. If gods can heal me, that is better. God says [what the illness entails] and I feel that way. He is Horh."

Continuing, Raute elder Daracho explained that Rautes propitiate local deities too, the kind of Hindu deities that I like to refer to as "borrowed gods." He noted, "We honor goddess Malika on a full moon day (*purni*), as well as honor the goddesses known to villagers as Kalika, Devi, and Seto. We call these goddesses by the names of Hune Mithu, Dudhe Mithu, Dudhe Bhainta, Seto Bhainta, and Kala Bhainta.[8] After doing rituals (*pujas*) to them, we can go hunting. We will hunt a young male rhesus and a young female rhesus monkey. For full-moon day, we might also hunt young langurs. The older ones are much tougher. We can't eat their bones." And, then, as if to lighten the gruesome image of chewing on monkey bones, he recited:

> We have to eat our fate.
> We'll die when death arrives.
> We eat the sweetest curd.
> And sing our father's name.

The poem reminded Daracho of his own fate and that of the monkeys as tied to inevitable life and death in the forests. For these foragers, lives are fated; death comes naturally to everyone and should not be an object of worry or fear.

Although death and illness are inevitable, Rautes like to keep themselves as healthy as possible, and sometimes it is important to propitiate all of the deities. Baby chicks can be sacrificed to Berh, baby goats offered to Doulikanato, and unhusked rice collected and given to Horh. Obtained from villagers, other paraphernalia are used as well, such as a brass bell, a brass cup, and ritual Bermuda grass. The Rautes' ritual paraphernalia are carried from camp to camp in a *piṭṭi*, a wooden box with dual compartments. The sacred box houses the respective sacred objects of each Raute patriclan, known as the Kalyal and the Raskoti.[9]

The Sacred Side of Animals

Rautes believe that there is a sacred side to the plants and animals of the forest. For example, they honor spirits associated with wild yams. On occasion, they personified yams in their drawings and made an analogy between the long spindly tubers and their own *tuni* hair lengths, which look like a trailing yam root. Also, their linguistic relatives, the Chepang, believe in a plethora of spirits, including spirits of yams, stones, and animals (Caughley 2000, 453). In speaking of their cosmological family, Rautes explained that the solar deity had created the stars, the forests, and then the first foods— yams and water. In these short explanations about creation, God did not create anything that lives outside of the Himalayan forests. Domesticated animals, such as buffalo, cattle, sheep, and goats, as well as Hindu villagers, are all absent from the Rautes' cosmological stories. Thus, regardless of how many divinities and spirits make up the Rautes' cosmological world, together they form an integral part of their family that inhabits the forest.

Rautes believe that, while various animals have a mundane, everyday existence, they also are sentient beings that have spirits and should be honored and respected. Monkeys, in particular, were discussed in their stories and conversations. For example, a Raute youth named Chandra said: "Rhesus monkeys used to be human before. The monkeys even went to weddings. In that time long ago, the rhesus had long tails, like langurs. But at one wedding, a man burned the rhesus monkey's tail in a bonfire. The upper part of its tail was burned away, leaving only the stump you see today. My father told me this."[10]

In this story, Chandra related that monkeys could do extraordinary things such as perform weddings. Yet similar as they believe them to be to humans, Rautes distinguish monkeys from human primates by referring to each species' distinctively shaped tails and social habits. Chandra pointed out that monkeys are not like Rautes because they lack speech (*khāma*) and they have different tails from the Rautes. Raute men and women wear a "tail," a length of twisted hair that grows to the floor in some cases. In contrast, langurs have a long tail, and macaques have a short one.

In many societies, humans and animals have special relationships. In India and Nepal, farmers worship particular birds, mammals, and reptiles. Rautes have heard some of these stories, especially those involving monkeys as told in the Hindu epic, the Rāmāyaṇa. For example, my research assistant asked Man Bahadur, "Why do you think the langur is black?" He responded with an allusion loosely related to the Rāmāyaṇa, saying: "In the town square of Lampa [this refers to Sri Lanka], a monkey was being

Chandraman removed
his turban to demonstrate
the length of his "tail."
His hair length almost
reaches the floor.

bad, making mistakes. The men wanted to kill it, but the monkey said, 'Do not kill me, I will kill myself instead.' So the monkey caught his tail . . . [to begin killing/hurting himself]. Just then came the goddess Sita. The goddess Sita hit the monkey with a black pan (*tāwā*), and the goddess Sita hit his rump (*pusi, puchar*) with a red pan." This, Man Bahadur explained, is why the macaque monkey is mostly black but has a short tail and a reddish rump. Although this story is not closely related to events recounted in the Rāmāyaṇa, it signifies that Rautes blend a little knowledge of the ancient epic with their own social rules and myths. In particular, the story contains the moral imperative in which the offender (the monkey) offers to punish himself. This markedly autonomous form of morality is indeed held by Rautes; in general they believe that people should be responsible for their own actions and misdeeds. They regulate behavior through agreement about the boundaries of morality, finding that immoral actions (*duši*) have to be corrected by the offender rather than by others.

In addition, the story also develops another mythical parallel involving the weapon used to punish the monkey. Note how the goddess Sita picked up an iron pan for this purpose. By analogy, an iron pan's shape, weight, and substance is similar to the Rautes' weapon of choice—the iron axe—used to dispatch monkeys. In both cases, the agents hit monkeys with these iron objects, and thus the story resonates with the integration of Sita into Raute ways of knowing the world.

When Rautes mythologize monkeys, they create a special relationship marked by a sacred bond of animal-to-human welfare. In other foraging societies, such as among the Iñupiats of circumpolar Canada, animals give themselves to the hunter, and they frequently communicate directly with humans under certain circumstances (Bodenhorn 1989, 2000; Brightman 1993). Barbara Bodenhorn cites an example of this conception of human-animal relations among Iñupiats, writing: "Whales, like all the other animals, offer themselves up to be killed. . . . This is a gift, again as with all animals, that is contingent upon proper human behavior" (2000, 33). Similarly, Rautes view their little brothers (monkeys) as sacrificial beings. They use the term *bilu* to signify meat as a sacrament. When they refer to monkey meat as *bilu* they mean that monkeys sacrificed themselves—with, however, divine intervention. As Chandra emphasized, "We will not leave alone the baby monkeys given by God." Thus, while the Rautes' little brothers sacrifice themselves, they do not "offer themselves" to hunters. The intervention of the hunting deity Berh is what ultimately allows successful hunts.

Further, Chandra noted: "Well, the Rautes' younger brothers are those who eat wild fruit in the thick forests. The Rautes' fodder (*ghãs*) is langur or rhesus. You make houses in neighborhoods and farm the land, hunt deer, that's your work."[11] In this way, Chandra classifies monkeys, Rautes, and villagers based on different types of consumptive behavior and production. Monkeys, Rautes, and villagers are distinguished by what they eat: monkeys eat fruit; Rautes eat monkeys; villagers eat deer. And, notably, only villagers are defined by human productive activity: they are busy making, farming, hunting, and working. Monkeys and Rautes, on the other hand, are not defined in this manner and, taken together with the fact that Rautes consider monkeys their "younger brothers," Chandra firmly identifies the Rautes more closely with monkeys than with villagers. As another Raute boy explained to me the relationship between Rautes and monkeys, "Well, we are brothers, but we split."

For Rautes, their cosmological system is a way of defining the boundaries of existence, and it depends on living in a morally right manner. Rautes were adamant that they must live in a virtuous way if their hunts are to be successful. If they act in an immoral or *duši* manner, the monkeys will disappear and the Rautes will "lose the taste of hunting." For example, my research assistant Bisnu and I wanted to kill the flies in our interview room since they were bothering us. But Man Bahadur said, no, that would be *duši*. Since the flies were not inflicting harm on us, he said, we should not inflict harm on them. This attitude of nonviolence was evident in their attitudes toward all animals—even monkeys, though they dispatch them with axes. Rautes rationalize their killing of monkeys by saying, "God gives us all the monkeys that come into our nets." Thus, from their point of view, monkeys are given to them, and it would be *duši* to leave any behind or discard any monkey meat after a kill.

Most of the sacred beings in the Rautes' cosmological world are kindhearted. Even the tiger, feared by villagers because they prey upon cattle, goats, and occasionally goat-herding children, is not feared by Rautes. A tiger is considered a kind of supernatural leader. When Raute drum leaders (*gurau*) become possessed, they sometimes transmogrify into the form of a tiger. But few of the supernatural animals are evil or malevolent, though Rautes acknowledge that malevolent spirits or ghosts do exist. However, they show little trepidation about ghosts, snakes, and the bodies of family members who have died in unfortunate circumstances (corpse, *šyiya*). Although people inevitably die, they noted, after a few years their spirits become gentle, no matter what actually killed them. Even in cases of premature death or accidents, Rautes did not show much fear of ghosts, nor did they seem to have any rituals to appease malevolent ancestors or snake spirits. The Banrajis, who follow most of the same cosmological ideas as Rautes, feel a bit differently about the deceased. Having adopted it from local Hindu farmers, Banrajis practice goat sacrifice (*pāṭhi puja*) to calm the malevolent spirits of the recently deceased. Banraji men, who sometimes have alcohol-related illnesses, may blame their uncontrollable outbursts of anger and violence upon being influenced by malevolent spirits of recently deceased kin. Such shifting beliefs among Banrajis may be a result of recent cultural changes rather than long-standing traditional beliefs.

Supernatural Forces

Although Rautes did not discuss the forces of wind, thunder, and earthquakes as deified forces, the neighboring Banrajis living along the Kali River did see these phenomena as forces in their lives. For the Banraji families, weather forces are collectively known as ancient ones—Ha'wa (from *ha'*, ancient one + *-wa*, pluralizer).[12] There are at least four of these forces that can hurt people. Laṭiyabar (from N. *laṭa*, to be dumb/deaf) is a harmful place of malevolent force; in it, Laṭiyabar can cause people to become deaf and dumb. Banrajis fearfully avoid such places, and believe that if people go there, they will be stricken mute, as was one unfortunate woman whom I interviewed. Unfortunately for Rajis, local Hindu authorities were unaware of these highly taboo places, and in one case the main school created for Banraji children was built on top of one! After many goat offerings and the raising of Siva's trident to ward off the maleficent forces, Banraji parents finally allowed their beloved children to enter the area. Afterwards, some sacred offerings were kept at the school to keep the area sanctified. If anyone were to steal the offerings, one Banraji elder predicted that the thief would be struck mute by Laṭiyabar.

Another maleficent force is Bandukiya-bar, meaning "gunshot deity," a force that peals across the sky in the form of thunder.[13] A third such force is known as Akāsh-bar, meaning "sky force," and it will also cause debilitation in the form of deafness or blindness. A fourth supernatural force, and the most deadly, is known as Baina Ha'wa, meaning "Great Force," since this one can cause a person to seize up and simply die. Sher Singh, an elder from the village of Kuṭachārāni, explained that Ha'wa are all around, everywhere, spirits in the air but not the air itself. He added that night especially represents a dangerous time when Ha'wa are present. This fear of supernatural forces was a noticeable distinction from Banrajis' neighboring nomadic Rautes, who generally expressed no fear of supernatural phenomena.

One might be tempted to see a connection between the Banraji Ha'wa and the Raute Horh deities. Both do share some features: Ha'wa and Horh deities are both figured as noncorporeal, multiple rather than a single deity, ethereal, composed of particles of matter, and omnipotent. But they have differences too. The Ha'wa are presented as malevolent and nonhuman, whereas Horh are described as human, judgmental, and able to heal. The Ha'wa were not described as having healing powers (much the opposite). More likely, these are two different groups of supernaturals. Ha'wa represent the Banraji way of relating the natural forces of thunder, lightning, and nighttime to the contingent dangers that these exert upon forest people.

It's All in the Family

The Rautes' large cosmological family may have different duties and characteristics, but all sentient beings—insects, monkeys, humans, birds, and so on—are equally valuable. I learned this when I asked Man Bahadur if Rautes were more important in any way than monkeys. He looked at me like I was an ignorant child and scoffed: "All of God's children are equally important. No, we are not better or worse than our little brothers." This ethos represents one of the most essential ways in which Rautes maintain equality among themselves and the world around them. Among foragers such as the Rautes, their relationships with supernatural beings are ones of equality or of elder to younger siblings, they are not hierarchically symbolized, as in technologically complex societies. Unlike a Judeo-Christian deity, Raute deities do not judge, condemn, or manage human affairs. Even Berh, the most powerful of beings, is a deity that Rautes honor but don't particularly fear. Rather, Rautes perform dances to let God know how much they love him and to make God happy. Raute ancestral spirits also are benevolent and not to be feared: their ancestors surround them, care about them, and guide them as they move through their sylvan surroundings.

It is important to focus not only on what Rautes do but what they *believe* about what they do. Societies like that of the Rautes are not only defined by the foraging work that they do but by their distinctive cosmological structures. The Rautes' animistic, egalitarian, and relational worldview is broadly characteristic of other foraging societies. Generally, the economic infrastructure of *any* society forms the basis for a culture's belief systems; belief systems arise from a culture's productive life. Pastoralists love and worship their cattle, agriculturalists are devoted to their complex hierarchies, and capitalists create commodity fetishisms. So it should come as no huge surprise that Raute foragers' system mirrors the material basis of their existence and forms the foundation for their belief that all of God's children reside within a sylvan home.

Often, religious beliefs in foraging societies can be conserved over time better than physical materials such as stone and bone artifacts. As the archaeologist Zarine Cooper writes in reference to the foraging Andaman Islander peoples: "It is interesting that customs relating to the socioreligious sphere, such as the preservation of animal skulls, as witness to successful hunts, have continued up to the present day, whereas objects concerned purely with subsistence strategies, such as clay pots and stone tools, were unhesitatingly dropped [from forager toolkits] despite having survived in the economy for over two millennia" (Cooper 2002, 180). While technologies may change, it seems that hunter-gatherers tenaciously hold onto and pass along their religious beliefs. The linguist Georg Van Driem refers to such enduring beliefs that survive the centuries as "memes"—units of thought, similar to genes, that are trying to preserve themselves over generations by causing us, as humans with language abilities, to encode them in stories, myths, songs, and especially religious codes of conduct (Van Driem 2001, 33). The Rautes' religious belief system may be the result of the generally tenacious nature of religious beliefs, or it may be part of their own cultural resilience so evident in the strategies they have adopted to preserve their way of life. One thing is certain: Rautes strongly resist assimilating into Hindu-based agrarian social life. Sometimes it seems as if nothing can stop the forces toward assimilation that pull foragers into complex agrarian societies. Rautes are not immune to this; but, in the big picture, it is their cultural resistance to such commercial forces that is extraordinary.

9

Cultural Resilience

The Big Picture

Everyone asks for the right to live.
You ask for agricultural fields, we ask for the forest.
　—Chandra

Cultural Diversity

The Raute people's right to pursue a life of nomadism represents one facet of larger issues concerning cultural diversity, resiliency, and human rights. Why is cultural diversity important? And why is Raute cultural autonomy important to those who read this book? Even though the term "cultural diversity" has become commonplace, small-scale societies are facing more challenges than ever before. They find themselves enmeshed in legal battles with powerful states. Their schools are unwilling or unable to meet their children's language needs. Laws are enacted that prevent them from hunting and gathering in protected forest reserves. Broadly, the forces of globalization influence decision makers in state societies, and their decisions often adversely affect small-scale societies.

Rautes are part of this political drama, and as one of the last full-time foraging peoples that has survived into the twenty-first century, they present a model of cultural alterity. To us living in technologically complex societies they represent everything that is "other," and from observing their otherness, we gain a new perspective on our own ways of living and being. Today advocacy groups such as the United Nations Permanent Forum on Indigenous Issues (UNPFII) plead for the preservation of endangered cultural groups. With a mandate to discuss issues related to development, culture, environment, education, and health and human rights, advocacy groups such as the UNPFII enable indigenous peoples to find commonality in their concerns no matter where they live. Yet, as we have seen from the continuing disappearance of endangered languages and eradication of many ethnic groups over the last century, advocacy work is not enough to preserve indigenous peoples and their cultures. Furthermore, many people from dominant sectors of society simply do not know about endangered cultures or are unaware of the positive aspects of cultural diversity. Why should an endangered language's survival really matter? Why should a minority group's cultural survival be so important?

The reasons for the importance of cultural diversity are complex, and many advocacy groups have not successfully provided clear explanations for and convincing arguments in favor of the preservation of minority peoples' cultures and languages. Too often the rationale seems to be that these cultures and languages are beautiful, astonishing, and rich. These humanistic reasons are certainly valid, but we must also demonstrate that the interests of majority populations can mesh with those of small-scale societies. Globalization may have made us more informed about many relevant foreign events, but the demise of a language or cultural group does not make headline news. When the last native speaker of a language disappears, many are unaware of this loss of a unique insight into the world. Different types of language and worldview can influence how we interpret the world around us, and language loss can even be dangerous when indigenous knowledge of plants and the environment is lost along with it. Endangered languages and cultures can shed light on early human migrations and interactions, but this chapter in our collective human history may be closed forever.[1]

Many people will mourn the extinction in the wild of species such as tiger, whale, condor, panda, or gorilla since, thanks to many researchers, the importance of biological diversity is better appreciated now than it was twenty years ago. It is now widely accepted that animals live in symbiotic relationships with others, and that any two species cannot live without the contributions of other interrelated species. Can we envision cultural diversity as being as complex and crucial to long-term human survival as biological diversity is to the maintenance of ecosystems?

Today, in fact, researchers are looking at this possibility. Ecologically diverse areas of the world such as the Himalayas are known as "biocultural diversity hot spots," places with an unusually high degree of mutually interacting ecological and cultural diversity (Deur and Turner 2005; Etkin 1994; Manandhar 2002). For example, in the Himalayan region that stretches for about 300,000 square miles, there are over 10,000 plant species, 3,000 of which are endemic, meaning that they grow nowhere else on earth. Ethnic and linguistic diversity is also exceptionally prevalent in the Himalayas. In

Nepal alone there are over a hundred distinct languages, and about three hundred languages are spoken throughout the region. This is comparable in many ways to the biocultural diversity of the North American California Floristic Province (CFP), which stretches about 100,000 square miles from Baja to Oregon. In the CFP, there are about 8,000 plants species (both introduced and native); 3,500 of these are native and about 2,000 endemic. Like the Himalayan biocultural diversity hot spot, the CFP's cultural diversity is also broad, with a hundred indigenous cultural groups continuing to speak a hundred Native American languages. It is important to recognize the correlation of flora, fauna, and people in biocultural diversity areas such as the Himalayas or California. These represent places where, until the advent of colonialism, human foragers have been able to live within the carrying capacity of their environments. The Himalayan foothills, for example, represent one of the last areas of continuous tiger habitat where humans and tigers have managed to coexist for thousands of years through the mutual division of their food resources. In geographical comparison, Nepal is 20 percent smaller than the state of Florida.

These ecological and cultural "edges" represent sources of environmental resilience to pollution and habitat destruction. Ecological edges, or fringe areas, are found in complex and fragile environments such as the biocultural hot spots, in places with countless small econiches defined by minute changes in elevation, slope angle, and direction. No wonder, then, that Nepal is home to the Ganges River dolphin (*Platanista gangetica gangetica*), red panda (*Ailurus fulgens*), pangolin (*Manis pentadactyla*), snow leopard (*Uncia uncia*), sloth bear (*Melursus ursinus*), and more than two hundred other mammals, many endangered. With forty different species of bats, the mountains have proved an ideal region for bat species diversification. Probably no people in the world understand the habits of bats better than hunter-gatherers such as the Rautes' ethnic relatives, the Banrajis, who live west of the Rautes, and the Chepang, living adjacent to and east of Raute territory. The hunting and tracking methods of these groups enable them to know more about bat habits than farmers, who seldom observe the habitats of these nocturnal mammals.

While we can readily appreciate the importance of biological diversity, cultural diversity is also important, for both scientific and humanistic reasons. Because they are forest-dwelling hunter-gatherers, Rautes, and their Raji and Chepang cousins, demonstrate symbiotic relations with other forest animals. For example, Rautes subsist upon prevalent fruits (figs, berries, jujube) and tubers (yams) that are also favorites of local prey species (deer, antelope, monkey, porcupine) as well as some predator species (bat, bear).

From an ecological perspective, prey and predator species together demonstrate complex interspecies interactions. Tubers get their roots dispersed through digging/disruption, and fruit-seed dispersal is facilitated by animal consumption and defecation. Thus predator groups such as the Rautes develop commensal relations with plants by helping them disperse and germinate. But, unlike farmers, who are also predator groups that hunt ungulates and other prey species, foragers do not overhunt species; they maintain no long-term storage facilities and are nomadic, moving after a short hunting foray to continually new forest locations. Thus foragers develop better triad prey–predator–plant species relationships than do farming populations.

In addition, the cultural diversity of small-scale societies like that of the Rautes is important for the preservation of human knowledge systems. Rautes and their relatives possess detailed and unique information about the natural environment. Chepangs, for example, have over fifty words for yams, due to their different ways of identifying the various parts, uses, and subspecies of *Dioscorea*. Botanists, on the other hand, have scientific names for only about five varieties of *Dioscorea* in Nepal. Foragers' knowledge of their environments is generally more intimate and is encoded in their languages with greater detail than we can hope to describe in one of the dominant spreading languages such as English. And while Rautes themselves may not be interested in how humans lived ten thousand or more years ago, their forest-collecting subsistence strategies, together with their egalitarian political structure, can teach us, by carefully delineated analogies, about how our human ancestors formed societies millennia ago. Scholars are starting to realize that ancient human experiences were marked by much more diversity than was previously assumed. We are starting to explore the possibility that even our Pleistocene-era ancestors engaged in very precise technological strategies in order to cope with specific environmental conditions. For example, fifteen thousand years ago, the people in northern India also ate jujube and figs, yet their skeletons and teeth indicate a taller, healthier population than that found today in most of northern South Asia (Lukacs and Pal 1993, 761). Foragers who continue to subsist on greater amounts of forest foods than farmers can help us to understand the human biology of past populations, if only by carefully constructed analogy.

Finally, the cultural diversity of small-scale societies like the Raute can provide us with new ideas and templates for planned social change. Rautes, for example, represent one of the most democratic societies on earth. Some elders have mastered rhetorical strategies that ameliorate conflict between members of their closely knit society. Their ways of reducing conflict serve as an example to societies, such as our own, where more militaristic conflict resolution strategies are employed. While many state-organized societies often use rhetoric based upon war metaphors, Rautes rarely resort to such hostile rhetoric. For example, when asked how Rautes deal with aggressive situations, a Raute headman said: "If two people are fighting then we should interrupt it. And if they're not listening, two to four people have to catch him and make him sit down. We have to really make him sit down. He has to sit down. We have to listen to everything; if something bad is going on in your heart, then you should imagine yourself stamping out that anger with your feet (*khuṭṭāle meṭāunu parcha*)." Many kinds of conflict resolution exist in the world, but it is notable that Rautes emphasize that people should avoid blaming others and try to take responsibility for their own actions.

Cultural Resilience

The Raute way of life does change over time, but rather than characterizing it as one marked by dynamic change, one might rather describe it as displaying a noticeable emphasis on perceived traditions and resistance to introduced change. I refer to this as "cultural resilience," a process marked by two notable features—active resistance to introduced changes and preservation of cultural practices. Cultural resilience applies to people who collectively and consciously resist and avoid changes that other groups, especially other agents such as development workers, view as expedient, good, correct, or necessary.

Notably, people who are culturally resilient direct their efforts toward preserving what they deem to be traditional practices. There is a marked emphasis on indigenous, original, and inherited beliefs and practices. Although things "traditional" do inevitably change over time, group consensus dictates which elements of their culture are preserved and sanctioned as paramount. Rautes, for example, stress their monkey hunting, declaring that "We have always hunted our brother monkey." They adamantly refuse to adopt complex hunting technologies such as guns, and they also refuse to broaden their meat obtaining strategies by hunting other animals such as deer. In the case of Raute hunting, these "traditional" hunting practices may appear to have remained static, when in fact they have been adjusted for contemporary political reasons. Rautes correctly intuit that if they were to practice broad-spectrum hunting, their capture of deer, pheasant, and other animals would create a conflict with farmers who hunt for sport and food. Furthermore, if they were to use gun technologies, they would enmesh themselves in trade inequities with farmers and so jeopardize their political autonomy. Rautes have thus come to the conclusion that adopting many exogenous materials and methods would have a deleterious effect on their way of life.

The Rautes' hunting and gathering is a large part of what they do, but it is not their only productive activity, and this is true of all foragers. Unfortunately, many academic studies perpetuate the myth of the full-time hunter-gatherer, neglecting to write about other aspects of indigenous peoples' lives. For example, foragers trade with others (either other foragers or farmers) in order to collect materials that they need or want, such as cloth, iron, tobacco, or "exotic" foods. Some foragers "produce" (collect for trade) resources desired by others. The Mbuti of central Africa collect bush meat for trade to villagers. The Batek of Malaysia collect rattan and malacca cane to trade to farmers. The most successful foraging groups gather only quickly renewable forest resources such as rattan, jute, wild yams, and renewable medicinals. They also learn to hunt in ways that avoid competition with farmers. The Rautes, for example, trade wooden bowls made from fairly easily renewable forest trees, and they hunt monkeys that farmers generally avoid hunting. Thus, contemporary foragers like the Rautes have created an economic niche that articulates smoothly with the dominant society. Foragers, especially in the modern world, cannot afford to be autonomous; they personify a state of economic, ecological, and ritual complementarity with the surrounding farmers.

But foragers and farmers seldom get along in such a smooth and seamless manner. Contemporary foraging peoples everywhere are engaged in everyday resistance to their surrounding dominant societies (Scott 1985). When they deal with sedentary employers during work and other interactions, this may take many forms of everyday "resistance," such as not showing up for work, work slowdowns, silence during interactions, running away, and so on. Subordinates seldom engage in overt forms of resistance such as union protests, letters of protest, or attempts to change laws; these actions generally lie beyond the abilities of marginal groups such as foragers and post-foragers. For Rautes to negotiate a law protecting them in their forested habitats, for example, would require them to lobby for change in government forums. A formal request for cultural autonomy is something that the Raute elders have made to the Nepalese government once or twice, but they speak at large public events with great reluctance. In the spring of 2005, for example, a handful of Raute elders allowed themselves to be transported to Kathmandu for a public event organized by an indigenous rights activist group. As one event organizer noted, "The Raute demand is that they should be able to exploit the forest resources free of interference because they have been doing so since time immemorial" (Lawoti 2005, 1).

The aim of some members of the hosting indigenous rights group, however, was to encourage Rautes to settle down and send their children to local schools. So when the Raute elders only announced that they "like their forested homes" and that "We wish to be left alone," the rights activists had mixed reactions. Another news report noted: "Unlike the Rautes, a pair of Lepcha tribals, who are also facing extinction, were well-informed and educated. Kumari Lepcha, who came all the way from Fikkal of Ilam, said she was pursuing [a] Bachelor's degree in Education. Professor Santa Bahadur Gurung, chairman of the National Foundation for Development of Indigenous Nationalities executive body, reinforced this idea, stating that 'the main objective of the visit was to motivate the Rautes towards development works.'"

The fact that indigenous rights leaders express mixed views about the Rautes and "development" reflects the general confusion over a complex issue—namely, the best strategies for guided social change in contemporary Nepal. While some indigenous groups have chosen to adopt the most recently introduced accoutrements such as cell phones and wireless computers, others such as the Rautes eschew such devices in favor of a conscious adherence to technologies and social practices perceived as traditional.

Because Rautes do not engage in physical resistance to introduced changes, their everyday resistance to change and "change agents" (especially development workers) takes the form of verbal duels, protesting statements, and elusive maneuvers such as "melting" into the forest. As I have mentioned in previous chapters, when people shower Rautes with questions about themselves, Rautes respond with evasive answers or even silence. When they fear that farmers will drive them out of a forest area, they quietly change camp, preferring to move along narrow goat paths on the forest edges rather than walk on the main paths used by farmers. When farmers suggest that they settle down and become farmers, Rautes respond by affirming that they are monkey hunters, not farmers. These subtle forms of everyday resistance are effective reminders of their profound need to be hunter-gatherers.

Together, these everyday acts form the Rautes' strategy of cultural resilience.[2] Though all cultures change over time, contemporary Rautes have survived with their cultural institutions intact whereas most other foragers throughout the world have not survived the encroachments of agriculture, deforestation, and loss of natural resources. As I reviewed the reasons for why this is so, I came to the conclusion that it is the resilient choices Rautes have made that have saved them from assimilating into the surrounding farming communities. Of course, it helps that Rautes traverse a region uncomplicated by the development of motorable roads, electricity, and airports. It helps that they never barter forest products that might compete with the part-time hunting of farmers who value deer, boar, and medicinals. And it helps that they choose to hunt the one animal that farmers are prohibited by religious taboo to hunt. But were these really coincidental factors or did Rautes make conscious choices that preserved their way of life?

My feeling is that Rautes did consciously choose to act in ways that increased their chances to survive, and that these choices constitute a form of cultural resiliency. For example, villagers in more easterly regions of Nepal—regions that now have motorable roads—recalled that Rautes hunted in their forest years ago but that they had not seen them for many years. This is because Rautes decided to limit their easterly territory, and they defend this decision by noting that "all of our sacred things are found to the west. We don't like to go too far east." While it is true that they value the Karnali River basin region, nevertheless they have chosen to discontinue their most easterly forays toward the Rapti River basin. As these examples demonstrate, Rautes pursue actions that amount to a program of cultural resiliency that, currently at least, enables them to avoid being assimilated into what would inevitably be the underclasses of the dominant society.

While Rautes are avoiding cultural assimilation, nonetheless an increasingly monolithic, global culture is taking shape that may have potentially harmful effects upon them, and even upon our human species in general. Do we really want all people on earth to conform to similar or common ideals, speak a limited number of languages, and share a limited number of beliefs? When indigenous knowledge bases are destroyed, who will know how to use specific forest resources? What happens when we need new perspectives on ethical and scientific solutions to new problems? If global cultural knowledge ignores indigenous knowledge systems, the lack of viable alternatives to environmental and ethical problems may have dangerous economic and environmental consequences. It might take decades for people to recognize the perils of monopolization and globalization of knowledge, economic systems, and languages, and the results will restrict humans' abilities to deal with environmental changes. As a species, we may be less prepared to adapt to those inevitable changes facing us in years to come.

It is important that we better understand and appreciate the uniqueness of people like the Rautes and the cultural richness of the Himalayas. To some people the project of learning appreciation of cultural difference may seem like a small, insignificant step. Yet countless times I have given lectures to audiences only to find that even educated adults question the wisdom of allowing the Rautes to live in their own way. Skeptics assert that Rautes live "like animals in the forest" and see them as primitive. It seems that many people, especially influential policy makers, are caught up in a worldview that champions commercial development and industrialization at the expense of other ways of living. This clash of worldviews lies at the heart of the Rautes' struggle for cultural survival.

The Rautes, like ourselves, are not some residual "caveman" culture; they are not stuck in a stone age. Rather, they represent a dynamic and contemporary people. Their society changes every year and with each passing event. Although it is true there were no researchers working with the Rautes one hundred years ago and no archaeological studies of Raute materials from previous generations and centuries exist, there is nevertheless no disagreement that Rautes, too, experience cultural changes over the generations.

Cultural Change

Despite the fact that archaeological work still needs to be done, we can surmise that the Rautes actually were different in the past than they are today. For example, historically they used to be more economically autonomous. Conceivably, Rautes in previous generations used to rely on rice and other grains much less than they do now; the percentage of foods, such as wild yams, that they gathered was higher than it is today;[3] and they likely relied not only on monkey but on a range of hunted game for their protein sources when human population levels in the Himalayas were lower and there was little or no competition with farmers for forest products. Further, Rautes used to produce fewer wooden wares for trading with farmers than they do today; but they did have wood-carving traditions even before intensive farmer–forager trade relations began. They were not bilingual in Nepali as they are today, but may have had to learn the language of local dominant polities of central Tibetan-speaking peoples who migrated into the cismontane region millennia ago. The nomadic Rautes and Rajis would have had political connections, and perhaps marriage alliances, in the past with other forest peoples such as Kusunda[4] and Chepang. They would have pursued tentative social connections with other Bodic-speaking groups such as Kham and Magar who reside in the greater region.

The nomadic Rautes may have had more patriclans than the two that exist today, and they probably sought out interactions and marriage alliances with others in their maximal language group—for example, the Raji and Banraji patriclans living along the Mahakali River. The Banraji have other clans, not just those of the Rautes' patriclans. When asked "What is your *jāti?*" a Banraji person will not give the patriclan names of the nomadic Rautes (Raskoti or Kalyal). They give other family names: Galdiyar, Barpelo, Khaniyale, Pacpaya, Patet(wa), and Rakhale. Members of each of these patriclans must marry a spouse from outside their patriclan. Thus, it is likely that there has been more cultural variability among Rautes in the past than there is today. There may have been a range of strategies, with some Rautes being sedentary and camping around rich riverine resource zones, others seminomadic, and yet others fully nomadic like those with whom I worked. It is even likely that the forest populations of Rautes were larger than today. British colonial literatures mention the decimation of the Ban Mānches by the local rulers of present-day Kumaun, India. As waves of Indo-Aryan–speaking Khasa, ancestors of today's western Nepali populations, immigrated into the region, they felled many forests and drove out or killed the *jaŋgali* Rautes. Access to forests would have become problematic, and forest peoples' populations would have decreased at the expense of the increasing and expanding agrarian populations.

Today, it is unfortunate that the nomadic Rautes, as well as their closely related brethren, must struggle to maintain their own cultural tradition. Constantly, when interacting with villagers, Rautes are called upon to defend their cultural heritage and practices. As Chandra replied to a village woman who wanted him to speak and live as she did:

> Since our language is given by God, we can't throw it away. In our language I have lived doing small things. What to do? You ask for big houses, buildings, agriculture, and paper to write. Since we are thrown in this forest by God, we make *koshi, madush, kăt*. That is our wish. You are thrown in homes while we are thrown in the forest. To eat forest greens and fruit is my share in life, while building houses and doing agriculture is your share. Oh God, I have my share to eat and my death to die. What can Chandra eat now? My work is to catch the monkeys and their babies and to become a shaman for the Rautes. We have no agriculture, so what can I eat? Chandra won't leave alone the baby monkeys given by God.

The issue of cultural resiliency is not as simple as complete rejection of all things Nepalese, however. Some Rautes adopt villager objects, while others favor maintaining the old ways: some welcome tennis shoes, jewelry, and tobacco available from farmers; others keep as distant from villagers as possible and eschew village accoutrements. Rautes are thus caught in an interplay between what Chandra described as a schism between the old Raute era and a new era, and they realize that they are part of a process of social change in the Himalayas. They are part of a larger political dynamic that grips Nepalese villagers and Rautes alike.

For several decades, Nepalese householders have been the object of development (*bikās*), exposed to the deeply held belief that their cultural practices are inferior to those of their neighbors in India and the people from countries that send Peace Corps volunteers and Volunteer Service Overseas youths.[5] Nepalese are taught to admire computer-age technologies, the English language, Radio India, the BBC, and posters of beautiful Japanese women. Is it any wonder, then, that Nepalese villagers eagerly discuss how to undertake their own cultural colonization, or "improvement," of the wandering, illiterate monkey hunters? The impulse is strong indeed. After years of being at the bottom of the development heap, here is a chance for the villagers of Nepal to tell another cultural group, the Rautes, the proper way to live.

Resisting such assimilation, Rautes have accomplished the feat of attaining cultural resiliency, not because they have clung to "caveman" habits and avoided the rest of humanity. To the contrary, they survive as contemporary hunter-gatherers because they have adapted their hunting techniques, foraging strategies, and even their songs and stories to meet the changing conditions of life in western Nepal. Raute cultural life is a work of art, a mosaic that the people have lovingly created from their deep knowledge of all their surroundings, both in the forest and as visitors in the Nepalese villages. The "real" Raute culture is not a monolithic structure of hunting, gathering, and trading, but something much more dynamic and interactive, containing bits of material gathered from many sources for incorporation into Raute social life. This is why, when we look at Raute society in comparative perspective, we must always bear in mind the particularity of each foraging group, acknowledging that each is based on its own history and political circumstances.

In conclusion, I would like to bestow an *āśik* blessing on the Rautes who helped me to understand the uniqueness of their way of life.

> May your sisters have lots of yams.
> May you have much salt and greens with your meat.
> May your sister's *dzhum* beer container always be plentiful.
> May you Rautes live like the *dubo* grass and never die out.
> I give this blessing and this book so that your people may
>   last through twelve generations of grandchildren.
> Thank you.

Appendix

Table 1. Ranked preference of common prey species

PREY ANIMALS		PREDATORS			
	Scientific genera	**Rautes**	**Banrajis**	**Hunting farmers**	**Tiger (*Panthera*)**[a]
Small-size prey					
Bats	*Megaderma, Pteropus, Rhinolophus, Hipposideros*		2		
Birds	10+ species		3	1	
Otter (2 species)	*Lutra*		4		n.a.
Large Indian squirrel	*Sciurus*		5	n.a.	
Fish	10+ species	3	6	caste specialized	
Monitor lizard	*Varanus*		n.a.	n.a.	n.a.
Indian Hare	*Lepus*			n.a.	n.a.
Medium-size prey					
Porcupine	*Hystrix*		1		4
Hanuman langur	*Presbytis*	1			3
Macaque monkey	*Macaca*	2			n.a.
Musk deer	*Moschus*			4	n.a.
Muntjac deer	*Muntiacus*			6	
Large prey					
Sambhār (large deer)	*Cervis*		7		2
Blackbuck (antelope)	*Antilope*				n.a.
Boar	*Sus*			2	5
Chital (Indian spotted deer)	*Axis*			3	1
Ghoral, wild goat	*Nemorhaedus*			5	n.a.
Swamp deer barasinghā	*Cervus*				n.a.

Notes: Wild prey species are ranked 1 to 7 according to reported hunted frequency with 1 denoting most preferred reported prey species, 2 denoting second most preferred reported hunted prey, etc. For tigers, preference is determined by hunt remains and fecal analyses. "N.a." indicates that prey is hunted but preference rank varies or has not been determined. A space is blank when a prey species is not purposely hunted for food, although opportunistic hunting may occur. Animals that farmers hunt for reasons other than food (as sport, to rid pests from field crops) are omitted.

[a] For frequencies of prey hunted by tigers, see McDougal 1977; for analysis of tiger scat, see Schaller 1967 and Shrestha 1997. Nepalese tiger feces studies find less than 7 percent cattle, buffalo, grass, eggshells, termites, and fruit. A recent study of tiger diet based on scats from Madhya Pradesh, India, revealed a similar range of tiger prey, including large deer (*Sambhār*), small deer (*chital*), cattle, wild pig, porcupine, four horned deer (*chausingha*), langur (plus blue bull [*nilgāi*], which is not reported for Nepal) (Karanth and Stith 1999). Data for Rautes, Banrajis, and Jajarkot hunting farmers are based on my own field notes.

Also note that leopards are endemic to the Raute and Banraji hunting territories. Both tigers and leopards are known as *bāgho* by Rautes and Banrajis. Leopards tend to eat more medium-sized prey—small deer, langur, porcupine, four-horned deer, jackals, reptiles, beetles, fish. They occasionally bring down large deer (*Sambhār*) too. Leopards are probably more common than tigers, so Rautes have to compete for prey against them more often than against tigers.

Table 2. Culturally significant plant uses by category

Use code	Food category	Edible plants per category
	Primary Foods:	
1	Roots, rhizomes, bulbs, tubers, corms eaten	11
2	Stems, leaves, sprouts, shoots, blossoms eaten	41
3	Fruit, nuts, seeds eaten	51
	Secondary Foods:	
4	Cambium, inner bark eaten	1
5	Mushroom, fungus eaten	2
6	Famine food	1
7	Beverage	3
	Other food-related uses:	
8	Sweetener, flavoring, chewing substance, nibbling, smoking	5
9	Aids in food preparation, cooking pits, food covering, wrapping	2
10	Notable animal forage for prey (monkeys)	37

Sources: This list, though incomplete, represents plants I recorded in Jajarkot District, Nepal, plus some plants recorded by other researchers, Fortier ethnographic field notes from 1986–1997 and 2004–2005, with secondary sources Howland and Howland 1984, Singh 1997, and Manandhar 1998, 2002.

Table 3. Edible forest plants consumed by nomadic Rautes

Scientific name	Common names	Uses[a]	Comment
1. *Alternanthe ra sessilis*	E. khaki weed; N. *gante phul, ākhle jhār*	2	Leaves and shoots edible as green vegetable
2. *Amaranthus blitum*	E. pigweed; N. *pahādi lunde*	2, 3	Similar to spinach; seed is cooked and used as a cereal substitute
3. *Amaranthus spinosus*	E. prickly amaranth; N. *bandani;* R. *māyaso*	2, 3	Like spinach; spines must be removed; very high in protein
4. *Ardisia solanacea*	E. marlberry; N. *damāi phul, khāli kāphal;* R. *halyune*	3, 6, 10	Lower-quality fruit
5. *Arisaema tortuosum*	E. jack-in-the-pulpit; N. *bãnko*	1	The tuberous herb's bulb or corm is boiled and eaten; must be thoroughly dried or cooked before being eaten
6. *Bassia butyracea*	E. Indian butter tree; N. *ciuri*	2, 3, 7, 8, 9	Nectar of flowers drunk like honey; flowers edible, seeds basis for alcoholic drink
7. *Bauhinia malabarica*	E. Malabar ebony; N. *tãnki*	2	Young, sour leaves cooked as vegetable, for flavoring
8. *Bauhinia purpurea*	E. butterfly tree; N. *tãnki*	2, 3	Young flower buds, young fruits cooked as vegetables; seeds eaten roasted
9. *Bauhinia vahlii*	E. camel's foot climber; N. *bhorla;* R. *mālu*	2, 3	Pods and leaves cooked as vegetable; seeds eaten raw, roasted, and fried
10. *Bauhinia variagata*	E. orchid tree, mountain ebony; N. *koiralo*	2, 3	Young leaves, flowers, and pods boiled as vegetable
11. *Berberis aristata*	E. Nepal barberry; N. *chutro*	3, 10	Delicious fruit, heavy composition, and easy to gather
12. *Berberis asiatica*	E. common barberry; N. *tilkuro*	3, 10	Heavy, easy-to-gather fruit
13. *Boehmeria rugulosa*	N. *githa;* R. *gethi*	4, 9, 10	Rautes use for bowl making, but may mix powdered bark with flour to make breads (like farmers)
14. *Botrychium lanuginosum*	E. grape fern; N. *jāluko sāg*	2	Fast-spreading, edible leaves
15. *Cassia fistula*	E. drumstick, golden shower; N. *rājbriksha;* R. *rājbrik*	2, 3	Leaves and fruits cooked
16. *Cassia tora*	E. fever weed; N. *chākramandi, chinchine, methighãs;* R. *tinkose*	2, 7	Vegetable; seeds ground for coffee-like drink; medicinal

Table 3. *(continued)*

Scientific name	Common names	Uses[a]	Comment
17. *Centella asiatica*	E. Indian pennywort; N. *ghortapre, golpāt*; R. *khocha*	2	Vegetable; medicinal
18. *Cinnamomum zeylanicum*	E. cinnamon; N. *dālchini*	8	spice
19. *Cirsium veratum* (*C. argyracanthum*)	E. thistle; N. *thākāilo, thākāl*	1	Roots chewed fresh, herb, medicinal
20. *Cissampelos pareira*	E. ice vine, velvet leaf; N. *bātula*; R. *musya belo*	1	Boiled roots ingested to alleviate constipation; treats gum swelling; taken internally for urinary tract infection, indigestion, colds
21. *Clerodendrum viscosum*	E. glory tree, Turk's turban; N. *tite, ghantosāri*; R. *titye*	2	Vegetable; medicinal
22. *Coelogyne ochracea*	E. silver orchid; N. *chandi gābha, changāri*	2	Calyces (flower buds) eaten as vegetable
23. *Colocasia esculenta*	E. *cocoyam, taro*; N. *kārkālo, pindalu*	1, 2, 10	Rhizomes starchy, edible; leaves cooked as a vegetable
24. *Commelina benghalensis*	E. day flower; N. *kāne jhār, ban kāne*; R. *kānema*	2	Vegetable; medicinal
25. *Crotalaria albida*	N. *bhedi phul*; R. *kose*	2	Medicinal; flowers cooked as vegetable
26. *Dioscorea belophylla*	N. *getha, ban tarul*; R. *nyuhri*	1	Tubers boiled and eaten
27. *Dioscorea bulbifera*	E. air potato, potato yam; N. *ban tarul, bhyākur, githa kukur tarul*; R. *ghār tyāur, nyuhri, dzyāhra, koi*	1, 10	Tubers boiled as vegetable
28. *Dioscorea deltoidea*	E. yam; N. *bhyākur, gune kauro, tarul, githa*	1, 10	Boiled with wood ash and cooked again for a vegetable
29. *Dioscorea pentaphylla*	E. yam; N. *chuinyan, jagate bhyākur, tyāguno*; R. *ghār tyāur, nyuhri, jyāhra, koi*	1, 10	Roots boiled like potatoes
30. *Drepanostachyum falcatum*	E. Himalayan weeping bamboo; N. *tite nigalo, tusa*	2	New roots/shoots cooked as vegetable
31. *Drepanostachyum intermedia*	E. [a type of]bamboo; N. *nigalo*	2	Shoot vegetable
32. *Dryopteris cochleata*	N. *liuro, nyuro, dāunre*	2, 10	Tender shoots and fronds are an edible fern that is cooked for vegetable
33. *Elaeagnus parvifolia*	N. *guyāli*	3	Fruit

Table 3. *(continued)*

Scientific name	Common names	Uses[a]	Comment
34. *Emblica officinalis, Phyllanthus emblica*	E. emblic myrobalan; N. *amala;* R. *aurya*	3, 10	Fruit rich in vitamin C
35. *Fagopyrum* spp.	N. *bhirin sag, bhade sāg*	2	Leaves cooked as a green vegetable
36. *Ficus hirta*	N. *khasreto*; R. *khahātya*	3, 10	Ripe figs eaten fresh, medicinal
37. *Ficus semicordata*	E. fig; N. *khãyu*; R. *kho'*	3, 10	Ripe figs eaten fresh; medicinal
38. *Flemingia strobilifera*	N. *barkauli jhar, gahate, chunetro ghans, bhatwasi;* R. *batya*	3, 10	Fruit
39. *Gonostegia hirta*	N. *chiple ghāns, chiple lahara;* R. *khasaruja*	1	Fresh root considered refreshing in summer; medicinal; soap
40. *Hippophae salicifolia*	N. *chichi, chugo*	3, 10	Ripe fruits are eaten fresh
41. *Holboellia latifolia*	N. *gulfa*	3, 10	Fruit
42. *Indigofera atropurpurea*	N. *sagino*; R. *hakunya*	2	Flowers used as vegetable; medicinal
43. *Indigofera pulchella*	N. *phusre ghāns, sakhino*	2, 3	Legume shrub with edible pods and flowers that can be eaten as a vegetable
44. *Jatropha curcas*	E. physic nut, purging nut; N. *arin, nimte, kadam;* R. *dekiro*	2	Shoots eaten as vegetable; medicinal
45. *Juglans regia* var. *Kumaunica*	E. thick-shelled walnut; N. *hade okhar*	3, 10	Kernels eaten raw
46. *Justicia adhatoda*	E. Malabar nut; N. *asuro, kālo basak*; R. *wašing*	2	Young leaves and flowers eaten as vegetable; medicinal
47. *Leptadenia reticulata*	N. *dabre, dore sag* (?)*, jibani*	1, 2	Edible leaves and roots
48. *Leucas lavandulifolia*	E. spiderwort; N. *kanthe jhar, galgabi* (?)	2	Leaves and shoots edible as green vegetable
49. *Medeola virginiana*	E. Indian cucumber; N. *kandmool*	1	Root tastes like cucumber
50. *Melastoma malabathricum*	E. Indian rhododendron; N. *thulo āyar, thulo chulesi;* R. *tupāri kāphal*	3	Ripe fruits edible; flowers adorn hair
51. *Mentha aquatica*	E. common mint; N. *pudina*	8	Spice

Table 3. *(continued)*

Scientific name	Common names	Uses[a]	Comment
52. *Morchella* spp.	E. morel mushroom; N. *guchi chyāun*; Rj. *bish*[b]	5	Eaten in June/July
53. *Morus bombycis, nigra*	E. mulberry, black mulberry; N. *kimbu*	3, 10	Fruit
54. *Mycopia* spp.	E. mushrooms; N. *Chyāu*	5, 10	About 13 types of mushrooms available; not a priority food for Rautes
55. *Myrica esculenta*	E. bayberry; N. *kāphal*	3, 10	Fruits eaten raw
56. *Ophioglossum vulgatus*	E. adder's tongue; N. *jibre sāg*	2	Vegetable
57. *Oxalis corniculata*	E. Indian sorrel; N. *chariamilo*; R. *chalmaro*	8	Leaves chewed like gum when fresh
58. *Phoenix humilis*	E. date palm; N. *thākal*	3, 10	Fruit
59. *Phytolacca acinosa*	E. poker weed, sweet belladonna; N. *jarionga sāg, jhāro*	2	Tender leaves and shoots used as vegetable
60. *Pinus roxburghii*	E. chir pine; N. *sāla*; R. *chyāri*	3	Nuts roasted and eaten
61. *Prunus pashia*	E. wild pear; N. *māyal*	3, 10	Fruit
62. *Pyracantha crenulata*	E. firethorn, Nepalese white thorn; N. *ghāngaru*	3	Ripe fruits eaten raw
63. *Remusatia vivipara*	E. hitchhiker elephant ear; N. *jaluka, kalo pidālu*; R. *pinda*	2	Young leaves cooked as vegetable; rhizome paste applied to muscular swellings; rhizome juice dripped on wounds against worms, germs
64. *Rheum australe*	E. rhubarb; N. *bhange chuk*	2	Leaf stalk dried and eaten as medicinal; rhizome used as stomach tonic
65. *Rhus javanica*	E. Nepalese sumac; N. *āmilo*	3, 10	Ripe fruits eaten raw; fruits are medicinal
66. *Rhus parviflora*	E. sumac; N. *sati bayār, dantya*	3, 8, 10	Ripe fruits eaten raw; leaves mixed with tobacco; bark paste used for muscle inflammation and injury
67. *Rorippa nasturtium aquaticum*	E. watercress; N. *sime sāg*; R. *dubākya*	2	Tender leaves cooked
68. *Rosa brunuonii*	N. *kuiyāsi*	3, 10	Fruit
69. *Rubus calycinus*	E. raspberry; N. *bhuin āselu*	3, 10	Ripe fruits eaten raw

Table 3. *(continued)*

Scientific name	Common names	Uses[a]	Comment
70. *Rubus ellipticus*	E. false blackberry, Himalayan yellow raspberry; N. *sunāulu āselu*	3, 7, 10	Ripe fruits eaten raw; roots, shoots, leaf buds, and fruit juice used as medicinals
71. *Rubus lineatus Reinus*	N. *ghempehel*	3, 10	Ripe fruits eaten raw
72. *Rubus niveus*	E. woolly-berried bramble; N. *Kalo āselu*	3, 10	Ripe fruits eaten raw
73. *Rubus paniculatus*	E. bear-berry, witch-berry; N. *bhālu āselu, boksi kanda, kāloāselu, phusre kanda, rukh āselu*	3, 10	Ripe fruits eaten raw; bark paste and leaf paste are medicinals
74. *Rubus rugosus*	N. *ban āselu, goruāselu*	3, 10	Ripe fruits eaten raw
75. *Rumex hastatus*	N. *kāpo*	2	Vegetable
76. *Smilax ovalifolia*	N. *kukurdāino, nadir*; R. *bhityāul*	2, 3	Fruit and vegetable; medicinal
77. *Solanum nigrum*	E. black nightshade; N. *bihi, kamāi, kamāri jhār, khursene*; R. *khajima*	2, 3	Shoots and leaves cooked for vegetable, ripe berries eaten fresh
78. *Solanum aculeatissimum*	N. *bhel*; R. *ban bāikal*	3, 10	Ripe fruits chewed as medicinal for toothache, headache
79. *Solanum erianthum*	E. potato tree; N. *dursul*; R. *khāuda*	3, 10	Fruit cooked and eaten; fruit applied to skin eruptions, other medicinal uses
80. *Sonchus oleracea*	N. *tite sāg*	2	Vegetable
81. *Syzygium cumini*	E. blackberry; N. *jamun*; R. *jabung*	3, 10	Fruit
82. *Taraxacum officinale*	E. dandelion; N. *dudhe jhār, phule jhār*	2	Leaves eaten raw or cooked as vegetable
83. *Terminalia bellirica*	E. belleric myrabolan; N. *barro*; R. *sidha*	3	Seed kernels edible, medicinal
84. *Terminalia chebula*	E. chebulic myrobalan, ink nut; N. *hārro*; R. *tupāri* (?)	3	Seeds edible, medicinal
85. *Thamnocalamus spathiflorus*	E. red Himalayan bamboo; N. *nigalo, tusha*	2, 3	Shoot vegetable; seed is cooked and used as a cereal
86. *Urtica dioica, U. ardens*	E. stinging nettle; N. *sisnu*	2	Tender shoots and leaves cooked as vegetable or soup; boiled with flour to make a porridge
87. *Viburnum mullaha*	N. *malāyo, kanda malāu*	3, 10	Fruit

Table 3. *(continued)*

Scientific name	Common names	Uses[a]	Comment
88. *Vigna sinensis*	E. cow pea; N. *bodi*	2	Vegetable
89. *Youngia japonica*	E. Japanese hawkweed; N. *chāulāne, dudhe*; R. *goibi*	2	Energy-giving shoots for a vegetable; medicinal
90. *Zanthoxylum armatum*	E. Winged Prickly Ash; N. *timur*	8	Spice used sparingly like black pepper
91. *Ziziphus incurva*	N. *hade bayer*	3	Ripe fruits eaten raw
92. *Ziziphus mauritiana*	E. Indian jujube; N. *bayer*	3, 10	Fruits are eaten; root, bark, and leaves used as medicinals
93. *Ziziphus oenoplia*	N. *boksi bayar, ā̄ule bayar, sita bayar*	3, 10	Ripe fruits are eaten; root juice applied to wounds

Notes: E = English, N = Nepali, R = Raute, Rj = Raji. Rautes sometimes gave the common Nepali name for plants, sometimes the name in their own language. Raute names are included when known. The total number of plant uses is larger than the number of species of plants because plants have multiple uses.

[a] See Table 2, Use code.

[b] About twelve edible mushroom species grow in Jajarkot. Rautes and Rajis only mentioned one type, which Rajis call *bish*. The other species that local farmers forage are from the following families: Agaricaceae, Auriculariaceae, Trichlomataceae, Clavariaceae, and Halvellaceae.

Table 4. Common cultivated plants foraged by Rautes

Scientific name	English	Vernacular names (N = Nepali; R = Raute)	Food types[a]	Comment
Amygdalis persica	Small peach	N. *chule āru*	3	Fruit
Cannibis sativa	Marijuana	N. *bhang, charas, gānja*; R. *bhānga*	2, 3, 8	Seeds roasted and eaten; resin, stembark buds, seeds, leaves used as intoxicant
Citrus reticulata	Orange	N. *suntala*	3	Fruit
Colocasia esculenta	Cocoyam, taro (wild also)	N. *kārkalo, pindālu*	1, 2	Rhizomes starchy, edible; leaves cooked as a vegetable
Dioscorea alata	Greater yam	N. *ghar tārul*	1	Root vegetable
Fagopyrum tataricum	Tatary, buckwheat	N. *tite phaphār*	3	Grain cooked as cereal
Pisum sativum	Garden pea, field pea	N. *thulo kerāu, sano kerau*; R. *kalāun*	3	Vegetable; medicinal
Prunus domestica	Common plum	N. *ālu bakhara*	3	Fruit
Prunus persica	Peach	N. *āru*	3	Fruit
Pyrus communis	Pear	N. *naspāti*	3	Fruit

Note: [a] See Table 2, Use Code.

Table 5. Estimate of (male) Raute food consumption

Food type	% Calories in monsoon (June–Sept.)	% Calories in dry season (Oct.–May)
Hunted meat[a]	25–30	25–30
Wild plants[b]	15–20	20–25
Fish	1–3	1–3
Domestic meat[c]	5–10	5–10
Grains[d]	30–35	25–30
Domestic plants[e]	5–7	5–7
Totals	81–105	81–105

Notes: Totals exceed 100 percent due to estimation range.

[a] Langur and rhesus macaque.

[b] Calorific consumption in the dry season relies on tubers, while in the monsoon/summer season fruits predominate; in fall, more calories come from nuts. Also, women consume more wild plants and fish than men, but there is insufficient data to estimate women's consumption patterns.

[c] Goat, sheep, pig, and chicken.

[d] Rice, wheat, millet, corn, and barley.

[e] These include the starchy potato and garden yam. Honey is not a significant source of calories according to nomadic Raute interviewees.

Table 6. Tree species used for Raute wooden wares and camp construction

Scientific name	Common English names	Common Nepali (N.) or Raute (R.) name	Raute uses	Uses in farm communities	Species density (kg./m^3)[a]
1. *Abies pindrow*	Fir	N. *salla*	Furniture[b]	Thatch, fuel, incense	300–400
2. *Abies spectabilis*	Himalayan silver fir	N. *bunga salla, talis pātra*	Furniture	Thatch, fuel, incense	300–400
3. *Acer* spp.	Maple	N. *phangaru, phirphire*	Furniture	Fodder, wooden drinking cups, agricultural implements	500–700
4. *Alnus nepalensis*	Nepalese Alder	N. *utis*	Furniture, wooden bowls, boxes	To relieve burns; erosion control; fuel, dye, fodder	320–590
5. *Bassia butyracea*	Indian butter tree	N. *ciuri*	Camp utensils	Wine, food, oil, fodder, fish poison, fertilizer, fuel, plates, soap, candles, medicinal[c]	600–950
6. *Bauhinia vahlii*	Camel's foot climber	R. and N. *mālu*; N. *bhorla*	Raute food bowls, walking sticks, nets, bags, ropes, thatching, plates, raincaps, edible seeds, pods, and leaves	Vegetable, medicinal, walking sticks, fibers, mats, fodder, containers	n.a.
7. *Bauhinia purpurea, B. malabarica*	Mountain ebony, Malabar ebony	N. *tānki*	Raute food bowls, walking sticks, rope	Dye, cordage, fodder, vegetable, edible seeds	670–820
8. *Bauhinia variegata*	Mountain ebony, orchid tree	N. *koiralo*; R. and N. *mālu*	Raute food bowls, walking sticks		670–820
9. *Boehmeria rugulosa*	False nettle	N. *githa*; R. *gethi*	Raute bowls from mature shrubwood, rope, bark; paste is medicinal	Medicinal, edible bark, tubers edible	n.a.
10. *Bombax ceiba*	Red silk cotton tree	N. *simal*	Rope making, wooden wares	Vegetable, medicinal, stuffing	300
11. *Toona cilata*	Red cedar	N. *tuni*	Furniture, wooden wares	Carving, medicinal, fodder	330–600

Table 6. *(continued)*

Scientific name	Common English names	Common Nepali (N.) or Raute (R.) name	Raute uses	Uses in farm communities	Species density (kg./m³)[a]
12. *Girardinia diversifolia*	Himalayan nettle	N. *āllo, āllo sisnu, lekh sisnu, thulo sisnu*	Rope making, net making, greens, cloth, ropes	Leafy edible greens, cloth, fishnets, rope	n.a.
13. *Diospyros embryopteris and D. kaki*	Indian persimmon and Japanese persimmon	N. *haluwa bet* R. *sāna*	Drums, fruit	Edible fruits	700–1,100
14. *Garuga pinnata*	—	N. *āule dabdabe*	Furniture, rope making, poles	Furniture, medicinal, twine	500–900
15. *Lyonia ovalifolia*	—	N. *āyār*	Bowls	Medicinal	n.a.
16. *Michelia kisopa*	(Magnoliaceae)	N. *chắp* R. *sirpo*	wooden-ware bowls, boxes	Construction, ritual flowers, fodder, flour from bark	500
17. *Mallotus philippensis*	Indian kamala dye tree	N. *rainu;* R. *rohinya*	Chests, medicine for indigestion, stems/leaves for hut-building material	Medicinal, fodder, dye	700
18. *Myrica esculenta*	Bayberry, boxberry	N. *kāphal*	wooden wares for trade, poles	Fruit, medicinal	900
19. *Persea odoratissima*	—	N. *Lāli, Kaulo;* R. *kāulo*	Wooden bowls	Leaves used for fodder	510–700
20. *Pinus roxburghii*	Three-leaf pine, chir pine, Himalayan long-leaf pine	R. *jhārro;* N. *Rani salla, khote salla, āule salla, salla dhup*	Boxes, medicine for cuts	Edible seeds, medicinal, needles used for keeping rodents out of grain	400–600
21. *Pinus wallichiana*	Blue pine	N. *khote salla, gobre salla*	Furniture	Fuel	300–600
22. *Rhododendron*	Rhododendron	N. *lāligurās*	Furniture, wooden-ware trade items, utensils; flowers used as hair ornaments	Medicinal, building material, fish poison, compost, insect repellent, ritual uses	575

Table 6. *(continued)*

Scientific name	Common English names	Common Nepali (N.) or Raute (R.) name	Raute uses	Uses in farm communities	Species density (kg./m³)[a]
23. *Sapium insigne*	Tallow tree	N. *khirro*	Furniture	Medicinal, fish poison	480
24. *Shorea robusta*	Sal tree	N. *Sāl*	Hut poles, walking sticks	Edible seeds, medicinal, timber, fuel, fodder, leaf plates, oil for lighting	930

Sources: Raute wood uses were compiled using my field notes and Singh 1997.

Notes: [a]Kg./m³ = kilo weight of a m (meter)³ sample of the wood species.
  [b]Singh lists all Raute wood uses as "furniture," which probably refers to wooden beds and boxes.
  [c]See Manandhar 1998 and 2002 for details of plant medicinal uses.

Notes

Introduction

1. The Raute language is generally called "Raute" by scholars, but a few use the name *Khāmci,* which means "our talk."

Chapter 3: Who Are the Rautes?

1. Naming foraging peoples is a politically contentious endeavor because many groups have been given derogatory names by surrounding populations (Albers and James 1986; Azoulay 1997; Gordon 1984).

2. As a form of impression management, Rautes (and Rajis) in far-western Nepal may adopt ruling high-caste surnames such as Bisht, Chand, or Pal.

3. In Nepali, the saying is *"Dullu ko bāsmati cāmal Dailekh pare bhokā; māyā bhannu sānu hoina, koṭ(h)ali kā rokha."*

4. I use the term "tribes" only when relating to literature that defines Rautes and other small-scale societies as such. The term is problematic for several reasons. First, "tribes" groups dissimilar peoples under one nebulous, poorly defined rubric. Second, "tribes" is a political concept used in contradistinction to the terms "chiefdom" and "state" to distinguish levels of political complexity. But the term "tribe" muddles our understanding of other aspects of a society (see Beteille 1986 and Southall 1969). Third, writers tend to use "tribe" as a euphemism describing a group as "unsophisticated," "uncivilized," or other derogatory terms. Fourth, at least one Nepali anthropologist correctly stresses that "tribe" is a term grounded in colonial relations that inaccurately describes the diverse people of Nepal (Dahal 1979).

5. The term *Dzanggali* refers to certain Tibetic-speaking peoples, but it conflates with the English "Janggali," meaning jungle people.

6. Chipula is still a Banraji forested hamlet today.

7. Reinhard revisited the nomadic Raute camp several times in later years as well.

8. The Raute terms for plus first-generation elders also are complicated by age grade. If Harka wishes to address his mother's elder sister, he will call her *yik-aiya.*

9. In the International Phonetic Alphabet, these terms are pronouced *jiya, ciniy,* and *ɲiya*. However, I transcribe Raute kin terms such as those for mother and aunt following transliteration conventions traditionally used for Tibetan, since the language of origin is Tibetan (or Proto-Tibetan). Also, Rautes have more complicated forms of address. There are more words to address a person according to their married status and to their position in the family as elder or younger among their sisters or brothers. Instead of calling his paternal aunt *ɲiya,* he could call her *yu-kuwa,* meaning "maternal uncle's wife." Instead of calling his mother "mother," he could call her an *u-ma,* "married woman."

10. I neglected to interview carefully enough in order to document terms for cross-cousins confidently. The only term in my notes when referring to MBS or FZS is either *lākha* (boy) or *pāya* (son). The only term in my notes for MBD or FZD is *pun* (girl) or *gar-hau* (daughter).

11. Ferry service increased when Maoists in Jajarkot removed the entryways to this suspension bridge. Between about 2000 and 2007, travelers needed to obtain permission from Maoists to have the stones replaced in order to cross the bridge.

12. Before 1950, the duties of the *katuwal* were to "execute official errands in the village" (Regmi 1978, 478). In contemporary Jajarkot, many villages still employ a *katuwal*. These messengers deliver information among villagers about marriage, political fights, agriculture, etc. They are paid a *khal,* a portion of household grain harvests, for their services.

13. For an origin story of Rautes descended from a Khas Malla king named Purwaj-Bahāti, see Nepala 1983. Also, many Scheduled Tribes in India likewise claim Kshatriya high-caste social status.

14. The Raute speaker provides a nonstandard version of one of the rural Nepalese folk origin stories. For example, the speaker does not describe the deity Maheswar as an incarnation of the god Shiva. Also, an alternate use of Braha by Kham-Magar living in Rolpa District describes Braha is a local ancestral god attached to a specific village territory; among the Kham-Magar, there are hundreds of local Braha deities (de Sales and Budha Magar 1994).

15. The word *bula* (*bhula, bulla, bhulla*) may come from a Tibetan source. This would possibly derive from *bu~bo-,* referring to the ancient kingdom and people of Bo (Tibet) plus the pluralizer *-la,* making the name mean in English something like "people of the land of Old Tibet." If the word is of Austroasiatic origin, however, *bhulla* means "nomadic" and would render their name as something like "the nomadic people." Since the Austroasiatic rendering is linguistically more simple, I intuit that the name refers to "nomadic people." Also, the Banrajis I spoke with did not pronounce Raute in quite the same manner as Nepali speakers. Instead of a dipthong, R*au*te, they used a glottal pause or stop—Ra'te.

16. In English usage, the adjective "Nepalese" is used to describe materials and social conditions related to Nepal. The adjective "Nepali" is reserved to describe the people and language. Nepali-language readers use the general modifier "Nepali" under all conditions.

17. Nepalis are also part of diasporas in which identity is based more upon imagined community than on physical place. For an example of Newar diaspora, see Lewis and Shakya 1988.

18. Voter registration lists are surprisingly accurate reflections of the actual population in *Jajarkot*. When I checked the population of villages from my field notes with the number of persons registered from 2046/47 b.s. (A.D. 1988) voter registration records in Kathmandu, 96 percent of my household population was recorded in registration lists. The remaining 4 percent were people of the Raut and Badi castes who were registered in the adjacent political ward. In addition, some Dalit low-caste people give a generic name; a fellow whom I interviewed named "Doté Bādi," for example, was registered under the surname "Nepali" as in "Doté Nepali." Doté was not trying to be deceitful, but among many Dalit low-caste groups using surnames is a fairly recent innovation in Nepal.

19. These statements occured in 1997, before the Nepalese state discontinued the monarchical form of government.

20. More material reasons for hegemony over foragers can be reviewed in Woodburn 1997.

Chapter 4: Forests as Home

1. Although note that in Hinduism some trees and plants are deified such as *tulsi, pipal, banyan*, etc.

2. Rodman's term "multilocality" is similar to the way the term "heterotopia" has been used by cultural geographers (Tuan 1977).

3. This is another name for the *rāni ban* forests that were instituted by the Rana government in the early twentieth century. Hunting was prohibited in such forests until the mid-century, when government changed hands (Stevens 1993, 203). Since then, *rāni ban* in Jajarkot have not been treated as protected but simply as government-owned forests.

4. For discussions of spirit possession see Hitchcock and Jones 1996; Maskarinec 1992; Stone 1976. A more detailed analysis of this Tamang man's situation is outside the scope of this book. Note however, that here "the forest" may be a metaphor for the man's state of social anomie. He had recently lost his job as a *maṇḍala* painter and felt socially lost and confused.

5. Rautes converse with villagers in Nepali, and they use the Nepali names *Bhāgvan, Bhuiyār*, or *Bārma* during discussions about God.

6. Among Mundic Austroasiatic speakers, *hor* is an important concept that refers to "man" in the sense of humanity and, in a narrower sense, to Mundic people and their ancestors (Bhattacharya 1970, 29). Among the Chepang, Tibetan speaking post-foragers, *horh* is defined as a genealogy, a line of descent, a clan (Caughley 2000, 284). Among Santals living in Nepal, their name for themselves is *Hor*.

7. The *twāāk twāāk* is the Rautes' onomatopoeic word for the sound of chopping wood. Rautes have many ethnopoetic terms to describe sounds in the forest.

8. Such pretenses among tribal peoples in India have a long-standing history. For example, the Austroasiatic-speaking Bhumij adopted the vegetarian model of caste behavior and proclaim themselves as having descended from Kshatriya lineages during their process of Kshatriyaization or Rajputization (Sinha 1962).

9. See Pandey 1997, 639–689 and Fortier 1995, 144–180 for overviews of Jajarkot history and architecture.

Chapter 5: Monkey's Thigh Is the Shaman's Meat

1. One exception is that Magar villagers in areas east of the Rautes do hunt monkey as food on occasion (Marie Lecomte-Tilouine, pers. comm.). There have also been recent unconfirmed reports of monkeys hunted and their meat dried to be sold in Nepalganj as "deer venison" to hotels and restaurants.

2. Rautes claim that they do not usually count things, as this plea for various numbers of chicks attests. In the Raute counting system, there are native words only for numbers one through six: *dā, ni, sum, pāri, pã̄*, and *turka*.

3. Kusundas are often called Ban Raja; both the names Kusunda and Ban Raja are exonyms. Their own name for themselves is Mihaq (for males) and Gemehaq (for females). With only a handful of speakers remaining, Kusundas represent a highly endangered language and cultural group.

4. While other researchers have reported that widows live on the fringes of the main camp (Singh 1997), I found a group of about five elderly widows inhabiting tents in the center. It is certainly possible, however, that some widows may have camped near their relatives on the fringes as well. One hunter who lived on the borders of camp regularly slept with his grandmother to keep her warm.

5. Anthropologists call sharing "reciprocity" and attach modifiers that describe its varieties, i.e., "generalized reciprocity," "delayed reciprocity," "negative reciprocity," etc.

6. For discussions of these exchange forms, see Blige-Bird and Bird 1997, Blurton-Jones 1987, and Peterson 1993.

7. The word *hit* literally means "kindness" or "friendship" in Nepali, but Rautes use it in its extreme form to mean a feeling of deep kindness that in English is best translated as "love." On the other hand, the word *mit* refers to friendship formalized by a ceremony in which two people exchange money, embrace, and become friends for life.

Chapter 6: Let's Go to the Forest and Eat Fruit

1. See Hildebrand 2002 for a discussion of *Dioscorea* use in Africa.

2. In contrast, Rajis of the Askot region, however, have recently begun trading yams to villagers. One Government of India official laughingly told me how a Raji woman offered to pay her land taxes to him in yams. Also, around the time of *šiva rātri*, Lord Shiva's birthday, Rajis provide villagers with wild yams from the forest.

3. The data for the 126 foraging societies is drawn from the *Ethnographic Atlas* (G. P. Murdock 1967). The data includes periods of ethnographic study prior to 1967, including "early contact" periods.

4. About 20,000 people, the Ituri Forest foragers are known in language literature as Bambuti and as Pygmies to the general public. They use smaller-grouped ethnic names such as the Mbuti, Efe, and Aka. The Ituri Forest foragers are located within the Democratic Republic of the Congo, formerly Zaire.

5. "*Dhārte rāmro ramṭori sāg, sagar rāmro jun / mānche rāmro dil baseko, tiun rāmro nun*." Another version of this proverb was recorded among Rautes in 1976, "Moon is beautiful in the sky. / Man is beautiful when you love him. / Salt is the best dressing [for food]" (no Nepali translation given; Bista 1978, 325).

6. US$0.38 in 1990 has about the same buying power as US$0.62 in 2008.

Chapter 7: Economy and Society

1. For related discussions of intracultural exchange in the hunting and gathering studies literature, see Bailey and Peacock 1988; Blige-Bird and Bird 1997; Blurton-Jones 1984; Burch 1991; Cashdan 1985; Gould 1982, Hawkes 1993; Kaplan and Hill 1985; Kent 1993; Peterson 1993; Sahlins 1965; Wenzel, Hovelsrud-Broda, and Kishigami 2000; Winterhalder and Smith 1981. For discussions of intercultural material exchange in the hunting and gathering studies literature, see Bahuchet and Guillaume 1982; Fortier 2001; Fox 1969; Gordon 1984; Lee and DeVore 1976; Morris 1982; Spielmann and Eder 1994. Discussions on spheres of exchange in general can be found in Piot 1991; Blau 1992; Bohannan 1955; Humphrey and Jones 1992.

2. For an overview of the classic characteristics of an egalitarian society, see Woodburn 1982. For discussions of variations in the political organization of egalitarianism, see Cashdan 1980, Kent 1993, and Wiessner 2002.

3. Rautes are known for digging their own water sources, not relying upon those made by farmers. In this case, Rautes retrieved water from a stream.

4. For a discussion of hidden exchange, see Berkovitch 1994; see Wenzel, Hovelsrud-Broda, and Kishigami 2000 for an overview of money use among foraging populations.

5. Rautes did not barter for millet or corn during my recorded observations. I did see one child in camp eating corn from the cob, and Raute traders were occasionally give a few corncobs as "tips" for their verbal performances and blessings bestowed on farmers during trade sessions.

6. I did not count transactions in Khalanga because of its large size. In rural villages, I found that most households owned at least one Raute bowl, but some of these bowls had been obtained many years earlier. Roughly, I estimate that in 1997 Rautes successfully traded a bowl with about 20 percent of the households in Karki-gaun, or about fifteen to twenty wooden-ware items.

7. I only massaged Sher's wife's sore neck and talked with her about her stress-

ful relationships. She had a sore neck that could have resulted from carrying heavy water vessels.

8. During June–October 1997, US$1.00 = Rs 50–60.

9. *Kalṭhākura* means "the Thakuri caste's forest reserves."

10. The suffix *–ji*, as in Karki-ji, represents an honorific that translates in English as "Mr. Karki" or "honorable Mr. Karki," and it is used during trading. When trading with villagers, Rautes like to be referred to as "–Mukhiya," as in "Mayn Bahadur Mukhiya," which translates as "Headman Mayn Bahadur." This honorific keeps the trade negotiations more equal and advantageous to the Rautes.

11. This fictive kinship blessing was also given to my research assistants, Rekha Lohani and Prakash Karki.

12. About US$2.00.

13. I only had the opportunity to observe interactions for three *mit* partners and record memories of several past ritual relationships. Each actually seemed contingent on the personality and circumstances of the partners. Some relationships seemed very friendly, while others were only for political purposes.

Chapter 8: The Children of God

1. The "borrowed gods" represent mostly Hindu deities such as incarnations of the goddess Devi, and local gods such as the Masta deities. They are written about in studies devoted to local Hindu and Buddhist deities; for more information about them see Bouillier and Toffin 1993; Gaborieau 1969; Hitchcock and Jones 1994; Kapur 1988; and Maskarinec 1995.

2. C. von Fürer-Haimendorf's 1938 ethnographic diaries can be accessed through www.digitalhimalaya.com/collection/haimendorf. This particular passage comes from Naga Diary One, 27.8.1936, p. 232, translated from the German by Ruth Barnes. Also note that there has been intensive Baptist missionary activity in this area since 1938.

3. In addition, one eighty-year-old Banraji woman told me that another deity was about as important as Diho and she called that deity Bujergalog. But she didn't elaborate, saying that I should speak with others who were more knowledgeable. The only reference I can think of concerning *Bujer-* is to a place due west at about latitude 30° north in the Pakistani Punjab named Bujer. Similarly, there is a city of about 40,000 population in Himalchal Pradesh called Galog, again at about latitude 31° north. Possibly, the deity Bujergalog refers to an important lineage deity or deity of place hailing from a time when Banrajis lived farther west than their present territory.

4. Among the Rajis of southwestern Nepal *Bhuiyār* is a collective term referring to all the deities of the village locale (Reinhard 1976, 284).

5. Daylight savings time is not observed in India and Nepal.

6. Rautes occasionally also "borrow" Nepali female deity names such as Malika, Kalika, Devi, Dudhe Bhainta, Seto Bhainta, and Kala Bhainta. Hunemithu and

Dudhemithu are probably also "borrowed" goddesses. They call upon these female deities when giving blessings to villagers during trade sessions.

7. The number seven is not explained. It is, however, the number used by shamans across Nepal, and also in the classic inner Asian tradition of shamanism.

8. All of these goddesses actually have the names of local Hindu deities. Kalika, for example, is an incarnation of the goddess Durga.

9. Note that the Banraji have different clans. When asked "What is your *jāti*?" a Banraji person will give patriclan names that include Galdiyar, Barpelo, Khaniyale, Pacpaya, Patet(wa), and Rakhale. Each of these patriclans will marry exogamously with a spouse from outside his/her own patriclan.

10. Rautes also tell versions of monkey fables from the Rāmāyaṇa for the benefit of villagers.

11. Note one exception experienced by Terence Bech when recording Raute songs in 1968 (pers. comm., April 23, 2002). After spending a day with Rautes tape recording their songs, he was told that he would have to leave. He writes that the Rautes threatened him that they would consider him the same as monkeys and treat him (kill him) in the same way if he continued to stay near their camp.

12. The *Ha'wa* can also be called by the Kumauni word, *Barari*, or the Nepali word, *Barāŋ*, when speaking with Hindu villagers.

13. Given that guns have been used in the region for about two hundred years, this term is a neologism. Possibly there was an older word that has been replaced by the Nepali word *banduk*, "gunshot."

Chapter 9: Cultural Resilience

1. There are a few remaining Kusunda speakers in Nepal, but they have assimilated into other cultural groups such as Rajis (Watters 2005).

2. A third strategy of cultural resilience, known alternately as revivalism or revitalization, plays an important part in reinforcing what are perceived to be "traditional" practices among some other endangered cultural groups. But in thinking about Raute dance, language, and other aspects of their expressive culture that might be amenable to revivalism, I found that Rautes do not really revive or revitalize any domains of their culture. They have not been proselytized by missionaries, for example, as other endangered cultural groups have been. Their language is used in all areas of social life, leaving no need to revitalize the language. In the next generation, a revitalization movement may become expedient, if Raute youths excessively drink alcohol produced by Nepali farmers, or if Raute women begin marrying Nepali farmers. At the time of this writing, however, neither of these early-onset culturally destabilizing practices has yet occurred.

3. A tangential but interesting debate concerns whether full-time yam foraging was possible in tropical rainforests (Bahuchet, McKey, and de Garine 1991; Bailey et al. 1989; Endicott and Bellwood 1991; and Headland 1987.) My feeling is that, since Rautes have lived in subtropical rainforests with 40–80 inches of rainfall per

year—ideal conditions for yams to grow in—long-term hunting and gathering was feasible during past millennia until conditions became cooler.

4. Despite some researchers' claims that Rautes were afraid of Kusundas, there seems to be scant evidence to support such antagonism. No defense of territories would be necessary and there was little overlapping of resources. Further, at least one Kusunda man was married to a Raji woman, and Rautes, Banraji, and Kusunda share at least one name for a hunting deity, suggesting that they at least occasionally intermarried and shared some similar cosmological views.

5. Literature on the political ramifications of development efforts is large; for a few relevant references, see Bista 1991; Ferguson 1994; Pigg 1992; Pigg 1993; and Stone 1989.

Glossary

This glossary consists of Nepali and Raute words that appear on more than one page in the book. Words are listed in order of the Roman alphabet, with long vowels following short ones and retroflex consonants following dental ones. Places and words with historically common English spelling remain in colloquial format. Botanical words may be found in the tables that make up the Appendix. Languages of origin are abbreviated as E. = English, R. = Raute, N. = Nepali.

achānu (N.). Wooden base or stump upon which wood-carving objects rest
ādhiyā̃ (N.). Half, a system of dividing harvests
bā̃dār (N.). Rhesus macaque monkey
ban (N.). Forest. See also *jaŋgal*
ban mānche (N. var. *ban ko mānche, ban vāsi, ban mānu*). Forest man or people
Banraji (N. var. **Raji, Rawat, Raut, Ra'te, Raute, B(h)ula**). Part-time foraging people, closely related to nomadic Rautes, who live along the Mahakali River basin and adjacent hills
bāsisthāne mānche (N.). People who stay or belong to a place; indigenous people
Berh (R.). Solar deity of the Rautes
bhulte (N.). A commercially traded plant with the scientific name *Nardostachys jatamansi*
bhut (N.). Ghost
bilu (R.). Meat strips; sacrificed meat
ciuri (N.; E. *chiuri*). *Bassia butyracea*, a valuble nut tree of Nepal
dāl-bhāt (N.). Lentil and rice meal
Dang (N.). District in western Nepal
dhāmi (N.). Type of shaman or religious specialist
ḍoko (N.). Large woven bamboo basket that is worn like a backpack
Doulikanato (R.). Female ancestral spirit
dubo (N.). *Cynodon dactylon*, a kind of Bermuda grass used in Hindu rituals
duši, dushi (R.). Morally wrong action
dzhākure (R.). Drinking cup (also *dāro*); the act of drinking
dzhum (R.). Raute wooden alcohol-storage container

gobar (N.). Fresh cow dung used in Hindu rituals

guna (N./R.). Langur monkey

Gurung (N.). Ethnic group of Nepal who speak the Gurung language

Horh (R.). Ancestral deities; human spirit

iya (R.). Completed mother, grandmother

Jajarkot (N.). Political district in Nepal

jaŋgal(i) (N.). Wild; uncultivated; from the forest (*jangal*)

jāt(i) (N.). Hindu social caste

jyuri, juri, jura (R./N.). Topknot of hair worn by men; likened to a langur tail

kãt (R./N.). Large wooden chest

Khalanga (N.). Capital of Jajarkot District

khāmci (R.). Raute term for their language; lit., "our talk"

koshi (R. var. *koshimāl*). Raute carved wooden bowls

Kumaun (N.). A historical region of India where Ban Raji communities live. Today Kumaun is comprised of four modern districts—Almora, Nainital, Pithoragarh, and Udham Singh Nagar—in the Indian state of Uttarakhand

madush (R.; N. *sandush*). Carved wooden storage box

maŋa (R.). Elder, village headman, elite person

mālu (R./N.). *Bauhinia* spp., a dark wood that Rautes favor for construction of household items

manāng (R.). Forest, upland forest

māta (R.). Rhesus macaque monkey

mit (N.). Ritual friendship

mukhiya (N.). Headman, village political head

Muluki Ain (N.). The legal code of Nepal

muri (N.). A measure of weight or volume equal to about 160 lbs.

Namaste N. from Sanskrit, meaning "Honor to you!"

nyuhri (R.). The mother root of a tuber; one word for a tuber deity

peṭṭi (R./N.). Sacred box, a box in general

prākrit(i) (N.). Natural, local, or unsophisticated behavior

puja (N.). Ritual ceremony

Rāji (N.). Name given to an ethnic group of western Nepal and northern India. The title derives from Raja, or king, and refers to a politically subordinate family of noble birth

Rawat (N. var. **Raut, Rāut**). A title of respect applied to various classes of people. The name Raute is related to this word

ropani (N.). A unit of land measuring about 70 square feet

roṭi (N.). Unleavened wheat bread, similar to a chapati or pocket bread eaten in the United States

sambhar (N.; E. var. *sambar*). *Cervis unicolor*, a deer equal in size to the American elk

sanskrit(i) (N.). Culture, cultural behavior

shikār(i), šikār (N.). To carry out a hunt

sisnu (N.). The plant *Urtica dioica*, which symbolizes poverty but is also a tasty cooked green vegetable

tāgādhāri (N.). One who wears the sacred thread

terai (N.). The southern lowlands of Nepal

ṭika (N.). A Hindu stamp or mark of blessing

varṇā (N.; var. *varṇāśram*). A Hindu social order that includes many social castes and patrilineages

References

Adhikary, Ashim K. 1999. Birhor. In *The Cambridge Encyclopedia of Hunters and Gatherers*, ed. Richard Lee and Richard Daly. Cambridge: Cambridge University Press.

Alavi, Hamza. 1973. Peasant Classes and Primordial Loyalties. *Journal of Peasant Studies* 1(1): 23–62.

Albers, Patricia, and W. James. 1986. On the Dialectics of Ethnicity: To Be or Not to Be Santee (Sioux). *Journal of Ethnic Studies* 14: 1–14.

Arnold, David. 1996. *The Problem of Nature: Environment, Culture and European Expansion*. Cambridge, MA: Blackwell.

Atkinson, Edwin T. 1882. *The Himalayan District of the North-Western Provinces of India*. 3 vols. Allahabad: North-Western Provinces and Oudh Government Press. Reprinted 1974 as *Kumaun Hills*. Delhi: Cosmo Press.

Azoulay, Katya Gibel. 1997. *Black, Jewish, and Interracial : It's Not the Color of Your Skin, But the Race of Your Kin and Other Myths of Identity*. Durham, NC: Duke University Press.

Bahuchet, Serge. 2006 (1999). Aka Pygmies. In *Cambridge Encyclopedia of Hunters and Gatherers*, ed. R. B. Lee and R. Daly, pp. 190–194. Cambridge: Cambridge University Press.

Bahuchet, Serge, and H. Guillaume. 1982. Aka-Farmer Relations in the Northwest Congo Basin. In *Politics and History in Band Societies*, ed. E. Leacock and R. Lee, pp. 189–211. Cambridge: Cambridge University Press.

Bahuchet, Serge, Doyle McKey, and Igor de Garine. 1991. Wild Yams Revisited: Is Independence from Agriculture Possible for Rain Forest Hunter-Gatherers? *Human Ecology* 19: 213–243.

Bailey, Robert, and R. Aunger. 1989. Net Hunters vs. Archers: Variation in Women's Subsistence Strategies in the Ituri Forest. *Human Ecology* 17(3): 273–297.

Bailey, Robert C., Genevieve Head, Mark Jenike, Bruce Owen, Robert Rectman, and Elzbieta Zechenter. 1989. Hunting and Gathering in Tropical Rain Forest: Is It Possible? *American Anthropologist* 91: 59–82.

Bailey, Robert, and Nadine Peacock. 1988. Efe Pygmies of Northeast Zaire: Subsistence Strategies in the Ituri Forest. In *Coping with Uncertainty in the Food*

Supply, ed. G. A. Harrison and I. de Garine, pp. 88–117. Oxford: Clarendon Press.

Bandhu, Cudamani. 1987 [2044 b.s.]. *Rauteharuko Sanskritik Adhyayan: Sankshyipta Pratibedan*. Kathmandu: Nepal Rājakiya prāja-pratishthanma prastut aprākāshiat anusandhāan pratibedan.

Barth, Fredrick. 1969. *Ethnic Groups and Boundaries*. Oslo: Universitetsforlaget.

———. 2007. Overview: Sixty Years in Anthropology. *Annual Review of Anthropology* 36: 1–16.

Benedict, Paul. 1972. *Sino-Tibetan, a Conspectus*. Cambridge: Cambridge University Press.

Bercovitch, Eytan. 1994. The Agent in the Gift: Hidden Exchange in Inner New Guinea. *Cultural Anthropology* 9(4): 498–536.

Berreman, Gerald. 1962. *Behind Many Masks: Ethnography and Impression Management in a Himalayan Village*. Ithaca, NY: Society for Applied Anthropology.

Beteille, André. 1986. The Concept of Tribe with Special Reference to India. *Archives of European Sociology* 27: 297–318.

Bhatt, Nina. 2003. Kings as Wardens and Wardens as Kings. *Conservation and Society* 1(2): 247–268.

Bhattacharya, Sudhibhushan. 1970. Kinship Terms in the Munda Languages. *Anthropos* 65(3/4): 444–466.

Biesele, Megan. 1998. Ju/'hoan Women's Tracking Knowledge and Its Contribution to Their Husbands' Hunting Success. Ms. 8th International Conference on Hunting and Gathering Societies, Osaka, Japan.

Bird-David Nurit. 1992. Beyond 'The Original Affluent Society': A Culturalist Reformulation. *Current Anthropology* 33: 25–47.

———. 1999. "Animism" Revisited: Personhood, Environment, and Relational Epistemology. *Current Anthropology* 40 (suppl.): S67–S91.

Bishop, Barry. 1990. *Karnali under Stress: Livelihood Strategies and Seasonal Rhythms in a Changing Nepal Himalaya*. Chicago: Chicago University Press.

Bishop, John, and Naomi Bishop. 1978. *An Ever-Changing Place: A Year among the Snow Monkeys and Sherpas in the Himalayas*. Kathmandu, Nepal, Centre for Action Research.

Bista, Dor Bahadur. 1978. Encounter with the Raute: Last Hunting Nomads of Nepal. *Kailash* 4(4): 317–327.

———. 1991. *Fatalism and Development: Nepal's Struggle for Modernization*. Calcutta: Orient Longman.

Blaikie, Piers, and Harold Brookfield. 1987. *Land Degradation and Society*. London: Methuen.

Blau, Peter M. 1992. *Exchange and Power in Social Life*. New Brunswick, NJ: Transaction Pub.

Blige-Bird, Rebecca, and D. W. Bird. 1997. Delayed Reciprocity and Tolerated Theft: The Behavioral Ecology of Food-Sharing Strategies. *Current Anthropology* 38: 49–78.

Blurton-Jones, Nicholas. 1984. A Selfish Origin for Human Food Sharing: Tolerated Theft. *Ethology and Sociobiology* 5: 1–3.

——. 1987. Tolerated Theft: Suggestions about the Ecology and Evolution of Sharing, Hoarding, and Scrounging. *Social Science Information* 26: 31–54.

Bodenhorn, B. 1989. 'The Animals Come to Me, They Know I Share': Niupaiq Kinship, Changing Economic Relations and Enduring World Views on Alaskan North Slopes. Ph.D. thesis, Cambridge University.

——. 2000. It's Good to Know Who Your Relatives Are. *Senri Ethnological Studies* 53: 27–60.

Bohannan, Paul. 1955. Some Principles of Exchange and Investment among the Tiv. *American Anthropologist* 57: 60–70.

Bouillier, Véronique, and Gérard Toffin. 1993. *Classer les dieux? Des panthéons en Asie du Sud.* Paris: Editions de l'école des hautes études en sciences sociales.

Brightman, Robert. 1993. *Grateful Prey: Rock Cree Human–Animal Relationships.* Berkeley: University of California Press.

——. 1996. The Sexual Division of Foraging Labor: Biology, Taboo, and Gender Politics. *Comparative Studies in Society and History* 38(4): 687–729.

Budhathoki, P. 1987. Importance of Community Forestry Management in Remote Areas: Experience in Jajarkot District. *Banko Janakari* 1(4): 24–29.

Burch, Ernest, Jr. 1991. Modes of Exchange in North-West Alaska. In *Hunters and Gatherers: Property, Power and Ideology,* ed. T. Ingold, David Riches, and James Woodburn, pp. 95–109. New York: Berg.

Cashdan, Elizabeth. 1980. Egalitarianism among Hunters and Gatherers. *American Anthropologist* 82: 116–120.

——. 1985. Coping with Risk: Reciprocity among the Basarwa of Northern Botswana. *Man* 20: 454–474.

Caughley, Ross. 1976. Chepang Whistle Talk. In *Speech Surrogates. Drum and Whistle Systems,* ed. Thomas Sebeok and Donna Jean Umiker-Sebeok, pp. 997–1022. The Hague: Mouton.

——. 2000. *Dictionary of Chepang: A Tibeto-Burman Language of Nepal.* Canberra: Australian National University.

Chagnon, Napoleon, and Timothy Asch. 1973. *Magical Death.* Film. Watertown, MA: Documentary Educational Resources.

Charnov, E. L. 1976. Optimal Foraging: The Marginal Value Theorem. *Theoretical Population Biology* 9: 129–136.

Chhetri, Ram. 1994. Indigenous and Community Forestry Management Systems: Reviewing Their Strengths and Weaknesses. In *Anthropology of Nepal: Peoples, Problems and Processes,* ed. Michael Allen, pp. 19–35. Kathmandu: Mandala Book Point.

Childers, R. C. 1876. Notes on the Sinhalese Language: Proofs of the Sanskritic Origin of Sinhalese. *Journal of the Royal Asiatic Society,* n.s. 8: 131–155.

Cooper, Zarine. 2002. *Archaeology and History: Early Settlements in the Andaman Islands.* Delhi: Oxford University Press.

Cozzi, Sergio. 1992. *Rautes: Les cent derniers nomades du Népal.* Barras, France: Les Grand Chemins.

Crooke, William. 1890. *An Ethnographical Hand-Book for the N.-W. Provinces and Oudh.* Allahabad: Allahabad, N.-W. Provinces and Oudh Government Press.

Dahal, Dilli Ram. 1979. *Tribalism as an Incongruous Concept in Modern Nepal.* Colloques Internationaux du C.N.R.S. 582: 215–221.

Dalton, Edward T. 1960 (1872). *Descriptive Ethnology of Bengal.* Calcutta: Office of the Superintendent of Government Printing.

Dash, Jagannatha. 1998. *Human Ecology of Foragers.* New Delhi: Commonwealth.

Deur, Douglas, and Nancy J. Turner. 2005. *Keeping It Living: Traditions of Plant Use and Cultivation on the Northwest Coast of North America.* Seattle: University of Washington Press.

Doniger, Wendy. 1980. *Women, Androgynes, and Other Mythical Beasts.* Chicago: University of Chicago Press.

Dove, Michael R. 1994. 'Jungle' in Nature and Culture. In *Social Ecology,* ed. Ramachandra Guha. Delhi: Oxford.

Ember, Carol, and Melvin Ember. 2004. *Introduction to Cultural Anthropology.* Upper Saddle River, NJ: Prentice-Hall.

Endicott, Kirk, and Peter Bellwood. 1991. The Possibility of Independent Foraging in the Rain Forest of Peninsular Malaysia. *Research in Economic Anthropology* 6: 29–52.

Etkin, Nina L. 1994. *Eating on the Wild Side: The Pharmacologic, Ecologic, and Social Implications of Using Noncultigens.* Tucson: University of Arizona Press.

Ferguson, Anne E. 1994. Gendered Science: A Critique of Agricultural Development. *American Anthropologist* 96: 540–552.

Fortier, Jana. 1993. Indigenous Labor Relations in Western Nepal. *Contributions to Nepalese Studies* 20(1): 105–118.

———. 1995. Beyond Jajmani: The Complexity of Indigenous Labor Relations in Western Nepal. Ph.D. diss., University of Wisconsin.

———. 2000. Monkey's Thigh Is the Shaman's Meat: Ideologies of Sharing among the Raute of Western Nepal. *Senri Ethnological Series* 53: 113–147.

———. 2001. Sharing, Hoarding, and Theft: Exchange and Resistance in Forager–Farmer Relations. *Ethnology* 40(3): 193–211.

———. 2002. The Arts of Deception: Verbal Performances by the Raute of Nepal. *Journal of the Royal Anthropological Institute* (n.s., formerly *Man*) 8: 233–257.

———. 2003. Reflections on Raute Identity. *Studies in Nepalese History and Society* 8: 317–348.

Foucault, Michel. 1986. Of Other Spaces. *Diacritics* 16(1): 22–27.

Fox, Richard. 1969. Professional Primitives: Hunters and Gatherers of Nuclear South Asia. *Man in India* 49: 139–160.

Fürer-Haimendorf, Christoph von. 1976. *Return to the Naked Nagas: An Anthropologist's View of Nagaland, 1936–1970*. New Delhi: Vikas Publishing House.

Gaborieau, Marc. 1969. Note préliminaire sur le dieu Masta. *Objets et Mondes* 9(1): 19–50.

Gardner, Peter. 1985. Bicultural Oscillation as a Long-Term Adaptation to Cultural Frontiers: Cases and Questions. *Human Ecology* 13: 411–432.

———. 2000. *Bicultural Versatility as a Frontier Adaptation among Paliyan Foragers of South India*. Lewiston, NY: Edwin Mellen Press.

Ghimire, Premalata. 1998. Crossing Boundaries: Ethnicity and Marriage in a Hod Village. In *Selves in Time and Place: Identities, Experience, and History in Nepal*, ed. Debra Skinner Dorothy Holland and Al Pach, pp. 195–218. Lanham, MD: Rowman and Littlefield.

Gilmour, D. A., and R. J. Fisher. 1991. *Villagers, Forests and Foresters: The Philosophy, Process and Practice of Community Forestry in Nepal*. Kathmandu: Sahayogi Press.

Gilmour, David, and M. C. Nurse. 1991. Farmer Initiatives in Increasing Tree Cover in Central Nepal. *Mountain Research and Development* 11(4): 329–337.

Godelier, Maurice. 1977 (1973). 'Salt Money' and the Circulation of Commodities among the Baruya of New Guinea. In *Perspectives in Marxist Anthropology*, ed. M. Godelier, pp. 127–151. Cambridge: Cambridge University Press.

Goodale, Jane. 1980. Gender, Sexuality and Marriage: A Kaulong Model of Nature and Culture. In *Nature, Culture, and Gender*, ed. C. MacCormack and M. Strathern, pp. 119–142. Cambridge: Cambridge University Press.

Goodman, Madeleine, P. Bion Griffin, Agnes A. Estioko-Griffin, and John Grove. 1985. The Compatability of Hunting and Mothering among the Agta Hunter-Gatherers of the Philippines. *Sex Roles* 12: 199–209.

Gordon, Robert. 1984. The !Kung in the Kalahari Exchange: An Ethnohistorical Perspective. In *Past and Present in Hunter-Gatherer Studies*, ed. Carmel Schrire, pp. 11–22. Orlando, FL: Academic Press.

Gould, R. 1982. To Have and Have Not: The Ecology of Sharing among Hunter-Gatherers. In *Resource Managers: North American and Australian Hunter-Gatherers*, ed. N. Williams and E. Hunn, pp. 69–91. Boulder, CO: Westview Press.

Guha, Ramachandra. 1990. *The Unquiet Woods: Ecological Change and Peasant Resistance in the Himalaya*. Berkeley: University of California Press.

———. 1999. *Savaging the Civilized: Verrier Elwin, His Tribals, and India*. Chicago: University of Chicago Press.

Gurung, Ganesh Man. 1989. *The Chepangs: A Study in Continuity and Change*. Kathmandu: The Author.

Hallowell, A. Irving. 1975. Ojibwa Ontology, Behavior, and World View. In *Teachings from the American Earth: Indian Religion and Philosophy*, ed. Dennis Tedlock and Barbara Tedlock, pp. 141–178. New York: Liveright Publishing Corporation.

Harako, R. 1981. The Cultural Ecology of Hunting Behavior among Mbuti Pygmies in the Ituri Forest, Zaire. In *Omnivorous Primates: Gathering and Hunting in Human Evolution*, ed. R. Harding and G. Teleki. New York: Columbia University Press.

Hart, J. A. 1979. Nomadic Hunters and Village Cultivators: A Study of Subsistence Interdependence in the Ituri Forest of Zaïre. M.A. thesis, Michigan State University.

Hart, John, and Terese Hart. 1984. The Mbuti of Zaire. *Cultural Survival Quarterly* 8(3): [on-line edition] www.cs.org/publications/csq/csq-article.cfm?id=232.

Hawkes, K. 1987. Limited Needs and Hunter-Gatherer Time Allocation. *Ethnological Sociobiology* 8: 87–91.

———. 1993. Why Hunter-Gatherers Work: An Ancient Version of the Problem of Public Goods. *Current Anthropology* 34(4): 341–361.

Hawkes, K., K. Hill, and J. O'Connell. 1982. Why Hunters Gather: Optimal Foraging and the Ache of Eastern Paraguay. *American Ethnologist* 9: 379–398.

Headland, Thomas. 1987. The Wild Yam Question: How Well Could Independent Hunter-Gatherers Live in a Tropical Rain Forest Ecosystem? *Human Ecology* 15: 463–491.

———. 1998. Hypergyny and the Future of a Philippine Negrito Post-Foraging Society: A New Mixed-Blood Population in the 1990s and Its Implications for Hunter-Gatherer Peoples in the 21st Century. Paper presented at the 8th International Conference on Huntering and Gathering Societies (CHAGS8), Osaka, Japan.

Hildebrand, E., S. Demissew, et al. 2002. Local and Regional Landrace Disappearance in Species of *Dioscorea L.* (Yams) in Southwest Ethiopia: Causes of Agrobiodiversity Loss and Strategies for Conservation. In *Ethnobiology and Biocultural Diversity: Proceedings of the Seventh International Congress of Ethnobiology*, ed. John Stepp, Felice Wyndham and Rebecca Zarger, pp. 678–695. Athens, GA: The International Society of Ethnobiology.

Hill, Kim, et al. 1987. Foraging Decisions among Aché Hunter-Gatherers: New Data and Implications for Optimal Foraging Models. *Ethology and Sociobiology* 8: 1–36.

Hirsch, Eric, and Michael O'Hanlon. 1995. *The Anthropology of Landscape: Perspectives on Place and Space*. Oxford: Oxford University Press.

Hitchcock, John, and Rex Jones, eds. 1976. *Spirit Possession in the Nepal Himalayas*. Warminster, PA: Aris and Phillips.

Hofer, Andras. 1979. *The Caste Hierarchy and the State in Nepal: A Study of the Muluki Ain of 1854*. Innsbruck: Universitätsverlag Wagner.

Hoffman, C. L. 1986. *The Punan: Hunter-Gatherers of Borneo*. Ann Arbor: University of Michigan Press.

Howell, Signe. 1996. Nature in Culture, or Culture in Nature? Chewong Ideas of Humans and Other Species. In *Nature and Society: Anthropological Perspectives*, ed. P. Descola and G. Palsson. London: Routledge.

Howland, A. K., and P. Howland. 1984. *A Dictionary of the Common Forest and Farm Plants of Nepal*. Kathmandu: Forest Research and Information Centre, Department of Forest [sic].

Humphrey, Caroline. 1995. Chiefly and Shamanist Landscapes in Mongolia. In *The Anthropology of Landscape*, ed. Eric Hirsch and Michael O'Hanlon, pp. 135–162. Oxford: Clarendon Press.

Humphrey, Caroline, and Stephen Hugh Jones, eds. 1992. *Barter, Exchange and Value: An Anthropological Approach*. Cambridge: Cambridge University Press.

Hutt, Michael, trans. and ed. 1993. *Himalayan Voices: An Introduction to Modern Nepali Literature*. Delhi: Motilal Banarsidass Publishers.

Ichikawa Mitsuo. 2006 (1999). Mbuti. In *Cambridge Encyclopedia of Hunters and Gatherers*, ed. Richard B. Lee and Richard Daly, pp. 210–214. Cambridge: Cambridge University Press.

Iltis, Linda. 1994. Women, Hindu Kings, and Goddesses in Newar Representations of Geopolitical Space. In *Anthropology of Nepal*, ed. Michael Allen, pp. 349–357. Kathmandu: Mandala Book Point.

Ingold, Tim. 1986. *The Appropriation of Nature: Essays on Human Ecology and Social Relations*. Manchester: Manchester University Press.

———. 1987. The Appropriation of Nature: Essays on Human Ecology and Social Relations. Iowa City: University of Iowa Press.

Jacobson, Calla. 1999. Sociable Poetics: Representing and Interpreting Culture and Difference in Nepal's Middle Hills. Ph.D. diss., University of Texas at Austin.

Jeffery, Roger. 1998. *The Social Construction of Indian Forests*. New Delhi: Manohar.

Kaplan, H., and K. Hill. 1985. Food Sharing among Ache Foragers: Tests of Explanatory Hypotheses. *Current Anthropology* 26: 223–245.

Kapur, Tribhuwan. 1988. *Religion and Ritual in Rural India: A Case Study in Kumaon*. New Delhi: Abhinav Publications.

Karanth, K. Ullas, and Bradley M. Stith. 1999. Prey Depletion as a Critical Determinant of Tiger Population Viability. In *Riding the Tiger: Tiger Conservation in Human Dominated Landscapes*, ed. J. Seidensticker, S. Christie, and P. Jackson, pp. 100–113. Cambridge: Cambridge University Press.

Kelly, Robert. 1995. *The Foraging Spectrum: Diversity in Hunter-Gatherer Traditions*. Washington, DC: Smithsonian.

Kent, Susan. 1989. And Justice for All: The Development of Political Centralization among Newly Sedentary Foragers. *American Anthropologist* 91: 703–712.

———. 1993. Sharing in an Egalitarian Kalahari Community. *Man* (n.s.) 28: 479–514.

Knauft, B. 1990. Violence among Newly Sedentary Foragers. *American Anthropologist* 92: 1013–1015.

Lawoti, Sagun S. 2005. Nepal's Last Hunter-Gatherers: Time Is Running Out for the Raute and Their Nomadic Lifestyle. *Nepali Times*, p. 1.

Lecomte-Tilouine, Marie. 2000. The Avataras of Varaha in the Nepal Himalayas. *Himalaya: Past and Present* 4: 127–172.

———. 2003. Le paysage népalais, exégèse et appropriation du pays. In *Perceptions et Representations des Milieux*, ed. D. Smadja, pp. 165–192. Paris: INRS.

Lee, Richard. 1999. Hunter-Gatherer Studies and the Millennium: A Look Forward (and Back). *Senri Ethnological Series* 23: 821–838.

Lee, Richard B., and Richard Daly, eds. 2006 (1999). *The Cambridge Encyclopedia of Hunters and Gatherers*. Cambridge: Cambridge University Press.

Lee, Richard B., and Irven DeVore, eds. 1976. *Kalahari Hunter-Gatherers: Studies of the !Kung San and Their Neighbors*. Cambridge, MA: Harvard University Press.

Lee, Richard, Irven DeVore, and Jill Nash, eds. 1969. *Man the Hunter*. Chicago: Aldine.

Lefebvre, Henri. 1995. *Introduction to Modernity*. London: Verso.

Lewis, Todd, and Daya Ratna Shakya. 1988. Contributions to the History of Nepal: Eastern Newar Diaspora Settlements. *Contributions to Nepalese Studies* 15(1): 25–65.

Luintel, Yuvaraja. 1993. *Bhramanasila Raute: Eka Samajasastriya Adhyayana*. Kathmandu: Nepala Rajakiya Prajha-Pratishthana.

Lukacs, John R., and J. N. Pal. 1993. Mesolithic Subsistence in North India: Inferences from Dental Attributes. *Current Anthropology* 34: 745–765.

Manandhar, Narayan. 1998. Native Phytotherapy among the Raute Tribes of Dadeldhura District, Nepal. *Journal of Ethnopharmacology* 60(3): 199–206.

———. 2002. *Plants and People of Nepal*. Portland, OR: Timber Press.

Manzardo, Andrew. 1982. Impression Management and Economic Growth: The Case of the Thakalis of Dhaulagiri Zone. *Kailash: A Journal of Himalayan Studies* 9(1): 45–60.

Marriott, McKim. 1976. Hindu Transactions: Diversity without Dualism. In *Transaction and Meaning: Directions in the Anthropology of Exchange and Symbolic Behavior*, ed. Bruce Kapferer, pp. 109–142. Philadelphia: Institute for the Study of Human Issues.

Martin, M. K. 1969. South American Foragers: A Case Study in Cultural Devolution. *American Anthropologist* 71(2): 243–260.

Maskarinec, Gregory G. 1992. A Shamanic Etiology of Affliction from Western Nepal. *Social Science Medicine* 35(5): 723–734.

———. 1995. *The Rulings of the Night: An Ethnography of Nepalese Shaman Oral Texts*. Madison: University of Wisconsin Press.

Matisoff, James. 2003. *Handbook of Proto-Tibeto-Burman*. Berkeley: University of California Press.

McDougal, Charles. 1977. *The Face of the Tiger*. London: Rivington Books.

McHugh, Ernestine Louise. 2001. *Love and Honor in the Himalayas: Coming to Know another Culture*. Philadelphia: University of Pennsylvania Press.

———. 2002. Encountering the Forest Man: Feminine Experience, Imaginary Others, and the Disjunctions of Patriarchy in Nepal. *Ethos* 30(1): 77–94.

Mintz, Sydney. 1963. Review of 'Behind Many Masks' by Gerald Berreman. *American Anthropologist* 65: 1362–1363.

Morris, Brian. 1982. *Forest Traders: A Socio-Economic Study of the Hill Pandaram*. London: Athlone Press.

Morrison, Kathleen D., and Laura Lee Junker, eds. 2002. *Forager-Traders in South and Southeast Asia: Long-Term Histories*. Cambridge: Cambridge University Press.

Muir, John. 1967 (1873). *Original Sanskrit Texts on the Origin and History of the People of India, Their Religion and Institutions*. Amsterdam: Oriental Press.

Murashko, Olga. 2000. The Concept of an International Ethnoecological Refuge. In *Hunters and Gatherers in the Modern World*, ed. Peter P. Schweitzer, Megan Biesele, and Robert K. Hitchock, pp. 183–191. New York: Berghahn Books.

Murdock, George. 1949. *Social Structure*. New York: Free Press.

Murdock, George Peter. 1967. *Ethnographic Atlas*. Pittsburgh, PA: University of Pittsburgh Press.

Naraharinath, Yogi. 1955/1956 [2013 b.s.]. *Itihas Prakash Mandal*. Kathmandu: Itihas Prakash Samgha.

Narayan, Vasudha. 1997. One Tree Is Equal to Ten Sons: Hindu Responses to the Problems of Ecology, Population, and Consumption. *Journal of the American Academy of Religion* 65: 291–332.

Nebesky-Wojkowitz, René. 1959. Kusunda and Chepang: Notes on Two Little-Known Tribes of Nepal. *Bulletin of the International Committee on Urgent Anthropological and Ethnological Research* 2: 77–84.

Nepala, Purna Prākasa [Nepali-Yatri]. 1983 [2040 b.s.]. *Raute: Lok Jivan*. Kathmandu: Government of Nepal Ministry of Communication, Department of Information.

———. 1997. *Raute Lokajivana*. Kathmandu: Ratna Pustak Bhandara.

Obayashi, T. 1996. The Kucong in Yunnan and Hunter-Gatherers in Northern Indochina: Do They Represent an Old Cultural Tradition or a Case of Cultural Devolution? *Senri Ethnological Series* 21(2): 345–389.

O'Brian, Denise. 1984. 'Women Never Hunt': The Portrayal of Women in Melanesian Ethnography. In *Rethinking Women's Roles: Perspectives from the Pacific*, ed. Denise O'Brian and Sharon Tiffany, pp. 53–70. Berkeley: University of California Press.

Oota, Hiroki, et al. 2005. Recent Origin and Cultural Reversion of a Hunter-Gatherer Group. *PLoS Biology* 3: e71.

Oppitz, Michael. 1983. The Wild Boar and the Plough: Origin Stories of the Northern Magar. *Kailash* 10(3–4): 187–225.

Owens, Bruce. 2002. Monumentality, Identity, and the State: Local Practice, World Heritage, and Heterotopia at Swayambhu, Nepal. *Anthropological Quarterly* 75(2): 269–316.

Pandey, Ram Niwas. 1997. *Making of Modern Nepal: A Study of History, Art, and Culture of the Principalities of Western Nepal.* New Delhi: Nirala.

Pant, [no first name]. 2004. Landless Rautes Returning to Jungle. *Kathmandu Post,* May 30, p 1.

Parajuli, Pramod. 2001. No Nature Apart: Adivasi Cosmovision and Ecological Discourses in Jharkhand. In *Sacred Landscape and Cultural Politics: Planting a Tree,* ed. Philip Arnold and Ann Grodzins Gold. Aldershot: Ashgate.

Parish, Steven. 1998. Narrative Subversions of Hierarchy. In *Selves in Time and Place: Identities, Experience, and History in Nepal,* ed. D. Skinner, A. Pach, and D. Holland, pp. 51–86. Lanham, MD: Rowman and Littlefield.

Parker, H. 1909. *Ancient Ceylon: An Account of the Aborigines and of Part of the Early Civilisation.* London: Luzac and Company.

Peet, Richard, and Michael Watts. 1996. Introduction. In *Liberation Ecologies: Environment, Development, Social Movements,* ed. Richard Peet and Michael Watts, pp. 1–45. New York: Routledge.

Peterson, Nicholas. 1993. Demand Sharing: Reciprocity and the Pressure for Generosity among Foragers. *American Anthropologist* 95: 860–874.

Pigg, Stacey. 1992. Inventing Social Categories through Place: Social Representations and Development in Nepal. *Comparative Studies in Society and History* 34(3): 491–513.

———. 1993. Unintended Consequence: The Ideological Impact of Development in Nepal. *South Asia Bulletin* 8(1): 45–58.

Piot, Charles D. 1991. Of Persons and Things: Some Reflections on African Spheres of Exchange. *Man* (n.s.) 26: 405–424.

Pirta, Raghubir Singh. 1993. Imperilled Western Himalaya and the Deteriorating Man–Nature Relationship: A Case Study of Hanuman Langur. In *Eco-Crisis in the Himalaya,* ed. Vir Singh, pp. 165–206. Dehra Dun: International Book Distributors.

Possehl, Gregory L. 2002. *The Indus Civilization: A Contemporary Perspective.* Walnut Creek, CA: AltaMira Press.

Rai, Nanda K. 1985. *People of the Stones, the Chepangs of Central Nepal.* Kathmandu: Centre for Nepal and Asian Studies, Tribhuvan University.

Regmi, Mahesh C. 1978 (1963). *Land Tenure and Taxation in Nepal.* Kathmandu: Ratna Pustak Bhandar.

Reinhard, Johan. 1974. The Raute: Notes on a Nomadic Hunting and Gathering Tribe of Nepal. *Kailash* 2(4): 233–271.

———. 1976. Shamanism among the Raji of Southwest Nepal. In *Spirit Possession in the Nepal Himalayas,* ed. Rex Jones John Hitchcock, pp. 263–292. Warminster, PA: Aris and Phillips.

Rival, Laura. 1996. Blowpipes and Spears. In *Nature and Society: Anthropological Perspectives,* ed. Philippe Descola and Giselle Palsson. London: Routledge.

Rodman, Margaret. 1992. Empowering Place: Multilocality and Multivocality. *American Anthropologist* 94: 640–656.

Roscoe, P. R. 1990. The Bow and Spreadnet: Ecological Origins of Hunting Technology. *American Anthropologist* 92: 691–701.

Ross, Anne Helen. 1978. *Catalog of the Terence R. Bech Nepal Music Research Collection*. Bloomington: Indiana University, Folklore Institute, Archives of Traditional Music.

Sahi, Krishna Bahadur, and Ganesa Bahadura Ji. 2000. *Raute Jati, Eka Choto Cinari*. Kathmandu: Gramina Utthana Samaja Nepala.

Sahlins, Marshall. 1965. On the Sociology of Primitive Exchange. In *The Relevance of Models for Social Anthropology*, ed. Michael Banton. New York: Routledge.

Sales, Anne de, with R. K. Budha Magar. 1994. Quand le chamane fait danser les sorcières: Un voyage en pays Magar. *Cahiers de Littérature Orale* 35: 85–121.

Sarasin, Paul, and Fritz Sarasin. 1893. *Ergebnesse naturwissenschaftlicher Forschungen auf Ceylon in den Jahren 1884–86*. Wiesbaden: C. W. Kreidel's Verlag.

Schaller, George. 1967. *The Deer and the Tiger*. Chicago: University of Chicago Press.

Scott, James C. 1985. *Weapons of the Weak: Everyday Forms of Peasant Resistance*. New Haven, CT: Yale University Press.

Seligmann, Charles, and Brenda Seligmann. 1911. *The Veddas*. Cambridge: Cambridge University Press.

Shields, Rob. 1991. *Places on the Margin: Alternative Geographies of Modernity*. London and New York: Routledge.

Shrestha, Tej Kumar. 1997. *Mammals of Nepal*. Kathmandu: R. K. Printers.

Singh, Nanda Bahadur. 1997. *The Endangered Raute Tribe: Ethnobiology and Biodiversity*. Kathmandu: Global Research Carrel for Ethnobiology.

Sinha, Surajit. 1962. State Formation and Rajput Myth in Tribal Central India. *Man in India* 42(1): 35–80.

Skaria, Ajay. 1999. *Hybrid Histories: Forests, Frontiers and Wildness in Western India*. Delhi: Oxford.

Southall, Aidan W. 1969. The Illusion of Tribe. *Journal of Asian and African Studies* 1–2: 28–50.

Spielmann, Katherine, and James F. Eder. 1994. Hunters and Farmers: Then and Now. *Annual Review of Anthropology* 23: 303–323.

Stevens, Stanley F. 1993. *Claiming the High Ground: Sherpas, Subsistence and Environmental Change in the Highest Himalaya*. Berkeley: University of California Press.

Stiles, Daniel. 1998. The Mikea Hunter-Gatherers of Southwest Madagascar: Ecology and Socioeconomics. *African Studies Monographs* 19(3): 127–148.

Stone, Linda. 1976. Concepts of Illness and Curing in a Central Nepal Village. *Contributions to Nepalese Studies* 3: 70–79.

———. 1989. Cultural Crossroads of Community Participation in Development: A Case from Nepal. *Human Organization* 48(3): 206–213.

Strathern, Marilyn. 1980. No Nature, No Culture: The Hagen Case. In *Nature,*

Culture, and Gender, ed. Carol MacCormack and Marilyn Strathern. Cambridge: Cambridge University Press.

Trail, G. W. 1828. Statistical Sketch of Kamaon. *Asiatick Researches* 16: 137–234.

Tuan, Yi-Fu. 1977. *Space and Place: The Perspective of Experience.* Minneapolis: University of Minnesota Press.

Turner, Ralph Lilley. 1931. *A Comparative and Etymological Dictionary of the Nepali Language.* London: K. Paul, Trench, Trubner. www.dsal.uchicago.edu/dictionaries/ turner.

Tylor, Edward Burnett. 1871. *Primitive Culture: Researches into the Development of Mythology, Philosophy, Religion, Art, and Custom.* London: J. Murray.

Valli, Eric. 1998. Golden Harvest of the Raji. *National Geographic Magazine* 193: 84–105.

Van Driem, George. 2001. *Languages of the Himalayas.* Leiden: Brill.

Watters, David. 2005. *Notes on Kusunda Grammar: A Linguistic Isolate of Nepal.* Kathmandu: National Foundation for the Development of Indigenous Nationalities.

Wenzel, George, G. Hovelsrud-Broda, and N. Kishigami, eds. 2000. *The Social Economy of Sharing: Resource Allocation and Modern Hunter-Gatherers.* Senri Ethnological Series, vol. 53. Osaka: National Museum of Ethnology.

Wezler, Albrecht, and Michael Witzel. 1995. Early Indian History: Linguistic and Textual Parameters. In *The Indo-Aryans of Ancient South Asia,* ed. George Erdosy, pp. 85–125. Berlin: de Gruyter.

Whatmore, Sarah. 2002. *Hybrid Geographies: Natures, Cultures, Spaces.* London and Thousand Oaks, CA: SAGE.

Wiessner, Polly. 1977. Hxaro: A Regional System of Reciprocity for Reducing Risk among the !Kung San. Ph.D. diss., University of Michigan.

———. 2002. Vines of Complexity: Egalitarian Structures and the Institutionalization of Inequality among the Enga. *Current Anthropology* 43(2): 233–269.

Wilmsen, Edwin, ed. 1989. *We Are Here: Politics of Aboriginal Land Tenure.* Berkeley: University of California Press.

Wilmsen, Edwin N., and James R. Denbow. 1990. Paradigmatic History of San-Speaking Peoples and Current Attempts at Revision. *Current Anthropology* 31: 489–524.

Winterhalder, Bruce, and E. Smith. 1981. Hunter-Gatherer Foraging Strategies: Ethnographic and Archaeological Analyses. Chicago: University of Chicago Press.

Wolf, Eric R. 1994. Perilous Ideas: Race, Culture, People. *Current Anthropology* 35(1): 1–12.

Woodburn, James. 1982. Egalitarian Societies. *Man* (n.s.) 17: 431–451.

———. 1997. Indigenous Discrimination: The Ideological Basis for Local Discrimination against Hunter-Gatherer Minorities in Sub-Saharan Africa. *Ethnic and Racial Studies* 20: 345–362.

Index

aboriginality, 3, 25, 30, 38, 41
Aché of Paraguay, 76, 95–96
Adhikary, Ashim, 150
adoption of agriculture, 109–112
altruism. *See* love
ancestral history of Rautes, 30–35
Andaman Islanders, 3, 157
Anishinabe, 3, 106, 143
arboreal classifications, 128–130
assimilation, 1–2, 9, 15, 28, 110–112,
    165–166, 193; through marriage,
    41–44
Austroasiatic languages, 31–32, 67,
    146–148, 188–190

Bailey, Robert, 87, 106–107, 125
Banraji, 4–5, 32–33, 35–38, 48, 78–79, 81,
    85, 188, 192–196; clans, 167–168;
    deities, 146–150, 155–156; fishing,
    104; hunting, 85, 91, 161, 173; trade,
    116, 190; settlements, 93, 187; yam
    gathering, 103
Batek of Malaysia, 3, 76, 164
Bech, Terence, 34
begging and blessings during barter
    sessions, 137–140
biculturalism. *See* impression
    management
biocultural diversity, 6–7, 160–162
Bird-David, Nurit, 96, 143
Birhor, 3, 25, 31, 39, 85, 150
Bista, Dor Bahadur, 35
blessings. *See* verbal art

Bodenhorn, Barbara, 154
Bourdieu, Pierre, 112
Brightman, Robert, 87, 143–144, 154
Bushmen of southern Africa, 2, 25, 101,
    107

California, 161; Baja, 62; Mission Indians,
    3, 101
camps. *See* forest camps
caste. *See* social status and caste hierarchy
Chepang, 49, 66, 78–79, 85, 91–93, 103,
    105, 146, 152, 161–162, 167, 189
collectors. *See* foraging
commoditization of wooden wares,
    126–127
communist parties, 52. *See also* govern
    ment of Nepal's politics and interests
controlled burning, 130
Cooper, Zarine, 157
cosmologies. *See* religious beliefs
cultural areas and territories, 25, 31–32,
    37, 166, 192, 194
cultural change, 167–169. *See also*
    cultural resiliency; globalization
cultural diversity, 159–163
cultural geography, 35–38
cultural resiliency, 2, 8, 163–169, 193
cultural reversion. *See* devolution

Dalton, Edward T., 30–31
dancing, 44, 55, 83, 102, 118–119, 122,
    125, 146–147, 157, 193
Dash, Jagannatha, 38–39

death, 151
deforestation, 4, 81, 165, 167
deities. *See* religious beliefs, about deities
development. *See* hegemonic change
devolution, 28, 38–41, 47–48, 81, 165
diet, 7, 10, 36, 95, 125–126, 173–181;
    choices, 112–113; complexity of,
    101–106; famine foods, 101; grains
    in, 17, 33, 95, 106–109, 121; vegetable
    proteins, 101–102. *See also* foraging
Dravidian language, 30–32, 67, 146

econiches, 4, 28–29, 105, 161, 164
edible wild plants, 100, 104–105, 175–180
egalitarianism, 8, 28, 36, 117, 140–141,
    191
encapsulation, 1, 38, 80
endangered languages, 160–162
exchange. *See* trade and exchange

fictive kinship, 95, 139, 192
ficus as keystone species, 101–103, 177
fire. *See* controlled burning
fishing, 27, 33, 44–45, 50–51, 78, 104–
    105, 107–108, 173
food collectors. *See* foraging
foragers: adaptive strategies of, 97, 161–
    162, 166–169; defined, 2; diversity of,
    30, 159–169; in history, 1–2, 30–35,
    42, 46–47, 54; horticulture and, 28,
    95, 104; political choices, 55–60, 159;
    Raute as, 3–4, 10, 24–26; religious
    beliefs of, 96, 142–144; social
    relations, 140, 154, 157; trade and,
    28, 134–135, 164
foraging, 18, 77, 175–181; broad-
    spectrum versus specialized strate-
    gies, 36, 78–80, 105, 163; among
    farmers, 63, 105, 180; and trade,
    106–109, 121
forest, 195–196; animals of, 26, 143,
    152–154; deciduous, 82; deification
    of, 14, 22, 68, 85, 142, 147; govern-
    ment interests in, 72–73, 122; as
    home, 17, 59; hunting in, 22, 36,
    77–78, 86, 91–92, 193; meanings of,
    58–63, 73–74; in prose and poetry,

63–64, 96, 102–103, 151, 168;
    reserves, 126, 192–193; as sacred
    or profane, 65–66; as signifying
    identity, 14, 27, 32, 45, 48, 51, 66–67,
    195; spirits, 150–151; subsistence
    foods, 69, 102–113; trade products,
    28, 190; types, 4, 18, 59; as wild
    places, 60–62
forest camps, 18, 21, 36, 45, 50, 69–72,
    165
forest management policies and politics,
    5, 52–53, 63, 68, 159, 164
forest medicinals, 14, 20, 55, 59, 78,
    101–102, 105, 166, 175–180
forest peoples, 4–5, 14, 16, 25, 30–31, 34,
    43, 49, 66–69, 167
forest resources, 5, 14, 107, 126, 164
Foucault, Michel, 62, 73
Fürer-Haimendorf, Christoph von, 146,
    192

Gardner, Peter, 28, 87
gifting, 83–84, 95, 124, 137, 140, 154. *See
    also* trade and exchange
globalization, 6, 159–160, 166
government of Nepal's politics and
    interests, 5, 26–27, 43, 50–51, 58, 63,
    72–74
Gurung, 43, 49, 196

Hadza of Tanzania, 111
Hart, John, 107
hegemonic change, 11–12, 26, 44, 54,
    59–61, 159–160, 165–167, 194. *See
    also* cultural resiliency
heterarchy, 27
Hill Kharia, 31, 146–147
Hindu religious traditions, 32, 46, 60–66,
    103, 137, 144, 151–152, 155, 189,
    192–193, 195–196. *See also* religious
    beliefs
Howell, Signe, 60
human rights. *See* cultural diversity
hunted animals, 31, 33, 36–37, 44–45,
    76–80, 82, 87–89, 143–144, 146, 151,
    163, 166, 173. *See also* foraging;
    monkey hunting

hunting preparations, 83–85. *See also* monkey hunting
hunting tools, 8, 14, 36, 78–81, 92–93, 104

identity, 24–26, 78, 112; emic forms of, 22, 25, 26–27, 130, 155; ethnic, 38–41; etic forms of, 25–26, 189; as monkey hunters, 72–75; politics and, 53–56; social roles and, 27, 115. *See also* ancestral history of Rautes; nationality
Iltis, Linda, 65
impression management, 9, 28–29, 46, 71, 145, 187
India, 4–5, 20–21, 27–30, 49–50, 53–54, 58–60, 68–69, 168–169, 173, 188
Ituri Forest Peoples, 86–87, 106–107, 164, 191

Jajarkot District, xi, 3, 7–8, 13–14, 43–45, 115–116, 120

Kalahari San. *See* Bushmen of southern Africa
Kelly, Robert, 98
kinship and marriage, 4, 22, 39–41, 95–96, 148, 167–168, 188; clan names, 24, 39–40, 45, 151, 168; hypergamy among caste Hindus, 42; with other sentient beings, 67–69, 74, 143–153, 157–158. *See also* fictive kinship
Kumaun (Kumaon), 32–33, 48–50, 85, 104, 116, 168, 193

language: Austroasiatic, 31; Banraji, 48; Chepang, 79; domination, 1, 4, 42, 159, 162, 169; Dravidian, 31; endangered, 160–161; indigenous knowledge of, 162; memes, 158; Nepali, 13, 50–51, 85, 188; Rautes', xi, 4, 6, 15, 27, 29, 33, 35, 37, 43, 59, 87, 167–168, 187–188, 193, 195; Tibeto-Burman, 32, 39
Lecomte-Tilouine, Marie, 65
Lee, Richard, 87, 144
Lefebvre, Henri, 53

love, 22, 29, 65–66, 97–98, 190–191
Luintel, Yuvaraja, 35

Magars of central Nepal, 47–49, 65–68, 167, 188, 190
Manandhar, Narayan, 35, 59, 174
Maoist activities and politics, 7, 53, 57, 63, 73, 188. *See also* communist parties; government of Nepal's politics and interests
marriage. *See* kinship and marriage
Marriott, McKim, 61
Mauss, Marcel, 84
meat sharing, 93–94. *See also* sharing
migration, 17, 20, 28, 36, 59, 77, 82, 85, 167–168
Mikea, 28
Mlabri of Thailand, 41–42
modernity, 53–54
money, 117–121; limited purpose monies, 118–120, 125–127
monkey hunting, 85–93. *See also* hunted animals
monkeys: demography, 82–83; drawings of, 88–90; as food, 93–96, 108; food choice ranking and, 76, 80, 105, 173; historical references to 33, 167; hunting, 3, 5, 7–9, 14, 36, 68, 77, 85–88, 91–93, 108, 190; kinship with, 4, 67–68, 143, 155, 163; pests, 6, 78; prose and poetry about, 13, 75, 151–154, 168, 193; Raute identity and, 25–26, 76–77, 165; ritual beliefs about, 14, 45–46, 58, 74, 83–84, 96, 147, 155, 157; as sacred, 14, 83, 154; as tabooed meat, 112–113; tracking, 22, 36
moral goodness, 154–155, 195

Naraharinath, Yogi, 34
nationality, 50–53
Nepala, Purna P., 35
nomadism, 4, 7, 14, 188; and diet, 101, 103; disparagement of, 54, 66, 73–74; ecology of, 92, 99; migration and, 77; Raute, 4–5, 18, 20, 25, 29, 35–38, 42, 51, 188; storage and, 162

Ojibwa. *See* Anishinabe

Paliyan, 28
Peacock, Nadine, 106–107
poetry. *See* verbal art
population: of agrarian communities, 26,
    76, 168, 189, 192; Dravidian speakers,
    31; dynamics, 81, 167; of foragers
    worldwide, 38; of Mlabri, 41; of
    monkeys, 18, 22, 77, 82–83; of Rautes,
    4, 33, 96, 125, 168
prey species, 173–174
primitivism, 8, 26, 53, 57, 62, 167
"pure" hunter-gatherer myths, 106–109

Raji of Nepal, 4–5, 30, 32–33, 36–38, 85,
    193–196; ceremony, 85, 148, 192;
    farming, 109; fishing, 78; hunting, 92,
    104–105; trade, 37
Rautini (Raute women), 15, 20, 42, 70,
    86–87, 94, 97, 117, 119, 122–123, 127,
    133–134
Rawat, 30–32, 41, 78, 195
Reinhard, Johan, 21–22, 34, 187
religious beliefs, 45–47, 60–61, 84–85,
    112, 129, 138; about ancestral spirits,
    68, 145, 155–156, 196; and animism,
    143–144; about deities, 63–65, 68–69,
    144–151; as relational cosmologies,
    157–158; about supernatural animals,
    152–156; about supernatural forces,
    156
resilience. *See* cultural resiliency
risk reduction models, 95–96
Rock Cree of Manitoba, 143–144
Roscoe, Paul R., 92

sedentism: and assimilation, 41–43, 109;
    forced, 4–5, 14, 27, 37; recent, 23, 38,
    45; resistance to, 115, 165; semino-
    madic, 29, 36; temporary, 19
sentient ecology, 11, 26, 58–68, 142–143,
    147–157. *See also* religious beliefs
settlements. *See* forest camps; sedentism
shamanism, 11, 34, 37, 47, 89, 93–94, 120,
    147–151
sharing, 7, 26, 55, 90; demand and

request, 111, 118–120; theoretical
    models of, 94–99; of tools, 116–117.
    See also gifting; meat sharing; trade
    and exchange
Singh, Nanda Bahadur, 35
singing, 10, 98–99. *See also* verbal art
social relations: with farmers, 6, 53, 121,
    140–141, 164–165; with other
    sentient beings, 143; among Rautes,
    6, 26, 141
social status and caste hierarchy, 45–49
society, defined, 26
storage systems, 122
supernatural forces, 156–157. *See also*
    religious beliefs

technology: complex, 54; as determinant
    of social life, 36–37, 92–93; and
    hegemony, 60–61, 169; simple, 54,
    62. *See also* hunting tools
territory. *See* cultural areas and territories
Tibetan languages and speakers, xi, 32, 47,
    49, 65, 132, 167
timber species, 131, 183–185. *See also*
    forest
trade and exchange, 3, 10, 20, 28–29,
    37–38, 57–58, 86, 95, 104–109, 116,
    120–121, 164, 165; internal versus
    external exchange, 116–121, 141;
    invisible, 116; materials, 184, 190,
    191; negotiations, 47, 114, 134–140,
    192; partners, 140; of wooden wares,
    121–126, 128–133. *See also* sharing
tuber-based subsistence, 9, 22, 45, 57,
    59–60, 103–104, 176; of Chepangs,
    162; in prose and poetry, 108, 152,
    169; in religion, 143–144, 147

Van Driem, George, 158
Vedda of Sri Lanka, 38–39
verbal art (*bhanne kala*), 29, 63–66,
    97–98, 138–139, 151

wage labor, 18, 37, 45, 125, 144
whistle speech in hunting, 91–92
Wolf, Eric, 37
women. *See* Rautini

wooden wares: blessings of, 29, 137–140; construction of, 71, 121–128; curation methods, 132–133; historical accounts of, 33, 35, 47–48; materials and tree species, 183–185; meanings of, 130–131, 141, 151; Raute's own objects, 44, 81, 117, 129–130; as special purpose money, 118–120; as traded objects, 3, 19–21, 86, 104, 114–116, 124–125, 133–136, 191, 195–196. *See also* trade and exchange

worldviews, 157–158

yams. *See* tuber-based subsistence

About the Author

JANA FORTIER received a Ph.D. in anthropology from the
University of Wisconsin, Madison. She was a tenured associate
professor at Southwest Minnesota State University until 2003
and is presently a visiting scholar at the University of California,
San Diego. She has published extensively on endangered
cultures and languages of the Himalayan region with support
from the Fulbright Foundation, the National Endowment
for the Humanities, and the Wenner-Gren Foundation for
Anthropological Research.

Production Notes for Fortier | KINGS OF THE FOREST

Cover design by Julie Matsuo-Chun
Text design by Paul Herr, University of Hawai'i Press
with text and display in Minion Pro

Text composition by Santos Barbasa Jr.

Printing and binding by The Maple-Vail Book
Manufacturing Group

Printed on 50 lb. Glatfelter Offset D37, 400 ppi